Multicultural Education
and the
Internet
Intersections and Integrations

Multicultural Education
and the
Internet
Intersections and Integrations

Second Edition

Paul C. Gorski
Hamline University

Boston   Burr Ridge, IL   Dubuque, IA   Madison, WI   New York   San Francisco   St. Louis
Bangkok   Bogotá   Caracas   Lisbon   London   Madrid   Mexico City
Milan   Montreal   New Delhi   Santiago   Seoul   Singapore   Sydney   Taipei   Toronto

The McGraw·Hill Companies

McGraw-Hill Higher Education

Multicultural Education and the Internet: Intersections and Integrations
Paul C. Gorski

Published by McGraw-Hill Higher Education, an imprint of The McGraw-Hill Companies, Inc.,
1221 Avenue of the Americas, New York, NY 10020. Copyright © 2005, 2001 by
The McGraw-Hill Companies, Inc. All rights reserved.

Cover image: Adam Crowley/Getty Images

This book is printed on acid-free paper.

8 9 0 DOC/DOC 9 0 9 8 7

ISBN-13: 978-0-07-301143-1
ISBN-10: 0-07-301143-6

www.mhhe.com

for Bob, Chuck, & Allen

Contents

Preface

Since finishing the manuscript for the first edition of *Multicultural Education and the Internet: Intersections and Integrations* in 2000 my practice and scholarship involving these phenomena have shifted dramatically. When I began writing about the Internet's role in multicultural education, I did so with great spirit and hope, extolling the exciting educational potentials of these new technologies. I naively assumed that, as many educational technology specialists insisted, computers and the Internet would ultimately contribute to education equity. But multicultural education pushes us to dig deeper, to push beyond our candy-coated assumptions and to understand emerging educational phenomena in a larger context of access and equity. So I dug.

What emerged from this process was a more critical examination of the role of these new technologies in the theory and practice of multicultural education. Before considering the ways in which the Internet can contribute to multicultural education, we must understand its relationship to the ways in which it may contribute to existing inequities. Before hopping on the Internet bandwagon, I must be sure that my teaching is grounded in sound multicultural pedagogy, not driven by the latest educational fad. We must collectively reflect on the implications of the growing reliance on computers and the Internet in education when there is little evidence that these technologies improve teaching and learning.

If we dedicate to engaging ourselves in individual reflection and collective dialogue about thoughtful and equitable employment of these technologies, I still believe that the Internet can be the most contributive, progressive, multicultural teaching and learning medium. In an effort to push the education community toward that reality, I have reframed parts of *Multicultural*

Education and the Internet to be more critical—to insist that the Internet is only as multicultural as the context in which it is employed. I have also included a new chapter on the digital divide (Chapter 3), believing an intensive discussion of this contemporary equity issue was sorely missing from the book's first edition.

I would like to thank Cara Harvey and everyone else at McGraw-Hill for giving me the opportunity to revise this book. Cara has been wonderfully supportive throughout the process.

Special thanks is extended to Christine Sleeter for writing a wonderful foreword for this book and for inspiring much of my work in multicultural education. Special thanks also go to Bill Howe, Morris Jackson, and Joy Wallace for contributing to Chapter 7.

I would also like to acknowledge my colleagues and friends who continue to support my work and challenge me to grow and rethink my biases, assumptions, and prejudices. My second family at the National Association for Multicultural Education provides the community of passion that energizes all of my work. The staff of the Office of Human Relations Programs at the University of Maryland, College Park, and the faculty and staff of the Curry School of Education at the University of Virginia are largely responsible for my growth as a multicultural educator. My new friends and colleagues at Hamline University have been incredibly supportive and inspirational as I have drafted, redrafted, and completed this book.

Charlene Green, Bob Covert, and Mr. Hill, my mentors, all of whom I love dearly, deserve most of the credit for anything I am fortunate enough to accomplish.

Several of the chapters in this book are based on articles I have previously written for *Multicultural Perspectives,* the quarterly journal of the National Association for Multicultural Education, published by Lawrence Erlbaum.

Biography

Paul Gorski is an assistant professor in the Graduate School of Education at Hamline University. He is an active consultant, conducting workshops and giving guidance to schools and educational organizations committed to equity and diversity. He created and continues to maintain the *Multicultural Pavilion* and the *McGraw-Hill Multicultural Supersite,* two Web sites focused on multicultural education. Gorski is actively involved in the National Association for

Multicultural Education (NAME), and serves on its board of directors. He is Associate Editor, Technology, for NAME's journal, *Multicultural Perspectives*, and Associate Editor, Multicultural Literature and Reviews, for *Multicultural Education*. Prior to his current position at Hamline University, Gorski taught for the University of Virginia, the University of Maryland, and George Mason University. He earned a doctorate in Educational Evaluation at the University of Virginia, where he spent four years facilitating multicultural workshops and dialogues for teachers and students and co-teaching several courses on multicultural education. He continues to publish and present in education-focused forums on topics ranging from whiteness and racism studies to multicultural curriculum transformation. He lives in St. Paul, Minnesota, with his cat, Unity.

Foreword

by Christine E. Sleeter

California State University, Monterey Bay

*I*n one of my graduate courses, students review literature that pertains to their thesis. As part of this process, I have them research an author whose work is most relevant to their own. Last semester a Chicana graduate student who was looking into high-achieving Chicano(a)s decided to find out more about the work of Patricia Gándara. An Internet search yielded some professional information, but the student also had questions she wanted to ask personally. I suggested the student e-mail her; the student was thrilled when she received a personal response. Another student who had discovered the concept of efficacy and the work of Albert Bandura spent hours reading about his life and some of his latest work on the Internet. In both cases, the students learned about and connected with role models they admired using the Internet. One was even able to establish personal communication with her role model.

In another course, my students were investigating the ideological orientations of several different curriculum documents. Most of the students in the course were classroom teachers who were feeling "boxed in" by the state standards they have to follow. The state standards were one of the curriculum documents we were investigating, but there were others, some of which were available on the Internet. Of particular interest to the class was the curriculum of the Oneida Nation, a description of which can be found at *http://schools.oneidanation.org/* and *http://www.4directions.org/resources/contributions/school/cache.pl.17.html*. These two sites offered an inspiring contrast to my state's curriculum standards and prompted an insightful discussion about culture and language in curriculum, and who has the power to define what children should learn. In this case, the Internet was particularly helpful because it connected students with a living vision in real schools that had been created by real teachers.

I begin with these stories to illustrate what Paul Gorski does so brilliantly in *Multicultural Education and the Internet.* Gorski shows teachers and teacher educators how to use the Internet as a tool for powerful teaching. He situates the Internet within a sound perspective about multicultural education, good pedagogy, and social justice. He is first and foremost a multicultural educator with a strong commitment to working for social justice. He happens also to be extraordinarily savvy about the Internet. He developed and continues to maintain the *Multicultural Pavilion* (*http://www.edchange.org/multicultural/*), which one of my graduate students described to her peers: "It has everything!"

In this book, Gorski demystifies the Internet for multicultural educators. He begins by acknowledging that technology does not necessarily strengthen teaching and learning, even though its advocates often push it as if it did. Although *Multicultural Education and the Internet* does a marvelous job of showing ways that technology can deepen learning in powerful ways, Gorski forthrightly cautions us that technology is not a panacea that will automatically improve education. And technology is bound up in the replication of inequalities that multicultural education seeks to address. Gorski offers an extensive discussion of the digital divide as a broad political and economic issue as well as a pedagogical issue. The digital divide is not an afterthought in this book, but rather part of the context in which we work and an inequity we can take action to address.

Multicultural Education and the Internet challenges teachers to develop what Paulo Freire referred to as ideological clarity. When a teacher chooses to use the Internet, who will benefit and in what ways? What vision of multicultural education guides the teacher's work? How might the Internet serve as a tool for empowering students? For connecting people? For helping teachers and students learn to hear historically subjugated voices? For facilitating social action? As Gorski shows throughout this book, the Internet has the potential to shift the locus of decision making about what is learned, who gets to decide, and what is done with learning. The Internet can extend corporate control (witness the amount of advertising Internet users must often wade through) and cultural hegemony (witness the predominance of the English language on the Web), but it can also serve as a tool for democratization (witness Internet organizations such as MoveOn.org). As Gorski shows throughout this book, teachers with a sociopolitical and historical consciousness can judiciously use the Internet in beneficial, just, and innovative ways.

But how? The educator who is already familiar with the Internet will benefit from the wonderful lists of sources in this book and the suggestions for analyzing and using them. And the reader who knows little about the Internet, and may even find it intimidating, will find this book marvelously helpful. Gorski provides tools that are clearly explained and easily accessible for beginners, while providing new resources for experienced Web surfers. For example, educators who are unsure what an e-mail discussion group or a listserv is will find a chapter explaining them in everyday language. At the same time, more technologically experienced educators who wish to start or facilitate an e-mail discussion group around sensitive issues will also find "words of wisdom" from people who have done just that.

For many young people today, the computer is a given. The question is not whether to use it, but how. Gorski helps us to see how, within a social justice consciousness and a passion for good teaching.

CHAPTER 1

Introduction

As I sat in a computer lab at the University of Virginia (UVA) in 1995, an instructional guide to creating Web sites in my lap, I had little notion about how important, both culturally and educationally, the Internet would be just a few years later. The people around me—primarily faculty, staff, and my fellow graduate students at UVA's Curry School of Education—were buzzing about electronic mail, which had not been widely used to that point, even though it had been available to everyone at the university for several years. My classmates were excited about this new way to contact previously inaccessible professors, and my professors were using the medium to track down large groups of students with a single message. The World Wide Web was a fairly new phenomenon at the time and had yet to make a big splash in either the K-12 or higher education arena. As I peered around the lab in search of a possible Web design tutor, I saw something that seems nearly impossible today: Nobody in the lab, other than me, was using the Web that day.

What made the situation especially strange was that I had no specific interest in Web technologies. In fact, my Internet incompetence had become a running joke among my classmates and professors, who virtually had to tie me to a chair and teach me how to access my e-mail. My computer use was limited to word processing and an occasional game of Tetris or Solitaire.

My passion—professionally, educationally, and personally—was (and is) multicultural education. I felt an intense sense of self-growth as I studied and discussed curriculum reform, multicultural organizational development, multicultural and critical pedagogy, and other aspects of this approach for educational transformation. But I most cherished the time I spent working directly with educators, engaging them (along with myself) in a process of examining our biases, prejudices, and assumptions, and how they inform teaching and affect students' learning. Relative to the personal nature and intimacy of this work, the Internet appeared to be a somewhat cold and impersonal place.

Then, in a single week, two of my professors invited colleagues into their classes to deliver presentations on educational uses of the Internet. The first presenter, visiting my Social Foundations of Education class, took my classmates and me on a tour of some of the resources available on the World Wide Web. He showed us online dictionaries, news sources, informational libraries, and other research tools. While this presentation alerted me to the potential of the Web as an effective information distribution medium, I failed to recognize—or the presenter failed to demonstrate—how it would contribute to the improvement of teaching and learning. Later in the week, a fellow student, Yitna Firdyiwek, visited my Advanced Multicultural Education class to share his Web project, *The Thomas-Hill Hearings Site*. Yitna, an English teacher by trade, had spent weeks putting the transcripts of the Anita Hill and Clarence Thomas hearings online. But his use of the Internet transcended that of employing its myriad informational resources. In addition to placing the hearings transcripts online, he created a series of what could be best described as electronic bulletin boards through which his students and other visitors to the site interacted, debated, exchanged ideas, and shared resources regarding the hearings and related topics. He essentially created an online community of collective and collaborative teaching and learning, inviting new and different voices and perspectives into his classroom via the Internet.

I began to recognize several important intersections between multicultural education philosophy and the capabilities and potentials of the Internet that day. As a multicultural educator, I deeply appreciated how Yitna, never wavering from a multicultural pedagogical approach that valued interactive, inclusive, and collaborative teaching and learning, employed an Internet technology to help put that philosophy into practice. I realized that when used to its full potential within a progressive educational context, the Internet could be one of the most important, most contributive media for the future of multicultural education and the continued push toward student-centered, interactive, inclusive, active, and collaborative teaching and learning (more on this in Chapter 3).

That Monday my attitude toward the Internet as an educational medium was dismissive at best. But there I was, by Thursday, inspired and energized, sitting in the computer lab with a guide to designing Web sites in my lap. It was

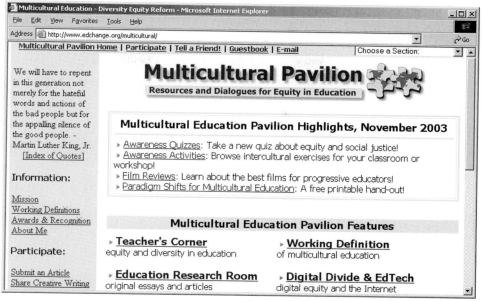

Figure 1.1   The Multicultural Pavilion
http://www.edchange.org/multicultural/

on that Thursday in the fall of 1995 that I initiated the creation of the first multicultural education Web site dedicated to facilitating the exchange of dialogue, ideas, and resources among teachers, students, and activists: the *Multicultural Pavilion* (see Figure 1.1).

In the years since, the Internet has literally exploded across the education scene. In December 1998, 32.7% of Americans used the Internet (National Telecommunications and Information Administration [NTIA], 2002). Between September 2001 and the middle of 2003, that figure lingered around 60% (Lenhart, 2003). By the beginning of the new millennium, most educational institutions in the United States, elementary through higher education, had taken notice of the potential value of the Internet as a teaching and learning tool, and a national push to "get wired" (or acquire access to the Internet) was in full effect. School districts were providing in-service Internet training for teachers, dozens of education conferences focused specifically on the role of the Internet in education, and many teacher education programs at colleges and universities added an educational technology requirement for pre-service teachers. Those who had not taken heed felt the pressure of No Child

Left Behind and other legislation insisting on deeper computer and Internet integration in education. If I walked back into that computer lab at UVA today, I would likely find more than half of the computers being occupied by Internet users, composing e-mail to a friend or colleague at another university, searching the Web for sources for a research project, or creating original educational Web sites.

A New Approach for Multicultural Education and the Internet

Unfortunately, despite the rapid growth of Internet use in and out of education, its multicultural capabilities remain largely unappreciated and untapped by teachers. Too many educational Internet workshops and books continue to present the Web and other Internet technologies as primarily informational resources. A new wave of print guides to multicultural education on the Internet have continued this trend, usually offering no more than an organized list of Web site references and failing to give ample attention to pedagogy, curriculum reform, or teaching and learning practices.

Multicultural Education and the Internet: Intersections and Integrations springs from my passion for multicultural education and a need to reframe an understanding of educational uses of the Internet in such a way that transcends a simple "resource guide" formulation. This book is designed specifically for classroom teachers, informed first and foremost by sound multicultural teaching and learning philosophy and a critical examination of Internet technology within that context. Although I have included annotated listings of many existing Internet teaching and learning resources, these serve only as examples and points of entry in relation to the primary purposes of this book, which are as follows:

- To provide a critical framework for examining ways in which the increasing reliance on educational technology will only recycle inequities if not considered in a wider and deeper sociopolitical context
- To illustrate ways in which the Internet can contribute to an existing multicultural context
- To highlight opportunities to expand resource bases using Internet technologies such as the World Wide Web and e-mail
- To provide strategies for locating, assessing, and using contributive Internet-based resources and materials to supplement multicultural teaching and learning practices

Consumers of this book should expect to develop a new appreciation for the Internet, informed not solely by the education technology field, but also, and more importantly, by sound multicultural teaching and learning principles. Along with that appreciation will come a new set of practical tools and strategies that can serve to enhance the overall educational experiences of teachers and students.

Outline of Remaining Chapters

Chapter 2, "The Multiculturality of the Internet," provides a framework for the rest of the book by describing the educational context in which educators are experiencing increasing pressure to infuse their curricula with computer and Internet technology. A conceptualization for multicultural education is provided, and intersections between multicultural education and the Internet are highlighted through a discussion of the educational opportunities and challenges presented by this cybermedium.

Chapter 3, "The Digital Divide," introduces the concept of digital equity through a thorough examination of research and data on inequities in access to computers and the Internet. Several dimensions of the digital divide are reviewed, including race, gender, socioeconomic status, language, and disability. I end the chapter by offering a new model for understanding and dismantling the divide.

Chapter 4, "Progressive Pedagogy and the Internet," examines ways in which, given an established progressive educational environment, the Internet can contribute to a variety of multicultural teaching and learning principles. These include critical pedagogy, collaboration, interaction, student engagement, and inclusivity.

Chapter 5, "Web Integration and Multicultural Curriculum Transformation," considers educational uses of the World Wide Web in the context of curriculum transformation philosophy. A continuum model for multicultural curriculum transformation is presented and supplemented by related strategies for integrating Web resources into classroom practice.

Chapter 6, "Bridges and Dialogues: Online Networking for Educators," emphasizes the importance and benefits of networking among teachers and explores forums through which the Internet helps facilitate these connections. Interactive forums including e-mail discussion groups, discussion boards, and chat rooms are highlighted.

Chapter 7, "Forging Communities for Education Change through E-mail Discussion Groups," provides a closer look at multicultural education e-mail discussion groups through the eyes of the moderators and facilitators of these online communities of dialogue, resource sharing, and collaboration.

Chapter 8, "Evaluating Educational Web Sites: A Multicultural Approach," critically examines existing Web site evaluation and assessment models from a multicultural perspective. The chapter offers a new framework for assessing online resources that takes multicultural teaching and learning principles into account.

Chapter 9, "Digging through the Dirt: Locating Contributive Online Resources," equips the reader with a set of strategies for maximizing the efficiency of time you spend searching for Internet-based multicultural education tools and materials.

Chapter 10, "A Guide to Online Resources: General," organizes hundreds of the best available Web sites related to multicultural education. Included items are carefully organized into categories including "Multicultural Education," "Organizations and Associations," "General Teacher and Curricular Resources," "Online Publications," "Articles and Essays," "Lesson Plan Databases," "Multicultural Classroom Activities," "Progressive Technology Integration," and "Site Indexes and Search Tools."

Chapter 11, "A Guide to Online Resources: Subject-Specific," organizes the best available sites into topic categories including "The Arts," "Bilingual Education," "History and Social Studies," "Language Arts," "Literature," "Math," "Science," and "World Languages."

Chapter 12, "A Guide to Online Resources: Issues in Multicultural Education," highlights Web sites about racism, sexism, *No Child Left Behind,* heterosexism, classism, ableism, high-stakes testing, and other contemporary educational issues.

Chapters 10 through 12 are not presented as exhaustive site listings. Instead, they are meant to provide examples of effective educational uses of the Internet. All resource references in this book should be seen as points of entry, not final destinations. Expanded resource lists can be found on the *Multicultural Supersite* at *http://www.mhhe.com/multicultural.*

It is my hope that this book will forge a new approach to finding connections and intersections between Internet technology and multicultural teaching and learning. As a multicultural educator by trade and training, I believe the opportunities presented by these new cybermedia can outweigh and overpower the challenges when—only when—understood and employed within a sound multicultural education framework.

References

Lenhart, A. (2003). *The ever-shifting Internet population: A new look at Internet access and the digital divide.* Washington, DC: Pew Internet and American Life Project.

National Telecommunications and Information Administration (NTIA). (2002). *A nation online: How Americans are expanding their use of the Internet.* Washington, DC: U.S. Department of Commerce.

CHAPTER 2

The Multiculturality of the Internet

Observing two of the students in my graduate Equity and Diversity in Education course sharing a private laugh, I sensed they had something insightful to share—insightful, that is, or funny, which can be equally valuable and well worth diverting the conversation. We were discussing various ways in which socioeconomic inequities impact schools. I introduced the concept of digital inequities—gaps due to socioeconomic status in students' access to computers and the Internet. I pleaded with the suddenly jovial teachers, coworkers at a middle school in northern Virginia, not to deny the rest of us a share of their fun.

Carol, a science teacher, still giggling, explained, "I just whispered to Fred that Mr. Johnson, our principal, had told the science teachers to make sure we leave our computers on every day, whether or not we're using them for anything."

Fred interrupted, "Apparently he's making the rounds, because he insisted the same from the English teachers. It doesn't matter that we have virtually no training on how to use them beyond creating electronic grade books and e-mailing each other. It's a funding stream, and Johnson doesn't want somebody in control of that stream to pop in on reality—that we may have computers in every classroom, but we don't have teachers in every classroom who know how to use them."

Carol chimed in, "Two of the computers in my room haven't worked in months. I asked him what do about those. He said to go ahead and turn them on, anyway. I'm sure we could do wonderful things with these machines if they worked, if we had some decent software, and if we had time to really learn how to use them well. But as far as I can see, for now, they're like giant digital flashcards."

Giant Digital Flashcards

The emergence of the digital information age has wrought upon educators a new set of pedagogical challenges and classroom complications. The pressure to incorporate computer and Internet technologies into teaching and learning is systemic, spelled out in local and national educational policy and related measures of accountability. This pressure filters through superintendents and school boards to principals and finally to teachers, who are expected to adapt their curricula, often without substantial preparation or ongoing professional development, particularly if they happen to teach at schools in poverty-laden communities or with a high percentage of students on free or reduced lunch.

Most recent and noticeable among these policies and accountability measures is No Child Left Behind. In this national legislation package, the George W. Bush administration identified the use of instructional technologies as a key component for providing quality education to all students. The sentiment is admirable; it is impossible to deny that we should be preparing today's students for a society and workforce that is increasingly reliant on computers and the Internet (a development that should be critically examined in and of itself), and that failing to prepare any student for this reality does, indeed, amount to leaving that student behind. Unfortunately, due to budget cuts and shifting economic priorities, fewer resources and programs are available to prepare educators to do that for which they are to be held accountable. And again, this is most deeply impacting low-income students, whose schools are less likely than those of financially privileged students to find other economic resources for teacher training, fixing ailing computers, and acquiring necessary software and hardware upgrades. Like other aspects of No Child Left Behind, the expectation ultimately seems to be that, without any additional resources or funding, schools will adequately prepare all teachers to incorporate Internet technologies into their classroom practice in pedagogically sound ways.

What we are left with is equality in school and teacher expectations, but glaring inequities in the process of providing all teachers, schools, or districts with the resources necessary for meeting them. In effect, we are leaving many teachers behind—not a very effective approach for ensuring that no child is left behind. Another complexity for educators trying to find their way in an increasingly technocentric society is the chasm between education technology development and effective teaching practice. Education technologists, in a rush (or race) to understand and employ new technologies, too often do so for the sake of technological advancement itself, with little thought to effective or theoretically sound pedagogy—where every decision about teaching and learning should start. In other words, when the question becomes "How do I incorporate this technology into my teaching?," instead of "What is the most effective way to teach this lesson or unit and how does this technology fit into that scheme, if at all?," it becomes crucial to reflect deeply on what drives our educational decisions.

The Internet is a prime example of this phenomenon. In fact, studies show that in most cases, the introduction of computers and the Internet to the kindergarten through twelfth grade (K-12) education milieu has done little to improve teaching and learning or to disrupt achievement gaps (Livingstone, 2003; Prain & Hand, 2003). Observation across the institutional landscape of schools in the United States reveals just the opposite: Overall, the technology boom is recycling these gaps at best and in many cases deepening them. Again, we must ask ourselves: Why, when this is the case, do educational decision- and policymakers continue to assign computers and the Internet such a high status in the present and future of schools and schooling? Should we not work out these disparities first, study the overall effectiveness of incorporating these technologies, and then decide their place in education?

To avoid the false assumptions about the educational magic of the Internet and misguided attempts to incorporate these technologies for the simple sake of incorporating them, and to effectively prepare educators to use computers and the Internet in ways that contribute to, instead of detracting from, positive teaching and learning experiences, these technologies must be understood in the greater context of the educational and societal framework in which they are to be employed. Moreover, products, resources, and materials incorporating these technologies must stand up to the same critical examination we apply to—or should apply to—textbooks, films, and every other educational medium. Likewise, we must engage in a critical consideration of the processes and methods through which we apply these new technologies with the same fervor with which educational technology enthusiasts exclaim the teaching and learning potentialities of the Internet.

What is clear among these complexities is this: Without a systemic and collective refocus among educational leaders, one that insists on good instruction first and the incorporation of technology, if it contributes to good instruction, second, these technologies will do as all aspects of education do when unchecked: contribute to the educational status quo. In other words, they will only contribute to existing inequities. Multicultural education, an approach for progressively transforming education based on a process for understanding, critiquing, and eliminating current shortcomings, discriminatory practices, and inequities in schools, provides an essential framework for this refocus and for assessing the present and future directions of computer and Internet technology implementation in our schools.

Conceptualizing Multicultural Education

The basis of multicultural education can be effectively expressed by a question: Does every student who walks into our schools or your classroom have an opportunity to achieve to her or his fullest, regardless of race, ethnicity, gender, sexual orientation, religion, socioeconomic status, first language, (dis)ability, national origin, or any other personal, social, or political identifier around which we have historically experienced and continue to cycle achievement gaps (including gaps in dropout rates)?

Research, literature, and even casual observation form an undeniable response to this question: Every student does not have an opportunity to achieve to her or his fullest. Girls and women continue to be systematically pushed out of academic pursuits in mathematics, the sciences, and computer science. Schools in which a majority of the students are people of color are much more likely to be overcrowded than schools in which a majority of students are white (National Center for Educational Statistics [NCES], 2002a). A recent study indicated that an alarming 23.6% of high schools students have heard homophobic comments from teachers and other school staff and 68.6% of lesbian, gay, and bisexual students do not feel safe in their schools because of their sexual orientation (Gay Lesbian Straight Education Network [GLSEN], 2001). Immigrant students of first languages other than English are still routinely assumed to have learning disabilities, regardless of how well they performed in the schools of their home countries. Socioeconomically disadvantaged students as well as African American, Latina(o), and Native American students drop out of school at rates that far exceed those of White and Asian

American and Pacific Islander students (NCES, 2001). These are just a few examples of the symptoms of continued educational inequities—a mere sample illustrating the desperate need to think deeply and critically about every future educational movement and reform.

Multicultural education insists upon a critical examination of these and other discrepancies across education. It is grounded in ideals of social justice and education equity and a dedication to facilitating educational experiences in which every student reaches her or his full potential as a learner. In this sense, multicultural education acknowledges that schools are essential to laying the foundation for the elimination of oppression and injustice in society. As such, the underlying goal of multicultural education is to effect social change. The pathway toward this goal incorporates three strands of transformation:

1. the transformation of self;
2. the transformation of schools and schooling; and
3. the transformation of society.

The transformation of self refers to the reflective responsibilities I take on as an educator, to engage in a critical and continual process of examining how my prejudices, biases, and assumptions inform my teaching and thus affect my students' educational experiences. I have a responsibility to myself to study and understand the lenses through which I see and experience the people and happenings around me. Only when I have a sense for how my own perceptions are developed in relation to my life experiences can I truly understand the world around me and effectively navigate my relationships with colleagues and students. I also have a responsibility to my students to work toward eliminating my prejudices, examining who is (and is not) being reached by my teaching style and relearning how my own identity influences their learning experiences. To be an effective multicultural educator, which is to say, an effective educator in general, I must be in a constant process of self-examination and transformation.

The transformation of schools and schooling involves the critical examination of all aspects of education, including teacher preparation, pedagogy, curriculum, educational materials, school and classroom climate, counseling practices, and assessment. How do these contribute to, or detract from, equitable educational experiences for all students? Who possesses the power to construct policy and accountability and make day-to-day decisions about each of these dimensions of education?

In a multicultural teaching and learning paradigm, traditional pedagogies are deconstructed to examine how they contribute to and support institutional systems of oppression. For example, how does the delivery of science instruction support the notion that girls and women are genetically inferior to boys and men in mathematics and the sciences? Multicultural pedagogy is student centered, purposefully drawing on the experiences and knowledge of students and making learning more active, interactive, and engaging. Emphasis is placed on critical and creative thinking, learning skills, and social awareness as well as facts and figures.

Multicultural curriculum transformation starts with the examination of all curricula for accuracy and completeness. It moves beyond a heroes and holidays approach to seamlessly incorporate diverse perspectives, including the voices of the students in the classroom. In addition, material is covered in a variety of ways, speaking to the diversity of learning and comprehension styles present in every classroom. (See Chapter 5 for a more detailed discussion of multicultural curriculum transformation.)

School and classroom climates grounded in a multicultural education philosophy foster a positive teaching, learning, and working environment for every member of the school community. Educators are provided with professional and personal development opportunities and work collaboratively to examine themselves and their school's culture. Together, they determine how oppressive practices might be cycled within school walls. Ultimately, a school is considered to be only as inclusive as its most alienated, disempowered students experience it to be.

Transformational evaluation and assessment includes a continual effort to measure the successes and failures of new and existing programs and to ascertain whether these programs worsen or improve conditions for all students. Current assessment and measurement practices, including the use of standardized tests, are continually examined while more just alternatives for measuring student "achievement," "ability," and "potential" are developed. Students demonstrate mastery and ability in a variety of ways, and this reality guides assessment.

In the end, the goal of multicultural education is to contribute proactively to the transformation of society and to the application and maintenance of social justice and equity locally, nationally, and globally. This is a logical progression, as the transformation of schools necessarily leads to social change in a society that puts so much stock in educational attainment, degrees, and test scores. In fact, it is particularly this competitive, capitalistic framing of the dominant mentality of the United States that multicultural education aims to challenge, shake up, expose, critique, and dismantle. If I do not understand the convergence of these issues in the larger society, I remain unprepared to recognize or respond to them in a school context.

To ensure equity and social justice in education, so that every student has an opportunity to achieve to her or his full potential, multicultural education must permeate our schools from top-level decision makers to each individual student and teacher. It is crucial to apply this critical lens to emerging educational trends, particularly those, like the growing reliance on computer- and Internet-based instructional technology, that have been sprung upon the educational community with little apparent consideration for their potential impact on effective and equitable teaching and learning. The somewhat sudden super-reliance on computer technology (especially the Internet), and false assumptions that it is, or can be, the "great equalizer" in education, serves as a powerful reminder of the need for multicultural education.

With this lens, we are better prepared to fully understand both the educational opportunities and challenges introduced by this relatively new, largely misunderstood, undeniably powerful, and, for better or worse, transformational cybermedium.

The Internet and Educational Opportunities

Beyond a relatively short learning curve, the resources and materials available via the Internet expand one's access to new and diverse resources to a virtually infinite degree (Trewern, 2001). The World Wide Web houses virtual libraries, up-to-the minute news sources, museums, reference works, research databases, collections of classic literature, archives of historic photographs and speeches, and countless other informational resources. As Internet use around the world climbs, these resources become increasingly diverse in perspective, language, scope, and worldview. Teachers can use these resources to enhance their own knowledge or to diversify the perspectives and voices dominating traditional educational media.

But the Internet's most potentially important educational and political contributions lie not in its power to connect educators and students to informational resources, but to connect us to the most important multicultural resources available: other people. Teachers and students are no longer constrained by what they can find in journals or their library shelves, or even in the aforementioned online informational resources. We have access to new voices, perspectives, and understandings—to other teachers, parents, students, researchers, and others. The key for unlocking this potential is in conceptualizing and using the Internet, not merely as an enormous compendium of information that we might otherwise find in print, but as an interactive medium that can connect people across national borders and cultural boundaries. It is this interactive nature of the Internet that makes it a potentially invaluable part of the multicultural education.

Imagine, for example, the added educational value of a textbook if the author's contact information—perhaps an e-mail address and a mailing address—was included on the inside cover so that you or your students could ask questions, request more information, or challenge her or him on information you believed to be biased, misleading, or incorrect. (As more studies reveal misleading information and blatant errors in many of the most often-used K-12 textbooks, perhaps the inclusion of author contact information should become a regular practice!) Better yet, imagine a vast network of teachers and students around the world and across myriad cultures and perspectives who have read a particular textbook gathering on an ongoing basis to share questions and exchange resources on a topic of common interest or trading lesson plans and teaching strategies. Or imagine an opportunity to facilitate a learning experience in which your students interact directly with someone who contributed to a certain scientific discovery or whose experiences are described in a section of a textbook. Imagine your students not only reading about the Holocaust, westward expansion, Japanese internment camps, and the Great Depression, but also having conversations with Holocaust survivors, Native Americans currently living on reservations, survivors of the internment camps, and individuals who lived through the Great Depression. Better yet, imagine connecting your students with their own peers across the country or around the world to discuss current events. These are just a few of the interactive opportunities made possible or easier by the Internet.

In short, employed thoughtfully and responsibly, the Internet can transcend the potential of many other educational media as a means to practice and supplement interactive, inclusive, active, and collaborative teaching and learning, each of which are fundamentals of multicultural education pedagogy. I will describe these fundamentals and how they meet at intersections between the Internet and multicultural education in Chapter 4.

The Internet and Educational Challenges

Where new and exciting educational opportunities exist, they are usually accompanied by a series of new challenges. The same is true with the effective incorporation of Internet technologies into classroom practice.

The most immediate challenge reappears with every new educational trend and technology: preparation and training. Although training programs and specially designed instructional materials have helped educators develop Internet competencies, recent research shows that teachers still identify a lack of computer or Internet skills as the primary reason for not incorporating these media into their teaching practice (NCES, 2002b). This situation is slowly changing as teacher education programs continue to require computer and Internet courses as part of the preservice process. But even when training does occur it often lacks sufficient practical or applicable context (Flake & Molina, 1995; Lai, 2001; Smith & Robinson, 2003; Wang, 2002). Instructional technology training and development programs must be improved so that teachers not only learn how to use the Internet, but also how to effectively, progressively, and equitably incorporate Internet resources into their teaching.

Additional challenges await even the most cybersavvy of all educators. For example, unlike textbooks and educational films, Web site content is usually not static. I have often returned to Web sites I used in my teaching only to find that the content or the design had changed considerably or that the site had disappeared altogether. This can be beneficial in certain contexts, enabling Web sites to offer up-to-the-minute news and information on current events. But it can also be disruptive to a carefully planned lesson, or, at worst, result in the redirection of students to a pornographic or white supremacist Web site.

Another constant challenge specific to Web media is that people who run Web servers (the computers that store the files that comprise Web sites) usually do not screen Web authors for credibility, expertise, or authority. Moreover, while the work of most educational book authors and contributors to education journals are subject to heavy review by publishers or peers, no such formal (or informal) review process exists for a majority of Web pages. This calls into question the accuracy and credibility of many educational Web sites. Like textbooks and other traditional educational media, Web sites designed for teachers and students often come with social and political leanings and biases. Unlike textbooks and other traditional media, the Web is so new that the social and political reputations of many Web sites are not well established. So unless I have read every word of content on every page of a Web site, I cannot be perfectly certain what my students will find during their own explorations.

The most troubling challenge to effective implementation of Internet-based instructional technology has been metaphorically and aptly coined the "digital divide." The divide has traditionally referred to gaps in physical access to computers and the Internet among various social and identity groups within the United States or around the world (Clark & Gorski, 2001). More recently, scholars have begun to broaden the conceptualization of "access" in reference to instructional technology. It is no longer sufficient to simply ensure that all schools have the same number of computers in classrooms, this scholarship insists. Instead, we must also examine gaps in access to effective and progressive incorporation of computers and the Internet into instruction, access to social and cultural support for valuing academic and employment pursuits related to technology, access to meaningful and nonoppressive online content, and access to the larger social dialogue about the importance assigned to these technologies for society and the school system (Gorski, 2002; The Children's Partnership, 2002). These gaps call into question the multiculturality of the Internet at the most basic level—that of inclusion and accessibility. (The digital divide will be explored in greater depth and detail in Chapter 3.) As an educator dedicated to equity and social justice in my classroom and in the larger education system, this challenge alone inspires me to think very critically about the implications of the assumption that the technology revolution in schools is, indeed, revolutionary, even though it recycles the same inequities that many assume it eliminates.

The trick, then, is to establish strategies and approaches for incorporating computers and the Internet into classrooms and the overall direction of schools and schooling that take advantage of the opportunities these media present. Meanwhile, we must concurrently refuse to succumb to the inevitably harmful outcomes of ignoring the sociohistorical and sociopolitical implications of blind digital faith. The first order of business in this process is to develop a deep and complex understanding of the chief barrier to multicultural education and the Internet—the digital divide. After all, there can be no progressive and equitable role for computers and the Internet in the larger educational landscape or in individual classrooms if that role is carried out inequitably across society or by individual educators.

References

The Children's Partnership. (2002). Online content for low-income and under-served Americans. Santa Monica, CA: Author.

Clark, C., & Gorski, P. (2001). Multicultural education and the digital divide: Focus on race, language, socioeconomic class, sex, and disability. Multicultural Perspectives, 3 (3), 39-44.

Flake, J., & Molina, L. (1995). Meeting pre- and inservice teachers' changing needs through technology: Considerations for curriculum, classroom, and teacher roles. In J. Willis, B. Robin, & D. Willis (Eds.), Technology and Teacher Education Annual (pp. 335-339). Charlottesville, VA: Association for the Advancement of Computing in Education.

Gay Lesbian Straight Education Network (GLSEN). (2001). 2001 national school climate survey. New York: Author.

Gorski, P. (2002). Dismantling the digital divide: A multicultural education framework. Multicultural Education, 10 (1), 28-30.

Lai, K. (2001). Professional development: Too little, too generic? In K. Lai (Ed.), E-learning: Teaching and professional development with the Internet (pp. 7-19). Dunedin, New Zealand: University of Otago Press.

Livingstone, S. (2003). Children's use of the Internet: Reflections on the emerging research agenda. New Media and Society, 5 (2), 147-166.

National Center for Educational Statistics (NCES). (2001). Dropout rates in the United States: 2000. Washington, DC: U.S. Department of Education.

————. (2002a). The condition of education 2001. Washington, DC: U.S. Department of Education.

————. (2002b). Beyond school-level Internet access: Support for instructional use of technology. Washington, DC: U.S. Department of Education.

Prain, V., & Hand, B. (2003). Using new technologies for learning: A case study of a whole-school approach. Journal of Research on Technology in Education, 35 (4), 441-507,

Smith, S., & Robinson, S. (2003). Technology integration through collaborative cohorts: Preparing future teachers to use technology. Remedial and Special Education 24 (3), 154-160.

Trewern, A. (2001). The World Wide Web: Education resources for teachers and students. In K. Lai (Ed.), E-learning: Teaching and professional development with the Internet (pp. 77-107). Dunedin, New Zealand: University of Otago Press.

Wang, Y. (2002). When technology meets beliefs: Preservice teachers' perception of the teacher's role in the classroom with computers. Journal of Research on Technology in Education, 35 (1), 150-161.

CHAPTER 3

The Digital Divide

*B*y August 2000, women had surpassed men to become a majority of the U.S. online population (National Telecommunications and Information Administration [NTIA], 2000) leading many instructional technology scholars to hail the end of the gender digital divide—gaps in computer and Internet access rates between women and men. If more women than men were using the Internet, the logic went, equality had been achieved. (The slightly larger overall number of girls and women, as compared with boys and men, using the Internet was consistent with the slightly larger overall number of girls and women, as compared with boys and men, in the U.S. population.) But girls and women continued to trail boys and men in educational and career pursuits related to computers and technology, due largely to a lack of encouragement, or blatant discouragement, from educators, peers, the media, and the wider society. And women remained virtually locked out of the increasingly techno-driven global economy. Meanwhile, men were much more likely to recognize computers and the Internet as tools for economic and professional gain at much higher rates than women, who were more likely to conceptualize these technologies as gateways for pursuing hobbies and friendly correspondence. The equalizing of Internet access rates between girls and boys and between women and men signified a significant step toward the elimination of the gender digital divide—a step toward equality. But if we looked through a different lens, one painted with the sociohistory of sexism in U.S. public schools, a much more complex conceptualization for "access," the heart of digital equity, began to emerge.

This conceptualization, which continues to emerge through the critical study of a fairly new media phenomenon, clarifies the lines between equality of access and equity of access, ultimately forcing us to think more critically about the richness of context and history in which all inequities are immersed. For example, if two thousand students attend a high school in which two sections of an advanced-level mathematics class are taught, does everyone have the same access to those classes? Assuming the school complies with standards set by the Americans with Disabilities Act, making the school accessible to students with disabilities, all students probably do, indeed, have physical access to the classes. In other words, I know where the class meets; I have physical access to the class. But consider the question broadly, contextually, and historically. Can we assume that each student has been encouraged equitably to pursue mathematics throughout her or his educational career? Can we assume that teachers have demonstrated expectations for mathematical achievement equally, regardless of gender, race, or socioeconomic status? What does it mean that research shows women and girls are systematically steered away from pursuits in mathematics and other technology-related subjects beginning as early as elementary school (Clark & Gorski, 2002a; Turkle, 1991)? When we begin to pose these types of questions, the fraudulency of the supremacy of equal access—of women and men enjoying the same rate of physical access to computers and the Internet—without equitable access is exposed as a mirage, a recycler of old inequities under a seemingly well-meaning but misleading reform attempt.

What is clear within this complexity is that an institutional paradigm shift is needed. The term "digital divide" has traditionally described inequalities in access to computers and the Internet between groups of people based on one or more social or cultural identifiers (Gorski, 2002). Accordingly, researchers tend to compare rates of physical access to, or rates of actual use of, these technologies across individuals or schools based on race, gender, socioeconomic status, education level, disability status, and first or primary language. The "divide" refers to the difference in access rates among one or more groups. For example, the racial digital divide is the difference in computer and Internet access and usage rates (at home, school, work, or other locations) between those groups with higher rates of access and usage (white people and Asian Pacific Islander people) and those with relatively lower rates of access and usage (Native American, African American, and Latina(o) people). But this traditional understanding of the digital divide fails to capture the full picture of inequity and alienation recycled by these gaps and the resulting educational, social, cultural, and economic ramifications, primarily for groups of people already educationally, socially, culturally, and economically oppressed. Meanwhile, such a limited view of the digital divide serves the interests of privileged groups and individuals, who can continue critiquing and working to dissolve gaps in physical access and use rates while failing to think critically and reflectively about their personal and collective roles in recycling old inequities in a new cyberform.

This chapter reformulates an understanding of the digital divide by building on a critical review of recent research and shifting the "access" paradigm toward one based not on equality, but equity. This, in turn, will facilitate a more meaningful discussion of strategies for eliminating the digital divide.

Shifting the Digital Divide Paradigm

A new understanding of the digital divide must provide an adequate social, cultural, and historical context, beginning with a dedication to equity and social justice throughout education. Multicultural education, a field of inquiry and transformation that enters every discussion about education with this dedication, provides a desperately needed framework for such an understanding (Gorski, 2002). Multicultural education insists that it is not enough to critically examine individual resources or programs. We must dig deeper and consider the medium and the content; the past, present, and future; the curriculum and the pedagogy; and how our assumptions, decisions, and practices contribute to, or challenge, systems of control and domination by people historically and presently privileged by the education system (such as white people, boys and men, first language speakers of English, heterosexual people, and able-bodied people). Multicultural education replaces an equality orientation with an equity orientation by considering this broader, more contextualized, picture of education and society. The result is a significant paradigm shift leading to a more complete and progressive understanding of the digital divide. The new paradigm differs from the traditional conceptualization based on at least seven principles, discussed next. (Each of these will be revisited in a later discussion on various dimensions of digital inequities.)

Most important, a new approach for framing the digital divide must be critical of digital inequities in the context of larger educational and social inequities. The race digital divide is a symptom of racism, and to understand it outside this context diminishes its significance and cripples our ability to address it effectively. The same is true of the gender, socioeconomic, and every other divide. As such, we must keep at the fore of the digital divide discussion the fact that the groups most disenfranchised by it are the same groups histor-ically and currently disenfranchised by curricular and pedagogical practices, evaluation and assessment, school counseling, and all other aspects of educa-tion (and society at large).

Second, we must broaden the meaning of "access" beyond that of physical access to, or usage rates of, computers and the Internet to include access to equitable support and encouragement to pursue and value technology-related fields, educationally and professionally. Educators, parents, the media, and society in general must continuously express expectations and assumptions that all students have an opportunity to achieve mastery of computer and Internet skills, regardless of race, gender, socioeconomic status, ability status, or any other dimension of their identity.

In addition, we must broaden "access" to include that to equitably non-hostile, inclusive software and Internet content and experiences. We must par-ticularly critique the movement to label the Internet the "great equalizer" when, for example, most of the gender inequities in society are replicated online, including conversation dynamics in online discussion groups, the pro-liferation of online pornography, cyberstalking, and cyberharassment.

Fourth, a new approach for understanding the digital divide must critical-ly examine both who has access to, or uses, computers and the Internet, as well as how these technologies are being used by various individuals or groups of people or by those teaching them. One way that expectations are communi-cated is through instruction—through the level of thinking skills with which I am expected to participate in my learning. Again, patterns in such expectations as expressed through traditional teaching methods are replicated by the approaches with which teachers employ instructional technology (NCES, 2001), a reality that must be dissected and abolished.

The paradigm shift must also lead us to consider the larger sociopolitical ramifications of, and socioeconomic motivations for, the increasing levels of importance assigned to information and instructional technology both in schools and society at large. How does the growing merger of cyberculture with wider U.S. culture privilege those who already enjoy social, political, and economic "access" in the broadest sense?

Sixth, this approach must expose capitalistic propaganda, like commercials portraying children from around the world announcing their recent arrival online, that lead people to believe that these technologies are available to anyone, anywhere, under any circumstances, who wants to use them. Such messages understate the severity of the digital divide and further demonize those who for various reasons do not have access to, or perhaps do not want to use, these technologies.

Finally, the new approach must reject any measure or program that purports to "close" the digital divide simply by providing more computers and more, or faster, Internet access to a school, library, or other public place. In addition to its offensively patriarchal nature, the suggestion that increasing or improving physical access to computers and the Internet will close the divide is simplistic and shallow—a Band-Aid approach to a remarkably ill social and educational system.

These seven principles provide a crucial starting point for examining the problem of the digital divide and formulating viable and far-reaching solutions in context. But more so, they demonstrate the complexity of the digital divide (as well as other equity issues) and the interrelatedness of its various components. This complexity and interrelatedness will become even more pronounced as we explore five dimensions of the digital divide: racism, sexism, classism, linguisticism, and ableism.

Racism and the Digital Divide

In 1999 the Economic Development Administration (EDA) conducted a study of technology infrastructure needs in Native American communities and found several sociohistorical and sociopolitical barriers to improving this infrastructure. Among these barriers was federal policy that fails to consider the severity of technology gaps faced by Native American people (EDA, 1999).

Their concern was justifiable. Since 1998 the U.S. government has collected and published an endless array of statistical reports on the digital divide and other technology issues through a variety of departments, including the National Center on Educational Statistics (NCES) and the National Telecommunications and Information Administration (NTIA). The most recent of these reports and the first to be released under the George W. Bush administration, *A Nation Online: How Americans Are Expanding Their Use of the Internet*, was released in February 2002. But for some reason not explained in any of these reports, the government stopped collecting or reporting information related to technology infrastructure, the digital divide, and computer and Internet use among Native Americans after 1999. According to Kade Twist,

The Bush administration is effectively removing Indians from the public discourse relating to the digital divide, placing them at a further disadvantage in the emerging economy. Furthermore, the exclusion of Indians leaves federal decision makers without evidence of a problem or a solution—it's simply an act of avoidance. (2002, p. 1)

This avoidance oppresses Native American communities in a variety of ways, two of which illustrate the larger complexity of the racial digital divide as a symptom of systemic racism: (1) it shields the federal government from the responsibility of addressing the technology infrastructure needs of many Native American communities, and (2) it strengthens the status quo by failing to provide Native American communities with data on any progress they have made or on successful strategies that could be replicated across these communities.

Any discussion of the racial digital divide in the United States must begin with a critical analysis of this omission, of this invisibility, of this most dangerous form of racial privilege that allows those in power to simply ignore a problem that is too large or complex or economically costly to understand. This serves as a powerful metaphor for the largeness and complexity of the racial digital divide overall, which may be best understood through an examination of three strands of access disparities: (1) gaps in computer and Internet access, (2) gaps in access to educational experiences that incorporate these technologies in progressive and pedagogically sound ways, and (3) gaps in access to support and encouragement to recognize technology-related fields as viable and attainable educational and professional pursuits.

Computer and Internet Access

Between August 2000 and September 2001 (the last period for which data are available), 55.7% of African Americans and 48.8% of Latina(o)s were regularly using computers. Both figures represent marked increases and important progress in just over a year. Still, both groups continued to lag behind when compared with the overall percentage of computer users in the U.S. population (66%), white people (70.7%) and Asian American/Pacific Islanders (71.2%). Similarly, by September 2001, about 60% of white people and Asian American/Pacific Islander people regularly used the Internet while only 39.8% of African American people and 31.6% of Latina(o) people did so (NTIA, 2002). Though these gaps have closed slightly, they continue to contribute sig-

Table 1   Rates of computer and Internet use by race between August 2000 and
September 2001

	Asian American/ Pacific Islander	White	African American	Latina(o)
Regularly used computers	71.2%	70.7%	55.7%	48.8%
Regularly used the Internet	60.4%	59.9%	39.8%	31.6%

Note. Based on data from *A nation online: How Americans are expanding their uses of the Internet* (NTIA, 2002). Parallel data for Native Americans does not exist for the time period.

nificantly to existing privilege and domination hierarchies in the United States (see Table 1).

An examination of where people access the Internet sheds some additional light on digital race inequities. Among people who identify themselves as Internet users, 55.2% of the Asian American/Pacific Islander population and 45% of the white population report accessing the Internet at home, at work, and at school. Only 29.8% of African American Internet users and 32.3% of Latina(o) Internet users access it from home, work, and school. Additionally, African Americans and Latina(o)s are much more likely than white or Asian American/Pacific Islander Internet users to have no access at home, school, or work, instead needing to find a different location, such as a public library, to go online (NTIA, 2002). These disparities raise crucial equity questions for classroom teachers. Undoubtedly, some of these "Internet users" are students who have been assigned work for which they need computer and Internet access. What does it mean that this access is much more easily attainable for some than for others? (This point will be discussed further in the section "Classism and the Digital Divide.")

Some suggest that these gaps can be explained by socioeconomic differences. Their explanation assumes, for example, that a study of economically disadvantaged Asian American/Pacific Islander people and similarly disadvantaged African American people would reveal similarly low rates of computer and Internet usership. But analysis of data from December 2000 shows that the most socioeconomically disadvantaged white and Asian American households are much more likely to own computers and have home Internet access than similarly disadvantaged Latina(o) and African American households (NTIA, 2000). In fact, no matter which other variables are held constant, whether socioeconomic status, education level, or geographic region (rural, urban, etc.), similar patterns of the racial digital divide emerge (Gorski & Clark, 2001).

One of the reasons for increasing computer and Internet usage rates across all racial groups is the widespread increase in exposure to these technologies in schools. For example, 95.9% of all 18- to 24-year-old high school and college students use a computer at home or at school. Of 5- to 9-year-old students, 84.3% use computers at home, at school, or both (NTIA, 2002). Virtually all schools are wired for Internet access, virtually all teachers have access to instructional computers somewhere in their schools (Smerdon et al., 2001), and nearly 80% of all P-12 public school instructional rooms in the United States are wired (NCES, 2001).

However, considerable gaps remain in school and classroom access to computers and the Internet across racial lines. By 2000, 85% of the instructional rooms in schools in which people of color comprised less than 6% of the student body were wired for Internet access. Meanwhile, in schools in which people of color comprised 50% or more of the student body, only 64% of instructional rooms were wired (NCES, 2001). Students in schools with high populations of people of color also enjoyed fewer computers per capita. What may be more alarming is that teachers who have access to these technologies in their classrooms are much more likely to use the technologies in other areas of their schools than teachers who do not have access in their classrooms (Smerdon et al., 2001). So even if a teacher without classroom access to these technologies has the option of using a state-of-the-art computer lab elsewhere in the building, they are less likely to do so than a colleague who already has computers and Internet access at their fingertips. The result is an additional loss for students of color, who are less likely to have the technologies in their classrooms.

In the end, white students are increasingly likely to build confidence and mastery over computer and Internet technologies, known as "net savvy." They are being prepared for the highly digitized global economy and pushed to understand technology in a complex way. Students of color, less likely to be exposed to these technologies, remain largely unaware of the power and complexity of the techno-society, and therefore outside the digital loop. And, as explored later, this exclusion can have social, cultural, and economic ramifications. Additionally, teachers who do not enjoy classroom access to these technologies lose the opportunity to develop comfort, familiarity, and proficiency with computers and the Internet, contributing to another strand of the racial digital divide: gaps in access to educational experiences that incorporate these technologies in progressive and pedagogically sound ways (Gorski & Clark, 2001).

Access to Progressive Learning Experiences

Teachers in schools with high enrollments of students of color are less likely to have access to the resources they need to incorporate the Internet into their instruction than teachers in schools with low enrollments of students of color. Compared with teachers in schools with less than 6% student of color enrollment, those in schools with 50% or more student of color enrollment are less likely to have training in the use of the Internet (82% compared with 70% having been trained) and less likely to have assistance in the use of the Internet, such as an on-site technology specialist (76% compared with 65%). They are nearly a third less likely to have training, assistance, and classroom-level Internet access than their counterparts at predominantly white schools (46% compared with 31%). As a result, teachers in schools with low student of color enrollments are more likely to actually use these technologies for instructional purposes in their classrooms. For example, 45% of teachers in schools with greater than 50% student of color enrollment report using the Internet in their instruction, compared with 56% of teachers in schools with less than 6% student of color enrollment (NCES, 2002).

Teachers in schools with high student of color enrollments cite an additional reason for not using computer and Internet technology in their teaching: outdated, incompatible, and unreliable computers. Like the lack of training and support, this problem is much more systemic in schools with high concentrations of students of color than in those with high concentrations of white students. Over 32% of teachers in the former cite this concern as a great barrier to their instructional use of computers, a rate nearly a third higher than that of the latter (Smerdon et al., 2001).

With these dynamics in place, it is not surprising that students experience technology in very different ways. Without the necessary training, support, and resources, teachers with classrooms full of students of color are more likely to use computer and Internet technology for a skills and drills approach to learning, similar to the "digital flashcards" mentioned in Chapter 2, or as a reward for good behavior. Meanwhile, consistent with the overall pattern of pedagogical differences regardless of the presence of technology, teachers in classrooms full of white students tend to use the technology for higher-level thinking skills such as critical analysis, construction of ideas and concepts, and research (Bigelow, 1999; DeVillar & Faltis, 1987; Solomon & Allen, 2003).

These trends are not revelations; they simply mirror gaps in instructional practices, preparation, and access to relevant professional development across the education system, with or without technology. But as our dependence on these technologies continues to increase, and as federal and local expectations related to the incorporation of computers and the Internet into day-to-day instruction increase, these discrepancies drive a more profound wedge between the information age haves and have-nots. An examination of the third strand of the racial digital divide, gaps in access to support and encouragement to recognize technology-related fields as viable educational and professional pursuits, further illustrates this point.

Access to Encouragement and Support

During a daylong panel on digital equity in education at the annual conference of the Society for Information Technology and Teacher Education, a fascinating discussion emerged from a participant's question: "Why, if we are looking at this through the lens of racism, do Asian American/Pacific Islanders have a greater rate of Internet and computer access than white Americans?"

One particularly passionate white presenter insisted, "The high computer and Internet access rates among Asian people are directly related to their proficiencies in subjects that dominated both early computer and Internet use: mathematics and science." This supposed digital divide expert, buying into an array of racial stereotypes and assumptions, aligned himself with attitudes prevalent in schools and society, among them the "model minority" myth, which also suggests intellectual, cultural, and social inferiority among other groups of color (Gorski & Clark, 2001). His line of thinking, and thus of being, contributes directly to the digital divide. Who would he, an adult educator, more likely encourage to pursue an interest in technology, an African American student or an Asian American student? Unfortunately, such attitudes are pervasive in U.S. schools, not only in terms of computers and the Internet, but also across the curriculum.

Considering the aforementioned gap in access to classroom experiences in which these computer technologies are incorporated in progressive, pedagogically sound ways, a symptom of institutional racist biases and assumptions, it comes as little surprise that people of color and white people tend to use computers and the Internet for different reasons. A study comparing the ways in which African American people and white people use the Internet shows that African American people are more likely to chat (38% compared with 33%), play a game (48% compared with 33%), listen to music (54% compared with 32%), or pursue other hobbies than white Internet users. In addition, African Americans report going online "just for fun" at a much higher rate than white people. White Internet users are more likely to seek financial, product, or health information online than African American Internet users (Spooner & Rainie, 2000). A different study, lending credence to this conclusion, reveals that Latina(o)s and African Americans are more likely to own a DVD player and a home theater than white people, but much less likely to own a home computer or have home Internet access than white people (Saunders, 2002). These disparities illustrate the results of a systemic lack of social and educational encouragement and support for people of color, particularly African Americans, Latina(o)s, and Native Americans, to pursue professional and educational interests in the information technology industry. Moreover, these differences must be understood in the context of racist education, socialization, and expectations of African American people in the United States and the connected maintenance of power and privilege among white people.

We must also remember that the model minority myth, and in this case, how it relates to computers and the Internet, is harmful to Asian American/Pacific Islanders as well, as it places undue social constraints and expectations on those who may feel alienated if they are not skilled with or interested in these technologies.

Other social, cultural, and political factors demonstrate a lack of support and encouragement for people of color to feel connected to the professional or educational dimensions of Internet technology. As mentioned earlier, the EDA (1999) found that several sociohistorical and sociopolitical barriers contributed to the complex challenge of building technology infrastructure in Native American communities. The first two of these barriers, a distrust of new technologies and a distrust of federal assistance, reflect the present and historical treatment of Native Americans by the U.S. and local governments. A related mistrust has been found in the African American community as well. For example, 72% of African American Internet users are very concerned about businesses and other people obtaining their personal information online, as compared with 57% of white Internet users (Gandy, 2001; Spooner & Rainie, 2000). In addition to reflecting another way in which the symptoms of systemic racism emerge in relation to what many mistakenly refer to as "the great equalizer," this collective distrust raises questions about whose interests are served by the techno-explosion and its social, cultural, and economic impact in the United States (Gorski & Clark, 2001).

Overall, an analysis of available data on the racial digital divide leads to an unmistakable conclusion: Though disparities in rates of physical access to computers and the Internet among racial groups are slowly shrinking (though they are still troublingly prevalent), when we employ a broader, more complex, conceptualization of "access," African American, Latina(o), and Native American people are being left on the sidelines while Asian American/Pacific Islander and white people are socialized and prepared to benefit from an increasingly technology-oriented society.

Sexism and the Digital Divide

In 1960, J. C. R. Licklider, a pioneer computer scientist in the United States, published a paper that constituted the groundwork for the next several decades of research in the field. He introduced concepts that would later be reformulated into the Internet as we know it today. The purposes of the paper, entitled "Man-Computer Symbiosis," were

> to present the concept and, hopefully, to foster the development of man-computer symbiosis by analyzing some problems of interaction between men and computing machines, calling attention to applicable principles of man-machine engineering, and pointing out a few questions to which research answers are needed. (p. 4)

Eight years later, Licklider expanded some of his ideas from "Man-Computer Symbiosis" in "The Computer as a Communication Device," a paper published in a 1968 edition of *Science and Technology*. He opened that paper declaring about the future of telecommunications: "In a few years, men will be able to communicate more effectively through a machine than face to face" (cited by Digital Systems Research Center [DSRC], 1990). Licklider's vision for the future of computer science, for using computing machines to facilitate human interaction, strikingly foreshadows the technocentric and Internet-dominated present.

But equally striking is the malecentric language in his work that, although common scientific practice by male scientists at the time, powerfully foreshadows the gender inequities, sexism, and malecentrism in today's digital community. The word "man," in its singular or plural form, appears fourteen times in the first four paragraphs of "Man-Computer Symbiosis" (Licklider, 1960). So even before the advent of personal computers and the Internet, the language associated with these technologies was uninviting to and exclusive of women. The man who invented the Internet also invented the gender digital divide.

Despite assumptions and contentions otherwise, the gaps continue to grow today. As mentioned earlier, U.S. women use computers and the Internet at roughly the same rate as men. But as with the racial digital divide, girls and women continue to experience techno-sexism in ways that closely mirror gender inequities in the wider society, leading to unique gaps in computer and Internet access. These include (1) gaps in access to support and encouragement to value and enter technology-related fields, (2) gaps in access to non-hostile and affirming computer and Internet content and software, and (3) gaps in access to a welcoming and safe cyberculture (Clark & Gorski, 2002a).

Access to Encouragement and Support

Like the narrowing of the racial gap in physical access to computers and the Internet, the disappearance of this gap between women and men represents an important step forward. However, an appreciation of such strides must be tempered by a consideration of lingering access inequities, if not to the technology itself, then to educational, cultural, and social norms that support and encourage pursuance of technology-related skills and interests. Furthermore, these inequities must be understood in relation to historical and present sexism in education, particularly in those fields, including mathematics, science, and engineering, from which these technologies emerged (Clark & Gorski, 2002a).

For example, of the 24,768 bachelor's degrees in computer and information sciences conferred during the 1996-97 academic year, fewer than 7,000 were earned by women. Fewer than one in six computer and information sciences doctoral degrees were conferred on women (NCES, 1999). In fact, despite popular belief, the number of women earning degrees in computer-related fields has been declining since 1986. Meanwhile, the gap in the percentages of women and men earning degrees in these fields continues to increase (Carver, 2000).

A full understanding of these disparities must begin with an examination of educational and socialization process as early as elementary school. A study conducted by NCES in 2000 highlights differences between boys' and girls' attitudes toward mathematics in fourth, eighth, and twelfth grades. The study reveals that, as girls progress through grade school, they become less likely to respond affirmatively to two statements: "I like mathematics" and "I am good at mathematics" (NCES, 2000). Though the rate of agreement to "I like mathematics" is virtually the same between boys and girls in fourth grade (69% and 70%, respectively), a disparity appears by twelfth grade (53% and 49%, respectively). But of greater concern is the gap in boys' and girls' agreement to "I am good at mathematics," starting at an alarming nine percentage points in fourth grade (70% and 61%, respectively) and increasing to twelve percentage points by twelfth grade (59% and 47%, respectively) (NCES, 2000).

Additional analysis of these data reveals other disturbing dynamics that suggest a pattern of discouragement and a failure to support girls and women in mathematics, and later, in computer science. In both grade-level samples, a bigger percentage of boys agreed with "I am good at mathematics" than "I like mathematics" (70% and 69%, respectively, in fourth grade and 59% and 53%, respectively, in twelfth grade). The reverse was true for girls—in both instances they showed lower levels of confidence in their mathematics abilities than in their fondness for the subject (61% and 70%, respectively, in fourth grade, and 47% and 48%, respectively, in twelfth grade). In addition, the agreement rates for both statements experience a more dramatic drop between fourth and twelfth grade for girls than for boys (NCES, 2000). These analyses support decades of research showing that boys are more likely to be convinced of their own mathematical competence than girls, regardless of interest in the subject.

An examination of patterns of mathematics and science course taking among high school girls and boys reveals similarly disturbing symptoms of institutional sexism. Data collected in 1998 show that, although a considerably higher percentage of high school girls than boys complete first-level advanced mathematics courses (15.7% and 13.2%, respectively), a higher percentage of high school boys than girls complete third-level advanced mathematics courses. The percentage point drop-off in completion of first- and third-level advanced mathematics courses among high school girls is more than three times that for boys (NCES, 2000). Similarly, while high school girls are more likely than boys to complete first-level chemistry and physics courses, boys are more likely to complete second-level courses in these subjects. Again, the percentage point drop-off for girls (30.9) far exceeds that for boys (21.9) (NCES, 2000).

The same pattern emerges in an exploration of computer science course and test taking patterns. By 2000, girls represented only 17% of computer science Advanced Placement test takers and less than 10% of the more advanced AB test takers (American Association of University Women [AAUW], 2000). So by the time students begin seriously considering their futures in the workforce or college, girls are losing confidence and interest in coursework related to technology, while boys are gaining confidence and interest in these fields (Clark & Gorski, 2002a; Kelly, 2000).

And the pattern does not stop there; it grows and intensifies in college and graduate school. Between 1996 and 1997, women earned 16.5% of bachelor's degrees in engineering, 37% of those in the physical sciences, and 46% of those in mathematics. During the same span, women earned 12.2% of all terminal degrees conferred in engineering, 22% of those in physical sciences, and 24% of those in mathematics, all well below the overall rate of conferred terminal degrees earned by women, 40.8%. In following with this pattern, women represented 27% of computer and information sciences bachelor's degrees conferees between 1996 and 1997 (NCES, 1999), a figure that has declined steadily since 1984, when women earned 37% of these degrees (AAUW, 2000). They earned 14.5% of all computer and information sciences terminal degrees conferred during the 1996-97 academic year (NCES, 1999; see Table 2).

Again, these patterns mirror those in the larger society privileging men economically and professionally and socializing women to stand clear of mathematics and the sciences. P-12 teachers, though largely women, have been socialized in this world and thus contribute to these disparities, often without intention. A male student is asked to help the teacher figure out why the television is not working. A female student is rarely exposed to women who contributed to scientific discoveries. Though, taken separately, these examples might be explained away by the suggestion that girls are genetically less interested in technology-related topics than boys, when considered together they form a web of sexist socialization that can have a long-term impact on everybody involved (Bolt & Crawford, 2000). Some information technology scholars argue that lifetimes of this sort of gender socialization lead women to actively resist masculinized technologies for fear that they undermine femininity (Jensen, de Castell, & Bryson, in press; Schofield, 1995).

TABLE 2   *Percentages of math- and science-related degrees conferred on women, 1996-1997*

Field	Bachelor's degrees (%)	Terminal degrees (%)
Engineering	17	12
Physical Sciences	37	22
Mathematics	46	24
Computer Sciences	27	15

Note. Based on data from *Higher education degrees* (NCES, 1999).

This dimension of the gender digital divide translates directly into present and future inequities between women and men in opportunities to participate in an increasingly global, increasingly digital, economy. As a result, women, much less likely than men to have been encouraged to value and pursue technology-related fields throughout their educational and social development, comprise only 20% of all information technology professionals (AAUW, 2000). Overall, the percentages of women pursuing educational interests and professional careers related to computer and Internet technology are dropping (Kramarae, 2001; Stabiner, 2003). Despite, or because of, recently equalized levels of physical access to computers and the Internet between women and men in the United States, this devastatingly more important divide persists, for the most part unexamined (Clark & Gorski, 2002a).

Access to Non-hostile and Affirming Content

Web-based pornography is the most lucrative Internet industry, earning more than $14 billion per year worldwide. In fact, Web pornography is as much as fourteen times more lucrative than its offline counterpart, largely due to its anonymous nature. But like its offline counterpart, Web-based pornography continues to derive from misogynistic dictates and is consumed overwhelmingly by men (Clark & Gorski, 2002a; Rich, 2001). Due to the enormous and growing proliferation of these sites, not only can a single mistyped character or Web site mis-click land an Internet user in a seemingly endless maze of pornographic Web sites and pop-up ads, but it has also become nearly impossible to avoid receiving unsolicited electronic mail advertising pornography (Clark & Gorski, 2002a).

Similarly sexist conditions are evident in another hugely profitable computer industry: video games. Increasingly, video game producers are relying on violent and sexual content to outdo their competitors. This has created a large-scale competition among video game producers to find new and more devastating ways to show death, destruction, and scantily clad women, who are often the "trophies" of male characters. A study by Children Now found that 89% of the top-selling video games contained violent content (Glaubke et al., 2001). Research has consistently shown that girls have little interest in the redundant violence of these games (AAUW, 2000; Gerrard, 1999; Jacobs, 1994; Kelly, 2000). Even games, like the best-selling *Tomb Raider*, that challenge norms by employing a strong, heroic female lead character tend to do so in a highly sexualized way, portraying her as a fantasy object for heterosexual male consumers. These characters typically have grossly exaggerated features of a stereotypical "beautiful" white American woman: an unhealthily small waist, unrealistically large breasts (particularly in proportion to that waist), and long, straight, but never messy, hair (Clark & Gorski, 2002a).

Since the 1980s several software companies have attempted, with varying degrees of effort, to produce games specifically for girls (Gerrard, 1999). Unfortunately, many of these feed into traditional gender roles and stereotypes, including *Barbie Fashion Designer*, the all-time best-selling video game marketed to girls (Glaubke, et al., 2001; Herz, 1999). Other titles, produced by feminist or girl-focused software companies in response to research showing different gaming habits between boys and girls, present strong female characters who use intelligence, not violence, to solve problems. But because boys, who remain the biggest consumers of video games, will not play games designed explicitly for girls, the market remains small and, as a result, an afterthought in the computer software industry (Gerrard, 1999).

Even more disturbing than the presence of sexism in video games is its presence in educational software. A study of a range of mathematics software programs designed for students from kindergarten through sixth grade revealed that only 12% of the gender-identifiable characters were girls or women, and these tended to play stereotypically female roles. And while both male and female students were able to identify games and programs that included male characters, only 6% could name one with a female character (Hodes, 1996).

Another study of thirty of the most used educational software packages showed that only 30% of the characters identified in graphics and text were female. Over 80% of characters with leadership roles were boys and men (Birahimah, 1993). Despite these overwhelming disparities, more than half of classroom teachers report noticing no noteworthy gender patterns in the content of educational software (AAUW, 2000), illustrating the depth and stronghold of sexism in education and society at large.

The usual approach for addressing these problems, adding a few software titles for girls and women, addresses only a symptom of a larger problem—that by every measure, girls and women are excluded from mainstream computer culture, in part by the hostile, sexist content they often find in computer and Internet content. The crucial step moves us beyond differentiating between software designed for girls and boys and developing software that challenges all users to think complexly, creatively, and critically. Video games are an important starting point for this process, as they remain one of the most important and most often-cited entry points into the techno-world, even among information technology professionals (Cassell & Jenkins, 1998). And although video game and software makers contend that their content is based on market demand (which, again, illustrates the need to understand these dynamics within a larger context of sexism), they continually fail to take responsibility for the fact that the mostly male population articulating that demand is defined, in part, by the women-hostile computing environment supported and maintained by their products (Clark & Gorski, 2002a).

Access to a Welcoming and Safe Cyberculture

Gaps in access to nonhostile and affirming content and gaps in access to support to pursue professional and educational paths related to technology have contributed to gaps in access to a welcoming and safe cyberculture for girls and women. Due to these disparities, girls and women looking for points of connection in technology-related fields find few female role models. And those girls and women who do overcome these barriers and pursue techno-interests often find that they must conform to a male centric, male-dominated environment (Clark & Gorski, 2002a). Cyberculture, constructed by men and for men, is at best unwelcoming to girls and women, once again challenging the notion that computers and the Internet are the facilitators of equality, inclusion, and equity that many claim them to be (Gerrard, 1999; Grigar, 1999; Herring, 1993).

For example, despite perceived potential for the Internet to facilitate democratic dialogue free of the sexist dynamics of face-to-face communication between women and men, research shows that these sexist dynamics are reproduced almost perfectly online (Castner, 1997; Herring, 1993). A study of online discussion forums reveals that, while men's posts are more likely than women's to receive explicit responses from both women and men, "women are discouraged or intimidated from participating on the basis of the reactions with which their posts are met when they do contribute" (Herring, 1993, p. 3). In addition, discussion topics introduced by women are less likely than those introduced by men to be taken up by the entire group of participants. And in those cases in which women initially participate equally and assert views that challenge those of men, they are often demonized by men exclaiming frustration with the discussion and threatening to leave the online forum altogether. It would be difficult to know, seeing these results out of context, if the researchers were studying online discussion forums or corporate boardrooms.

Another way that the Internet and computer culture remains unwelcoming to women is the persistent threat of cyberharassment and cyberstalking. While increased media attention of this problem has led to improved training and monitoring by law enforcement agencies, this attention has also led to a heightened sense of insecurity and vulnerability among female Internet users (Brail, 1996; Clark & Gorski, 2002a). According to Stephanie Brail, a survivor of the terrors of online harassment, "stories of online harassment are told and retold partially because of their 'car wreck fascination' factor, but more importantly because we all keenly feel our vulnerability in the new medium of computer-mediated communications" (1996, p. 143). That is not to say that better policing and media coverage is *causing* the divide. But like in the offline world, whether an individual woman or girl experiences harassment, the threat is enough to limit women's mobility through a heightened sense of vulnerability. In some cases, these dynamics are intensified online due to the added trauma of being violated in the supposed comfort and safety of one's home (Crary, 2001). Again, offline sexism is replicated in an online form.

These gaps are reinforced through the media's continual cycling of the message that women are not welcome in cyberculture (AAUW, 2000). A study of technology industry advertisements reveals that men are typically depicted as confident, tech-savvy executives while women are depicted as insecure typists or secretaries (Marshall & Bannon, 1988). Such depictions are consistent with an overall picture of gender socialization and education in the United States and the other gaps that comprise the gender digital divide.

They are also consistent with, and supportive of, economic sexism, as women continue to be excluded from the globalized cybereconomy. Like women who, despite institutional sexism, climb the ranks of corporate America, women who fight their way into technology-related fields and technoeconomic opportunities often find that they have ventured into an unwelcoming, unaffirming, and hostile environment. Meanwhile, men, conditioned to value and pursue technological competence, and more easily welcomed into the cyberculture they created, maintain their power and privilege through technologies many assumed would help dismantle these barriers.

Classism and the Digital Divide

In February 2001, the United States General Accounting Office (GAO) released *Telecommunications: Characteristics and Choices of Internet Users*, exploring a wide array of issues related to technology access and the digital divide. Although its data painted a clear picture of the divide, the summary of the report minimized, if it did not wholly dismiss, an analysis of digital inequities:

> *Some of these findings suggest the existence of a "digital divide" at this time. However, it is often the case that individuals with greater education and income are the first to adopt new technologies, and individuals in rural areas are the last to be reached by the deployment of new telecommunications infrastructure. Because the Internet is still in a relatively early stage of commercial deployment, these socioeconomic and geographic differences in Internet usage are not surprising and may not be long lasting. (p. 7)*

Like the racial and gender divides, the socioeconomic digital divide must be understood in a larger sociopolitical and sociohistorical context. Unfortunately, like most scholarship on the problem, the GAO report fails to consider critical political and economic concerns that underlie existing class structures—conditions that will persist whether or not physical access to computer and Internet technologies is provided (Clark & Gorski, 2002b). Although the GAO report (2001) broadly identifies the contextual frame of the digital divide, suggesting that, "it is often the case that individuals with greater education and income are the first to adopt new technologies" (p. 7), it remains devastatingly silent about the ramifications of this observation. It fails to make the connection between the socioeconomic digital divide and the maintenance of existing structures of class power and privilege in schools or the larger society (Clark & Gorski, 2002b).

The report's summary illustrates at least three ways in which flawed or shallow scholarship on the digital divide perpetuates inequities. Most important, such scholarship, like the GAO's summary, flows from the oppressively erroneous assumption that socioeconomically privileged people are entitled to quicker access to new technologies than socioeconomically disadvantaged people. Second, though the report was produced by the U.S. government, an entity with the power to eradicate such inequities, it fails to problematize the fact that "individuals in rural areas are the last to be reached by the deployment of new telecommunications infrastructure" (GAO, 2001, p. 7). Third, mirroring the lack of depth in much of the digital divide research, the report minimizes the complexity of the socioeconomic divide by measuring it only by rates of Internet usage, quelling any sense of urgency for reform by suggesting that the divide will close "naturally" in due course: "these socioeconomic and geographic differences in Internet usage are not surprising and may not be long lasting" (p. 7). If indeed these differences "are not surprising," it is because of the institutional nature of classism, which the report assumes to be the natural order of things instead of an inequity to be eradicated. Once again, research purporting to address inequities has simply recycled them.

A more complex view of the socioeconomic digital divide includes at least three gaps in computer and Internet access: (1) gaps in physical access to computers and the Internet, (2) gaps in access to teaching and learning experiences that incorporate computers and the Internet in pedagogically sound ways, and (3) gaps in access to relevant Internet content.

Computer and Internet Access

Children living in high-income households are more than twice as likely to have home computer and Internet access than children living in low-income households (Corporation for Public Broadcasting [CPB], 2003). Among adults, less than 25% of those with annual incomes below $25,000 have Internet access at home, compared with more than 75% of those with annual incomes above $50,000 (Cooper, 2002). Particularly troubling is that the socioeconomic group with the most quickly growing rate of Internet access is composed of people in the $100,000 to $150,000 household income range (up twenty percentage points between 2001 and 2002), followed by those in the $150,000-and-up bracket (up fourteen percentage points between 2001 and 2002). Meanwhile, people in households making less than $25,000 per year experienced the smallest increase in Internet access, with only a two percentage point increase between 2001 and 2002 (CyberAtlas, 2002). Consistent with these gaps, people in lower income brackets are much less likely than people in upper income brackets to enjoy high-speed Internet access from home. According to Mark Cooper, Director of Research for the Consumer Federation of America,

> while lower income households have been gaining access to the narrowband Internet, the Internet has not been standing still. Upper income households have moved on to high speed Internet service. The percentage of upper income households (incomes above $75,000) that already take high-speed Internet is as large as lower income households (incomes below $25,000) that take narrowband Internet at home. In other words, lower income households have fallen a full generation of technology behind. (2002, p. 5)

Among households that have never had Internet access, 17.3% identify cost as the primary reason for not connecting, ranking it higher than a lack of time, access to the Internet elsewhere, a lack of computer knowledge, and concerns about children accessing certain online material. When compared with the total sample, nearly twice as many respondents from households with incomes under $15,000 cite cost as their primary reason for not connecting (32.6%). Meanwhile, only 9.4% of people from households with incomes over $75,000 select cost as their primary deterrent. However, challenging assumptions of complacency among the socioeconomically disadvantaged, people from households in the lowest income bracket are less likely to respond that they do not want Internet access—that the primary reason they do not have access is that they do not want it—than the average respondent (26.6% and 30.8%, respectively) (NTIA, 2000). Across all socioeconomic groups, computer and Internet technologies are in high and desperate demand. The problem is that access to these technologies is not equitably distributed (Clark & Gorski, 2002b).

These disparities are also prevalent in schools, despite years of presidential propaganda and programs aimed at dismantling the digital divide. In 1997, the President's Committee of Advisors on Science and Technology (PCAST) determined that, for effective learning, schools must achieve a student-to-computer ratio of four or five to one (1997). But as late as 2001, though the average U.S. public school had achieved a ratio of five students to one computer, the poorest schools had, on average, nine students per computer (NCES, 2001). Likewise, by 2001, 82% of classrooms in schools with low proportions of students on free or reduced lunch plans were wired for the Internet while only 60% of those in schools with high proportions of students on free or reduced lunch were wired (NCES, 2001). Overall, 32% of students from low-income households report using the Internet at school, compared with 47% of students from high-income households (CPB, 2003).

An analysis of students' points of Internet access within schools reveals similarly disturbing classism. Only 14% of low-income students report accessing the Internet from more than one classroom, compared with 28% of high-income students. Likewise, whereas 33% of low-income students report using the Internet from their school library or media center, 48% of high-income students report doing so. All groups of students are more likely to access the Internet in a computer lab than in the library or a classroom, but low-income students (66%) are still less likely to do so than high-income students (70%) (CPB, 2003). So, even when low-income students experience the Internet during school, they are much more likely to do so in a computer lab, where teaching and learning can often feel disconnected from the overall educational experience.

It often has been suggested that the way to bridge this divide is to provide students with computer and Internet access before school, after school, and on weekends. But wealthier schools are more likely than schools with high rates of poverty to provide Internet access to students outside of school hours (NCES, 2001), despite the fact that a far greater percentage of students at wealthier schools already enjoy home access than those at lower-income schools. Once again, these dynamics perpetuate cycles of poverty around which the lines of access are already firmly drawn.

Access to Progressive Learning Experiences

Adding complexity to this inequitable equation, teachers in low-income schools, less likely than their peers at high-income schools to have computers and Internet access in their classrooms, are thus less likely to develop comfort, competence, and confidence with the technology (Clark & Gorski, 2002b). In addition, like teachers in schools with high proportions of students of color, teachers in schools with high proportions of students on free or reduced lunch are less likely than those at high-income schools to have the other resources they need to develop needed technology skills (McAdoo, 2000; NCES, 2002). Whereas 90% of teachers in schools in which less than 11% of the students are on free or reduced lunch report that they have been trained on how to use the Internet in their classroom, only 67% of teachers in schools in which 71% or more of the students are on free and reduced lunch report such training. Likewise, 82% of teachers at high-income schools report assistance in using the Internet in their classrooms compared with 62% of teachers in low-income schools (NCES, 2002; see Table 3).

When this lack of training and support is compounded by the low expectations teachers and the education system in general confer to socioeconomically disadvantaged students, the result is predictable: even when teachers of predominantly low-income students incorporate computers and the Internet into their teaching, they tend to do so in pedagogically unsophisticated ways. Teachers at high-poverty schools are more likely to use these technologies for skills and drills and menial, lower-level thinking skills tasks. Meanwhile, those at low-poverty schools are much more likely to use computers and the Internet for creating instructional materials, conducting research, and

TABLE 3   *Percentage of teachers reporting availability of Internet resource needs by socioeconomic status, 1999*

Students eligible for free or reduced lunch (%)	Classroom access to the Internet (%)	Training in classroom uses of the Internet (%)	Assistance in classroom use of the Internet (%)	Training, assistance, and classroom access to the Internet (%)
Less than 11	57	90	82	48
11-30	60	85	79	49
31-49	56	86	79	44
50-70	44	72	72	33
71% or more	44	67	62	36

Note: Based on data from *Beyond school-level Internet access: Support for instructional use of technology* (NCES, 2002).

engaging students in higher-level thinking skills activities (Fulton & Sibley, 2003; McAdoo, 2000; NCES, 2001; Riel, 2000; Solomon & Allen, 2003). According to Maisie McAdoo (2000),

> the public schools may turn out a group of Internet geeks capable of not just accessing but actually creating vast frontiers of knowledge, but, at the same time, may effectively limit access to a techno-class, narrow and rich and white.

Again, these dynamics do not simply add up to a new inequity for educators to understand and dismantle. Instead, they reflect, recycle, and strengthen existing inequitable pedagogical approaches and assumptions related to socioeconomic status and educational capability (Resta & McLaughlin, 2003). Teachers who incorporate these technologies into the teaching and learning environment are not merely making a short-term instructional decision. They are beginning the process of defining students' points of educational relation and connection to computers and the Internet. If students' only point of connection with these technologies is established through lower-level thinking experiences and rote learning, they are cheated out of both more effective learning opportunities that may or may not include computers and an understanding of the educational, social, and economical potentialities of these media. And while some instructional technologists continue to hail computers and the Internet as equalizing media that recognize no gender, racial, or socioeconomic distinctions, the reality simply reestablishes and reinforces the status quo: rich students are prepared to take full advantage of new technologies and opportunities while poor students are left out of the digital loop (Clark & Gorski, 2002b).

Access to Relevant Internet Content

Even when the necessary infrastructure and supports are in place, socioeconomically disadvantaged Internet users often find that the online world is not created with their needs in mind (Clark & Gorski, 2002b). A 2003 study by The Children's Partnership (TCP), supporting previous findings by TCP (2000), identifies four primary barriers to contributive online information faced by various populations of low-income Internet users in the United States: (1) a lack of pertinent information about their local community; (2) a lack of resources accessible to people who do not read at an advanced literacy level; (3) a lack of meaningful documents in languages other than English; and (4) a general lack of cultural diversity among the resources, information, and documents that do exist. An earlier study estimates that over fifty million people in the United States face at least one of these barriers (TCP, 2000).

According to TCP (2003), the resources low-income Internet users most want to find online are virtually non-existent. These include local job listings (including entry-level positions), local housing listings (including low-rent apartments and homes in foreclosure), and general community information about schools and healthcare services (TCP, 2000; 2003).

Due to the interrelatedness of socioeconomic status and literacy (part of the larger picture of institutional classism of which the digital divide is a contemporary symptom), many low-income Internet users find very few Web sites accessible. Some of the limited-literacy resources they seek, but rarely find, include preparatory materials for working toward a high school equivalency degree, sites that incorporate graphics and other non-text tools for improving reading skills, and computer and Internet tutorials to help them realize the day-to-day benefits of these technologies (TCP, 2003). Nearly all of the limited-literacy Web content (roughly 1% of all Web sites) is created for young children, not adults (TCP, 2000).

Another substantial low-income group still in search of relevant Web content includes those for whom English is not a first or primary language. The resources sought by this group include online translation tools, English language tutorial programs, and general information in multiple languages.

Although several large online information portals including *Yahoo!*, *MSN*, and *Lycos* contain substantial amounts of content in a few languages other than English, most of this content focuses on entertainment as opposed to life needs and human services (TCP, 2003). (The language digital divide will be addressed in greater detail in the next section.)

The fourth barrier that low-income Internet users searching for relevant Web content face is a general lack of cultural diversity among the resources, information, and documents that do exist (Bolt & Crawford, 2000). These users seek platforms to share information and dialogue about heritage and cultural practices and accessible and culture-specific health information. Though information about culture and history is relatively easy to find, content related to health and human services for low-income people is sparsely available (TCP, 2003).

Due to these disparities and other content gaps, even those socioeconomically disadvantaged people who do have computer and Internet access become frustrated with their online experiences more often than socioeconomically privileged people. In fact, over 80% of low-income Internet users report that it takes them too long to find pertinent information on the Web (TCP, 2000). As a result, low-income users, rarely finding themselves or their interests reflected online, remain unlikely to recognize the technology industry or related technology competencies attainable, valuable, or desirable. A long list of technology world millionaires who never finished high school reminds us that one does not need a terminal degree or any formal education to develop deep levels of computer and Internet literacy; the potential for some economic equalization exists through the techno-world. But it remains nearly impossible for low-income Internet users, socialized to believe that cyberculture and the computer world are not and have no plans to be inclusive, to find the motivation to build the necessary techno-literacy for this upward mobility (Clark & Gorski, 2002b).

Linguisticism and the Digital Divide

Most research reports, articles, and books about the digital divide focus exclusively on race, gender, disability, and socioeconomic status, with no mention of access disparities related to language (Gorski & Clark, 2002a). Nearly all of the available research and literature on the relationships between language and Internet access have been produced by marketing firms that help online companies decide who, other than native speakers of English, they should target and how they should use language to target them (CommerceNet, 2000; Global Reach, 2001; Pastore, 1999; Vilaweb, 2000). But even a cursory examination of the data collected and distributed by these firms elicits access and equity concerns, both key elements of the digital divide. The concerns include gaps in access to first language Web content and gaps in access to culturally relevant online resources.

Access to First Language Web Content

Current or potential Internet users who do not speak English or for whom English is not a native language may find the Web to be a very lonely place. Over 57% of Internet users worldwide are native speakers of languages other than English (Global Reach, 2001). However, less than 32% of all Web pages are in languages other than English (Vilaweb, 2000; see Table 4). Over 68% of all Web content is in English despite the fact that first language English speakers comprise only 14% of the world population. Among Web pages not in English, 63% are in other European languages (French, Spanish, Italian, and German, among others). Asian languages dominate Web sites that are not in European languages (Global Reach, 2001). Of the ten most popular Web site languages, seven are European and three are Asian, a situation consistent with and reinforcing the racial digital divide (Gorski & Clark, 2002a; Vilaweb, 2000).

Despite growing language diversity, the language digital divide flourishes among U.S.-based Web sites, too. According to a TCP study of one thousand U.S.-based sites "selected from the best portals on the Web rather than what was typically available" (2003, p. 10), only 2% offer any multilingual content. Nearly all of these sites incorporate some resources in Spanish, but rarely any other languages. All in all, an estimated 70% of Web documents originating in the United States are available only in English, even though more than forty-five million Americans speak languages other than English at home (TCP, 2003).

These disparities, like those related to other dimensions of the digital divide, cannot be understood fully outside the context of existing linguisticism. Just as some schools and other social, cultural, political, and educational institutions are translating materials into a variety of languages, hiring translators, and finding other ways to serve a linguistically diverse society, the linguistic digital divide ensures the maintenance of inequity and exclusion.

TABLE 4   *The twenty most highly represented languages on Web pages, 2000*

Language	Web pages (in millions)	Percentage of total
English	241.250	68.39
Japanese	18.336	5.85
German	18.070	5.77
Chinese	12.114	3.87
French	9.263	2.96
Spanish	7.573	2.42
Russian	5.901	1.88
Italian	4.883	1.56
Portuguese	4.291	1.37
Korean	4.046	1.29
Dutch	3.162	1.01
Swedish	2.929	0.93
Danish	1.375	0.44
Norwegian	1.259	0.40
Finnish	1.199	0.38
Czech	0.991	0.32
Polish	0.849	0.27
Hungarian	0.499	0.16
Catalan	0.443	0.14
Turkish	0.431	0.14

Note. Based on data from *Web pages by language* (Vilaweb, 2000).

Access to Relevant Online Resources

Like socioeconomically disadvantaged Internet users, speakers of languages other than English who find their way online are unlikely to find culturally relevant resources there (Resta & McLaughlin, 2003). As mentioned earlier, the limited non-English content offered by popular Internet portals such as *Yahoo!* tends to focus on entertainment rather than daily life needs. Additionally, commercial sites rarely offer information about human services in a language other than English (TCP, 2003), especially those originating in the United

States. Even *LatinoWeb*, perhaps the most popular Latina(o)-focused Web portal, reinforces these dynamics and the resulting stereotypes. While its links to business, industry, health, and even bilingual education resources are in English, those to shopping Web sites are in Spanish.

Another significant barrier for non-English-speaking Internet users is English-centric search engines. When Internet users seek non-English Web content by employing U.S.-based Web search engines, they often find the results of their searches irrelevant. But even Spanish-language search engines pale in comparison with English-language engines. A TCP study shows that users of English language search engines have a one in five chance of finding information relevant to the search whereas users of Spanish language engines have only a one in eight chance of finding relevant information or resources (TCP, 2003).

Again, these disparities are directly connected to larger issues of linguisticism both in the United States and around the world. Instead of challenging the norms of power and colonialism, the current configuration of the Internet confers additional status and power to English speakers (Gorski & Clark, 2002a). And both of these factors—status and power—are linked by research to educational underachievement among language minorities (Cummins, 2000).

Ableism and the Digital Divide

The Internet is capable of having a profound impact on the lives of people with disabilities. About 48% of adult Internet users with disabilities report that the Internet significantly improves the quality of their lives, a rate nearly double that of adult Internet users without disabilities. Accordingly, adult Internet users with disabilities spend twice as much time online as those without disabilities (Taylor, 2000). According to adult Internet users with disabilities, by providing electronic opportunities to connect with other people, the Internet broadens their "mobility." As a result, they are more likely to indicate that the Internet significantly increases the extent to which they feel connected to the world around them and that it significantly increases their ability to reach out to people with similar interests and experiences than adult Internet users without disabilities (Taylor, 2000).

Unfortunately, while computer and Internet technologies have proven to be valuable resources for those who have access to them, the digital divide remains a wedge between this potential and the digital reality for most people with disabilities (Gorski & Clark, 2002b; Staples & Pittman, 2003). (In most of the digital divide literature, "disability" is conceptualized roughly parallel to the criteria spelled out in the Americans with Disabilities Act [ADA]: (1) He or she has a physical or mental impairment that substantially limits one or more of his/her major life activities; (2) he or she has a record of such an impairment; and/or (3) he or she is regarded as having such an impairment [1990].) Like the race, gender, socioeconomic status, and language divides, the disability digital divide can be observed and understood as a series of access gaps between people with and without disabilities, including (1) gaps in physical access to computers and the Internet, (2) gaps in access to affordable computer and Internet equipment, and (3) gaps in access to a nondiscriminatory and supportive information technology (IT) culture.

Access to Computers and the Internet

People with disabilities, regardless of what disabilities they have, are less likely to own, have home access to, and use computers and the Internet than people without disabilities (Lenhart, 2003; NTIA, 2002). Even when people with disabilities live in a household that has a computer, they are less likely to use that computer or the Internet than people without disabilities in the same situation. Depending on the disability or combination of disabilities, the rates of home computer use among 25- to 60-year-old people with disabilities living in a household with a computer range from 67.8% (for people with multiple disabilities) to 77.1% (for people who have difficulty leaving home), compared with 83.4% for those without disabilities. (Some of the reasons for this will be explored in the following section.) Similarly, between 56.4% (multiple disabilities) and 68% (deafness or severe hearing impairments) of 25- to 60-year-old people with disabilities living in a home with a computer use the Internet, compared with 75.1% of those who have no disabilities (NTIA, 2002).

This gap is equally observable and equally troubling among the younger U.S. population. People who are between 3 and 24 years old and have one or more disabilities are almost as likely to live in a household with a computer than those with no disabilities. However, whereas the rate of home Internet use among 3- to 24-year-old people with disabilities ranges from 26.6% to 32.4%, people without disabilities enjoy a 43.8% rate of home Internet use. Overall, only 38% of U.S. people with disabilities use the Internet, a rate significantly lower than that of the overall U.S. population (58%) (Lenhart, 2003).

The gap in computer and Internet use among people with and without disabilities, like parallel gaps, is a symptom, a point in the cycle of institutional ableism (Gorski & Clark, 2002b). The symptom must be understood in its larger context because that context informs and helps explain the symptom. For example, one reason people with disabilities enjoy less computer and Internet access than people without disabilities is that they are more likely to be unemployed, more likely to live in poverty, and more likely not to have completed high school than people without disabilities (Lenhart, 2003; NTIA, 2002). These factors, like the gap in computer and Internet use and the disability digital divide in general, are symptoms of the larger problem of ableism in the United States.

Access to Affordable Equipment

People with disabilities are more than twice as likely to live in a household with less than $20,000 annual income than people without disabilities (29% and 12%, respectively) (Lenhart, 2003). Add to this the cost of adaptive software and hardware (programs and equipment that help facilitate computer use among people with disabilities such as hearing and visual impairments), and these technologies become inaccessible to many people (Kearns, 2001; Lenhart, 2003). According to Amanda Lenhart's report, *The Ever-Shifting Internet Population* (2003),

> it can cost thousands of dollars to buy adaptive technologies such as magnified or large monitors, hands-free mice and keyboards, and speech synthesizers. A head-mounted mouse can cost 10 times what a normal mouse costs, and a large button keyboard can run 5 times the cost of a normal keyboard. Braille interface machines cost over $3,000, and magnified screens are selling for nearly $2,000. Considering that people with disabilities have, on average, significantly smaller disposable incomes, the cost of adaptive technology in addition to the normal costs of computers and Internet access can be a significant barrier to getting online. (p. 32)

The situation is equally bleak in schools. Public computer labs as well as public and private schools are frequently ill-equipped for students needing adaptive technologies to access computers and the Internet. And even in those schools that have adaptive resources, most teachers do not know how to use them (Ability Hub, 2002).

A lack of access to adaptive technologies renders many people with disabilities entirely locked out of the computer and Internet world. But even those who have overcome these barriers often find that the battle for equitable access has only begun.

Access to a Nondiscriminatory and Supportive IT Culture

If the prohibitive costs of adaptive technology in addition to the regular costs of computers and Internet service are not enough to dissuade people with disabilities from taking full advantage of these technologies, an unsupportive, often discriminatory IT culture often is. For example, because the majority of computer and Internet workshops are not designed to accommodate people who need adaptive resources (Kearns, 2001), people with some disabilities are forced to seek out educational opportunities developed specifically for people with such needs. As a result, they often pay more for technology-related workshops and classes (Gorski & Clark, 2002b). And again, the disability/poverty cycle stays in motion.

Another way ableism leads to an unsupportive and discriminatory IT culture for people with disabilities is based on the assumption that people with disabilities do not need access to educational or professional resources because they cannot, or do not want to, achieve what people without disabilities achieve (Gorski & Clark, 2002b). A study by the International Center for Disability Resources on the Internet shows that many people without disabilities assume that people with disabilities have no reason to access the Internet (Kearns, 2001). The institutionalization of these attitudes leads people with disabilities to be "hesitant to use the Web for fear of seeming ignorant or unknowable" (p. 4). This may be particularly true for people with learning or psychological disabilities, who already often approach new learning experiences with caution.

Following logically but devastatingly from these assumptions is a widespread lack of compliance with disability accessibility standards. Contemporary graphical and script-based Web site designs present great challenges to those producing and using adaptive technologies. Most Web site designers are more interested in flash—in competing with other Web designers to use the newest technologies to impress the newest generation of Web viewers (who can see the screen)—than in accessibility. The U.S. government insists that all of its Web sites follow accessibility standards that make them functional for people with disabilities. Unfortunately, most Web sites do not comply with these standards, making them partially or fully inaccessible to many people with disabilities. Until the culture underlying this thoughtlessness changes and the cyberworld begins to police itself more stringently, a large percentage of the information and resources that some take for granted will be practically nonexistent to others, even if they have access to the Internet.

Many facilities that house public use computers and computer labs, built before the passage of the ADA, are partially or practically inaccessible to people with some disabilities (Gorski & Clark, 2002b), exacerbating these access issues and raising questions about decision makers' understandings of and sensitivity to the inequities faced by the disability community. And due to prohibitive costs and other factors, most public computer locations do not have adequate adaptive equipment for people with disabilities (Kearns, 2001). The assumption again seems to be that certain people are entitled to access to these technologies and that certain others must fend for themselves, or make due with the leftovers—an attitude that simply reflects institutionalized and systemic ableism.

Digital Divide Summary

Considered independently, any one aspect or angle of the digital divide should raise serious concerns about equity, social justice, and cycles of oppression. Considered together, they weave a complex web that mirrors patterns of power, privilege, and oppression in the larger society and the U.S. education system. We will never fully understand the breadth and depth of the digital divide if we do not examine it within these contexts. And we will never end the digital divide if we do not fully understand it.

The first step in this process is to recognize the race, gender, socioeconomic status, language, and disability digital divides as symptoms of racism, sexism, classism, linguisticism, and ableism. The divides are a set of problems that cannot be fixed by introducing more computers or more, or faster, Internet access into an inherently inequitable system. Adding these resources does not transform teachers' attitudes and expectations of different students or the pedagogical gaps that have been observed with or without the presence of these technologies. The digital divide, like gaps in expectations and pedagogy, is sociohistorical, sociopolitical, and sociocultural in nature and can only be dismantled through movements that address it on those levels.

Until the digital divide is understood, critiqued, and addressed though this lens—the lens of multicultural education—these technologies, which some refer to as social and educational equalizers, will at best uphold current inequities and at worst deepen them.

Dismantling the Divide

In order to dismantle the digital divide, we must first develop a progressive understanding of what equitable access might look like. This is a difficult task in a society which remains inaccessible.

What Equitable Access Looks Like

Equitable access, where "access" is broadly defined, and the end of the digital divide can be conceived as those actions that maintain a present and lead to a future in which all people, regardless of race, ethnicity, sex, gender, sexual orientation, socioeconomic class, disability status, age, first language, education level, or any other social, political or cultural identity

1. enjoy equitably safe, comfortable, encouraged and encouraging, non-hostile, and valued physical, cultural, and social access to information technology including software, computers, and the Internet;
2. enjoy equitably safe, comfortable, encouraged and encouraging, non-hostile, and valued physical, cultural, and social access to educational pursuits in technology-related fields including mathematics, science, computer science, and engineering;
3. enjoy equitably safe, comfortable, encouraged and encouraging, non-hostile, and valued physical, cultural, and social access to career and professional pursuits in these technology-related fields;
4. enjoy equitably affordable access to the resources they need, including adaptive and assistive tools, to take full social, cultural, educational, and economic advantage of computer and Internet technology;
5. play an equitable role in determining the sociocultural significance of computers and the Internet and the overall social, educational and cultural value of these technologies; and
6. are guaranteed that these conditions will be constantly monitored, examined, and ensured through a variety of perspectives and frameworks.

Practical Needs for a Systemic Shift

Clearly, these are not minor shifts; they are major changes that call for a systemic shift in thought and action. One way to set that shift in motion is to begin putting measures in place to address the root of the problem (as opposed to adding more computers to a classroom or school). These actions should include the following:

1. Provide more effective and more complete teacher training on how to use computers and the Internet in progressive, pedagogically sound ways.
2. Inform educators at all levels about the complexity of the digital divide so that they can develop strategies for examining their own employments of technology for inequities.
3. Ensure that all students and teachers have equitable access to up-to-date software and hardware, and relevant training for how to use them.
4. Limit costs of computers, Internet access (including high-speed access), and adaptive technologies through sliding scales, government subsidies, or other means.
5. Reestablish government-funded digital divide research that includes all disenfranchised groups and establishes a broader interpretation of "access."
6. Extend government Web accessibility standards to all Web sites, perhaps even charging Web developers who do not comply a tax or fee to help support those who do.
7. Draw on existing legislation such as ADA and Title IX to insist on greater access to computer instruction and courses for people disenfranchised by the digital divide.
8. Place educational technology specialists in every school to provide support and computer and network maintenance.
9. Increase the amount and scope of research on ways in which the application of computer and Internet technologies can enhance teaching and learning for all students.
10. Pressure popular Internet portals like *Lycos* and *MSN* to provide more non-English and limited literacy level content.

If these and other strategies are employed to diversify the online community, the dynamics of supply and demand would necessarily change, at least to some degree, leading to better online content and communities for people of all racial, ethnic, gender, socioeconomic, language, and disability groups.

What Classroom Teachers Can Do

As we work toward these bigger shifts, what can we, as individual classroom teachers, do to minimize the impact of the digital divide on our students and in our practice?

1. When I use computers and the Internet in my classroom, I will make sure that I have included all necessary adaptions for students with disabilities.
2. Recognizing the digital divide as a symptom of larger inequities, I will constantly reflect on the assumptions and expectations I have of different students and how that impacts the relationship I try to develop between them and computer and Internet technologies.
3. I will particularly encourage girls and women, students of color, students with disabilities, students for whom English is not a first language, and socioeconomically disadvantaged students to recognize the educational and professional potential of computer and Internet technologies.
4. Before I incorporate computers and the Internet into a lesson plan or unit, I will reflect on how, or whether, doing so will improve teaching and learning, ensuring that I am not using technology for its own sake rather than to provide the best possible learning experience for my students.
5. I will not replace opportunities for face-to-face communication and interaction with computer-facilitated communication and interaction.
6. I will use technology for progressive, pedagogically sound teaching and learning, not to mimic rote learning techniques.
7. I will engage my students in critical discussions about the digital divide and the role of computers and the Internet in education and the larger society.
8. Until I am sure that all of my students have equitable access to these technologies, I will not assign any homework or out-of-school-time assignments that require computers or Internet access.

Though we should not fool ourselves into believing that these individual shifts will end the digital divide, we have a responsibility for improving conditions for the students in front of us while the larger shifts take shape. However, we must not become complacent. The most important thing we can do to end the digital divide is to confront every instance of racism, sexism, classism, linguisticism, ableism, and any other form of discrimination and oppression, that we witness or experience, or to which we contribute, whether or not it is directly related to computers and the Internet.

Equipped with a deeper understanding of the digital divide and the resulting context in which we teach and learn, we can begin to think more practically about how computers and the Internet can contribute to progressive, engaging, multicultural education.

MORE ON THE DIGITAL DIVIDE

Center to Bridge the Digital Divide

http://cbdd.wsu.edu/

The University of Washington has organized its efforts to dismantle the divide and offers many of the resulting resources through the Center's Web site.

Digital Divide

http://www.pbs.org/digitaldivide/

PBS hosts this companion site to its film on the digital divide. The site includes learning tools and classroom resources.

The Digital Divide Network (DDN)

http://www.digitaldividenetwork.org/

DDN, dedicated to examining the digital divide from a variety of perspectives, brings together the research and work of people from many fields working to end digital inequities.

The Digital Divide's New Frontier

http://www.childrenspartnership.org/pub/low_income/

The Children's Partnership presents its research and commentary on the lack of access to relevant online content for underprivileged and underserved Americans.

EdTech and the Digital Divide

http://www.edchange.org/multicultural/net/net.html

The Multicultural Pavilion's contribution to the international digital divide dialogue includes a fact sheet of important statistics, a model for a new understanding of the divide, and a list of related resources.

References

Ability Hub. (2002). *Assistive technology solutions.* Available: *http://www.abilityhub.com/*.

American Association of University Women (AAUW). (2000). *Tech-savvy: Educating girls in the new computer age.* Washington, DC: AAUW Educational Foundation Research.

Americans with Disabilities Act of 1990 (ADA) Public Law 101-336. July 26, 1990. 104 STAT. 327. (1990).

Bigelow, B. (1999). Why standardized tests threaten multiculturalism. *Educational Leadership, 4* (13), 37-40.

Birahimah, K. (1993). The non-neutrality of educational computer software. *Computer Education, 20* (4).

Bolt, D., & Crawford, R. (2000). *Digital divide: Computers and our children's future.* New York: TV Books.

Brail, S. (1996). The price of admission: Harassment and free speech in the wild, wild west. In L. Cherney & E. Weise (Eds.), *Wired women: Gender and new realities in cyberspace* (pp. 141-157). Seattle, WA: Seal.

Carver, D. (2000). *Research foundations for improving the representation of women in the information technology workforce.* (unpublished paper).

Cassell, J., & Jenkins, H. (1998). *From Barbie to Mortal Kombat: Gender and computer games.* Cambridge: MIT Press.

Castner, J. (1997). The clash of social categories: What egalitarianism in networked writing classroom? *Computers and Composition, 14,* 257-268.

The Children's Partnership (TCP). (2000). *Online content for low-income and underserved Americans: The digital divide's new frontier.* Washington, DC: Author.

―――. (2003). *Online content for low-income and underserved Americans.* Washington, DC: Author.

Clark, C., & Gorski, P. (2002a). Multicultural education and the digital divide: Focus on gender. *Multicultural Perspectives, 4* (1), 30-40.

Clark, C., & Gorski, P. (2002b). Multicultural education and the digital divide: Focus on socioeconomic class background. *Multicultural Perspectives, 4* (3), 25-36.

CommerceNet. (2000). *Worldwide Internet population.* Available: *http://www.commerce.net/research/stats/wwstats.html.*

Cooper, M. (2002). *Does the digital divide still exist?: Bush administration shrugs, but evidence says "yes".* Washington, DC: Consumer Federation of America.

Corporation for Public Broadcasting (CPB). (2003). *Connected to the future: A report on children's Internet use from the Corporation for Public Broadcasting.* Washington, DC: Author.

Cummins, J. (2000). Beyond adversarial discourse: Searching for common ground in the education of bilingual students. In C. Ovando & P. McLaren (Eds.), *The politics of multiculturalism and bilingual education: Students and teachers caught in the crossfire.* Boston: McGraw-Hill.

CyberAtlas. (2002). *Affluent Americans lead web growth.* Available: *http://cyberatlas.internet.com/big_picture/demographics/print/o,,5901_1428031,00.html.*

DeVillar, R., & Fatis, C. (1987). *Computers and cultural diversity: Restructuring for school success.* Albany, NY: State University of New York Press.

Digital Systems Research Center (DSRC). (1990). *In memoriam: J. C. R. Licklider.* Palo Alto, CA: Author.

Economic Development Administration (EDA). (1999). *Assessment of technology infrastructure in Native communities.* Washington, DC: U.S. Department of Commerce.

Fulton, K., & Sibley, R. (2003). Barriers to equity. In G. Solomon, N. Allen, & P. Resta (Eds.), *Toward digital equity: Bridging the divide in education* (pp. 14-24). Boston: Allyn & Bacon.

Gandy, O. (2001). African Americans and privacy: Understanding the black perspective in the emerging policy debate. In J. Barber & A. Tait (Eds.), *The information society and the black community* (pp. 59-73). Westport, CT: Praeger.

Gerrard, L. (1999). Feminist research in computers and composition. In K. Blair & P. Takayoshi (Eds.), *Feminist cyberscapes: Mapping gendered academic spaces* (pp. 377-400). Stamford, CT: Ablex.

Glaubke, C., Miller, P., Parker, M., & Espejo, E. (2001). *Fair play?: Violence, gender and race in video games.* Oakland, CA: Children Now.

Global Reach. (2001). *Global Internet statistics by language.* Available: *http://www.glreach.com/globstats/index.php3.*

Gorski, P. (2002). Dismantling the digital divide: A multicultural education framework. *Multicultural Education, 10* (1), 28-30.

Gorski, P. & Clark, C. (2002b). Multicultural education and the digital divide: Focus on disability. *Multicultural Perspectives, 4* (4), 28-36.

————. (2002a). Multicultural education and the digital divide: Focus on language. *Multicultural Perspectives, 4* (2), 30-34.

————. (2001). Multicultural education and the digital divide: Focus on race. *Multicultural Perspectives, 3* (4), 25-35.

Grigar, D. (1999). Over the line, online, gender lines: E-mail and women in the classroom. In K. Blair & P. Takayoshi (Eds.), *Feminist cyberscapes: Mapping gendered academic spaces* (pp. 257-281). Stamford, CT: Ablex.

Herring, S. (1993). *Gender and democracy in computer-mediated communication.* Available: *http://dc.smu.edu/dc/classroom/Gender.txt.*

Herz, J.C. (1999, February 14). Girls just want to have fun: When it comes to children's software, Barbie rules. *New York Times.*

Hodes, C. (1996). Gender representations in mathematics software. *Journal of Educational Technology Systems, 21* (1).

Jacobs, K. (1994). RoboBabes: Why girls don't play videogames. *The International Design Magazine, 41* (3), 38-45.

Jensen, J., de Castell, S., & Bryson, M. (in press). Girl talk: Gender, equity, and identity discourses in a school-based computer culture. *Women's Studies International Forum.*

Kearns, T. (2001). *Using partnerships to bridge the digital divide within the disability community.* Raleigh, NC: International Center for Disability Resources on the Internet.

Kelly, K. (2000). The gender gap: Why do girls get turned off to technology? In D. Gordon (Ed.), *The digital classroom: How technology is changing the way we teach and learn* (pp. 154-160). Cambridge, MA: Harvard Education Letter.

Kramarae, C. (2001). *The third shift: Women learning online.* Washington, DC: AAUW Educational Foundation.

LatinoWeb. Available: *http://www.latinoweb.com.*

Lenhart, A. (2003). *The ever-shifting Internet population: A new look at Internet access and the digital divide.* Washington, DC: Pew Internet and American Life Project.

Licklider, J. (1960). Man-computer symbiosis. *IRE Transactions on Human Factors in Electronics.* Volume HFE-1, pp. 4-11.

Marshall, J., & Bannon, S. (1988). Race and sex equity in computer advertising. *Journal of Research on Computing in Education, 2,* 115-127.

McAdoo, M. (2000). The real digital divide: Quality not quantity. In D. Gordon (Ed.), *The digital classroom: How technology is changing the way we teach and learn* (pp. 143-153). Cambridge, MA: Harvard Education Letter.

National Center for Education Statistics (NCES). (1999). *Higher education degrees.* Washington, DC: U.S. Department of Education.

————. (2000). *The condition of education: 2000.* Washington, DC: U.S. Department of Education.

————. (2001). *Internet access in U.S. public schools and classrooms, 1994-2000.* Washington, DC: U.S. Department of Education.

————. (2002). *Beyond school-level Internet access: Support for instructional use of technology.* Washington, DC: U.S. Department of Education.

National Telecommunications and Information Administration (NTIA). (2002). *Falling through the net: Toward digital inclusion.* Washington, DC: U.S. Department of Commerce.

————. (2000). *A nation online: How Americans are expanding their use of the Internet.* Washington, DC: U.S. Department of Commerce.

Pastore, M. (1999). *The language of the web.* Available: *http://cyberatlas.internet. com/big_picture/demographics/print/0,,5901_150171,00.html.*

President's Committee of Advisors on Science and Technology. (1997). *Report to the president on the use of technology to strengthen K-12 education in the United States.* Washington, DC: Author.

Resta, P., & McLaughlin, R. (2003). Policy implications of moving toward digital equity. In G. Solomon, N. Allen, & P. Resta (Eds.), *Toward digital equity: Bridging the divide in education* (pp. 211-228). Boston: Allyn & Bacon.

Rich, F. (2001, July 8). Under wraps, porn business thrives in U.S. *The Baltimore Sun.*

Riel, M. (2000). A Title IX for the technology divide? In D. Gordon (Ed.), *The digital classroom: How technology is changing the way we teach and learn* (pp. 161-170). Cambridge, MA: Harvard Education Letter.

Saunders, C. (2002). *Latinos outpace other groups' online growth.* Available: *http://cyberatlas.internet.com/big_picture/demographics/print/0,,5901_1428231,00.html.*

Schofield, J. (1995). *Computers and classroom culture.* Cambridge: Cambridge University Press.

Smerdon, B., Cronen, S., Lanahan, L., Anderson, J. Iannottie, N., & Angeles, J. (2001). *Teachers' tools for the 21st Century: A report on teachers' use of technology.* Washington, DC: National Center for Educational Statistics.

Solomon, G., & Allen, N. (2003). Introduction: Educational technology and equity. In G. Solomon, N. Allen, & P. Resta (Eds.), *Toward digital equity: Bridging the divide in education* (pp. xxvi-xxiv). Boston: Allyn & Bacon.

Spooner, T., & Rainie, L. (2000). *African-Americans and the Internet.* Washington, DC: The Pew Internet and American Life Project.

Stabiner, K. (2003, January 12). Where the girls aren't. *New York Times.*

Staples, A., & Pittman, J. (2003). Building learning communities. In G. Solomon, N. Allen, & P. Resta (Eds.), *Toward digital equity: Bridging the divide in education* (pp. 99-114). Boston: Allyn & Bacon.

Taylor, H. (2000). *The Harris Poll #30: How the Internet is improving the lives of Americans with disabilities.* Creators Syndicate, Inc. Available: *http://harrisinteractive.com/harris_poll/index.asp?PID=93.*

Turkle, S. (1991). Computational reticence: Why women fear the intimate machine. In C. Kramarae (Ed.), *Technology and women's voices* (pp. 41-61). New York: Routledge & Kegan Paul.

Twist, Kade. (2002). *A nation online, but where are the Indians?* Available: *http://www.digitaldividenetwork.org/content/stories/index.cfm?key=215.*

United States General Accounting Office (GAO). (2001). *Telecommunications: Characteristics and choices of Internet users.* Washington, DC: Author.

Vilaweb. (2000). *Web pages by language.* Available: *http://www.vilaweb.com.*

CHAPTER 4

Progressive Pedagogy
and the Internet

There is virtually no evidence that, across the board, computers and the Internet strengthen teaching or student achievement (Lai, 2001; Livingstone, 2003). This raises a myriad of important questions, particularly if part of our goal for education is to provide every student with the best possible teaching and learning experience. Why has there been such an unrelenting push for technocentric education reform without proof that it improves what happens in schools? Why has the U.S. government advocated this agenda through federal legislation such as No Child Left Behind when there is abundantly more evidence that these technologies are driving a deeper wedge between the educational haves and havenots than evidence suggesting they improve classroom practice? Why has much of society seemingly bought into the false promise of the computer-driven education revolution?

Effective teaching and learning emerge from strong pedagogy, high levels of expectations for all students, and a classroom approach that centers and empowers those students, not any particular technology or medium. Without these elements, no single medium or resource, removed from a context of progressive pedagogy, can improve teaching and learning. With these elements in place, all media, including computers and the Internet, can contribute to and support positive experiences for all members of the education community (Goddard, 2002). Glenn M. Kleiman (2000, p. 8), exploring the line between potential and practice, asserts:

Computers are powerful and flexible tools that can enhance teaching and learn-
ing in innumerable ways. However, the value of a computer, like that of any tool,
depends upon what purposes it serves and how well it is used. Computers can be
used in positive ways—such as to help make learning more engaging, to better
address the needs of individual students, to provide access to a wealth of informa-
tion, and to encourage students to explore and create; or in negative ways—such
as to play mindless games, access inappropriate materials, or isolate students.

Kleiman (2000) discusses five myths—misunderstandings about the contemporary relationship between computer technology and K-12 schools in the
United States. These include the following:

1. Putting computers into schools will directly improve learning; more
   computers will result in greater improvements (p. 8).
2. There are agreed upon goals and "best practices" that define how computers should be used in K-12 classrooms (p. 9).
3. Once teachers learn the basics of using a computer, they are ready to put
   the technology to effective use (p. 11).
4. The typical district plan is sufficient for putting technology to effective
   use (p. 12).
5. Equity can be achieved by ensuring that schools in poor communities
   have the same student-to-computer ratios as schools in wealthier communities (p. 13).

The fallacy underlying each of these myths is the same: the assumption
that computers, regardless of software or Web site content (Fulton & Sibley,
2003) and despite whatever else is happening in a given educational context
(Sprague, 1995; Wang, 2002), can improve teaching and learning. Developing
a firm understanding and critical lens regarding this fallacy is a crucial first
step toward considering how, when a progressive, multicultural context exists,
the Internet can contribute to effective and progressive teaching and learning
in the classroom.

Once such an understanding and lens are in place, an exciting vision for the
potential educational role of the Internet emerges. Indeed, the Internet holds
the potential to contribute to progressive education practices in profound ways
that push boundaries, engage students, and empower all learners. In fact, in
many ways, the Internet, when used thoughtfully, can complement multicultural teaching and learning in ways unfathomable without this technology. It

can contribute to the realization of many of the most important principles of multicultural education—principles that define effective teaching and learning—including critical pedagogy, interaction, inclusion, collaboration, engagement, and the flexibility to feed diverse learning styles (Gorski, 1999; Schrum & Bracey, 2003; Weasenforth, Biesenbach-Lucas, & Meloni, 2002).

Critical Pedagogy

As discussed in Chapter 2, one outcome of multicultural education is the development of critical thinking skills among students through the consideration of divergent viewpoints and perspectives. This, in turn, empowers students with more complex decision-making and social action competencies. The philosophical paradigm that centers this approach, in which all members of the educational community apply critical thinking skills to all information they take in, is called *critical pedagogy*. In addition, the critical pedagogy paradigm draws on students' current knowledge and perspectives as building blocks for continued growth and development. As such, it values and centers diversity and divergence in the classroom for the benefit of all learners (Nieto, 2001).

For those who have access to it (physical access, language access, and cultural access), the Internet is an unprecedented compendium of viewpoints and perspectives. The sheer volume and divergence of these lenses immediately challenges any assumption that there is one *correct* way to understand an issue or solve a problem—a key value of critical pedagogy (Tetreault, 2001). For example, when I use *Google.com*, the most popular Web search engine, to search for information on "manifest destiny," I discover that more than 286,000 Web pages at least mention the topic. If I focus only on the first five, I find a wonderfully diverse cross section of perspectives and angles on manifest destiny:

1. *Manifest Destiny*, a page hosted by the Public Broadcasting System (PBS), includes a collection of illustrated essays and interviews that explore various experiences and significances of westward expansion. Perspectives include those of white Americans, Native Americans, and Mexicans.
   http://www.pbs.org/kera/usmexicanwar/dialogues/prelude/manifest/manifestdestiny.html

2. *From Revolution to Reconstruction*, developed and maintained by the Department of Humanities and Computing at the University of Groningen

in the Netherlands, includes this hypertext exploration of manifest destiny. The essays are fairly critical, though the last piece tries to justify the philosophy as "human nature."

http://odur.let.rug.nl/~usa/E/manifest/manifxx.htm

3. *Manifest Destiny: The Dragoon Expeditions,* part of the National Park Services' Fort Scott Web site, provides a government-sponsored historical discussion of expeditions along the Oregon Trail. The content here is neither critical or celebratory of westward expansion or the manifest destiny philosophy.

http://www.nps.gov/fosc/mandest.htm

4. *John L. O'Sullivan on Manifest Destiny* is an online version of O'Sullivan's powerful 1839 speech exclaiming the U.S. destiny to fill the continent with its freedoms and equality. Its lack of attention to westward expansion's impact on Native Americans' freedom and equality illustrates a lack of philosophical and actualized consistency in the application of supposed U.S. rights, making it a great individual tool for encouraging critical thinking skills.

http://www.mtholyoke.edu/acad/intrel/osulliva.htm

5. *Manifest Destiny 1841-1848,* a site created in 1998 by a high school teacher, is a directory of links to other online resources on the topic.

http://www.madbbs.com/~rcw/US_History/manifest_destiny.htm

So, in the first five listings of a *Google.com* Web search, I have located a perspective representing the U.S. government's Park Services, a view from an organization outside the United States, a first-person account from a staunch supporter of manifest destiny thought, diverse contemporary perspectives from a fairly liberal media outlet (PBS), and a directory of links assembled by a fellow educator—a wonderfully diverse cross section of ideas.

Of course, it is not an exhaustive set of perspectives. In fact, after looking through the top thirty *Google* listings, I find none that provides a strong, historic, Native American perspective on the topic. And, as a critical pedagogist, I must constantly take into account ways in which schools perpetuate inequalities (Gay, 1995); for example, I must always consider whose voices I am missing simply because most of the world's population cannot afford the technology. I must remember that my employment of the Internet does not in and of itself constitute critical pedagogy or multicultural education, though when used with a critical consciousness, it can contribute to a classroom in which these philosophies are already in place (Goddard, 2002).

Equally important to the divergence of perspectives to be found online, then, are the ways in which the technology is incorporated into the teaching and learning process. If I simply print two or three of these Web pages and distribute them to my students as "other" or "alternative" perspectives on manifest destiny, I recycle a hierarchy of voices and re-center the textbook. Instead, I might ask my students to work in groups, scouring the Web to find a variety of perspectives and viewpoints on manifest destiny. They will then build on each other's current knowledge as they collaboratively develop strategies for finding the information. They will broaden their knowledge base by reviewing similarities and differences among a variety of views and accounts of the topic. And they will develop a deeper critical consciousness as we discuss why such divergence exists and why people with different experiences and histories might have experienced manifest destiny in different ways. How did you decide which search terms to use? Which resources did you assume were more accurate? How might political leanings have influenced the angle of the resources you found? Why did your textbook authors fail to include some of the information you found? Whose voices have you still not heard? What connections can you make between these historical accounts and news reports in newspapers, magazines, or television programs?

Without question, the Internet introduces opportunities for such activities unlike any other educational medium. In the spirit of critical pedagogy, students on the Internet can become researchers with greater access to more voices and perspectives than afforded by textbooks, films, or entire libraries (Weis et al., 2002). But too often, these opportunities are unrealized because the context for critical pedagogy—an appreciation for divergent perspectives (without an ultimate centering of a single perspective), the empowerment of students, and the encouragement of critical thinking—is not present (Arvedson, 2003). When it is present, a few guidelines can help ensure that my use of the Internet is consistent with an overall critical, multicultural, pedagogical framework:

1. I must encourage my students to think critically about all information they receive, including that which they read on the Internet. Who built this Web site? Who funded it? Whose voice is it pushing forth?
2. I must not diminish voices and perspectives from resources other than the textbook by referring to them as "alternative" or "other" perspectives.

3. I must empower students by facilitating experiences in which they develop their own questions and learning strategies and use the Internet to facilitate the process of researching those questions.

4. I must challenge my students to consider the significance of the divergent perspectives available online and the relationship between these perspectives and their own.

5. I must openly discuss the digital divide with my students so that they recognize and reflect critically about whose voices are absent from the online education milieu.

In many ways, these are some of the guidelines I should follow regardless of whether or not I use the Internet in a particular lesson plan. But because of the relative novelty of the Web in education, and because of the mounting pressure to incorporate it into my teaching, I sometimes find myself failing to apply the same criteria to the Internet that I apply to textbooks, films, and other media. If I follow these guidelines within a larger critical pedagogy framework, the Internet can be an invaluable teaching and learning tool in my classroom.

Interactive Teaching and Learning

Interactive teaching and learning refers to the facilitation of social, cultural, and intellectual interaction among students and between students and educators. Such interaction encourages skills and competencies in teamwork and collective problem solving, but also gives students an opportunity to learn from one another's experiences, perspectives, and ideas.

During the recent emergence of digital educational media, the term "interactive education" has taken on new meanings. Today, the term often is used to describe the relationship between a person and a piece of software or the hypertext nature of Web sites. For example, by this conceptualization of interaction, if I can click my way around a Web site or a piece of software, controlling, to some degree, the relationship between myself and the content I see on the screen, I am experiencing interactive learning. Although this conceptualization of interactive learning can help make education software and Web sites more engaging for users and provide opportunities for more active learning than a textbook, it ignores the fundamental power of Internet technology—its ability to facilitate interaction among people (Meyer, 2003). It is this ability that separates the Internet from other educational media.

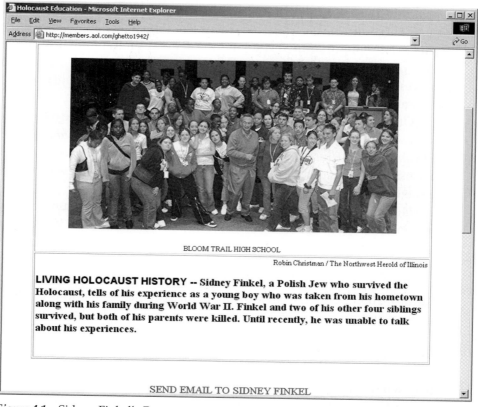

Figure 4.1   Sidney Finkel's Page
http://members.aol.com/ghetto1942/

For example, the Internet helps connect students to first-person sources, many of whose experiences and perspectives are, accurately or inaccurately, described in students' textbooks. Most Web site authors, unlike their textbook author counterparts, provide an e-mail address or other contact information so that teachers, students, and others can contact them with questions, challenges, critiques, or requests for further information. Some, such as Holocaust survivor Sidney Finkel of *Sidney Finkel's Page* (see figure 4.1), specifically encourage site visitors to send their questions and comments.

A similar brand of sites facilitates the exchange of questions, answers, and discussion among students and experts in a variety of fields. *Ask Dr. Math* provides this service for those seeking expert opinions or exchanges regarding mathematics. *Pitsco's Ask an Expert* connects teachers and their students to professionals in fields ranging from acting and entertainment to law and business. These sites give students a new way to investigate a problem and may be particularly important for students who have a budding interest in a profession or field to which they see few points of connection. In addition, the process of posing their question and interacting with somebody "in the field" enhances communication skills.

Other Web sites are designed to host discussion and dialogue on a certain topic. Some, including the *Multicultural Pavilion's Community Dialogue Forums*, facilitate interaction among educators through Internet media such as discussion boards and electronic mail discussion groups. These forums are discussed more fully in Chapter 6.

Dozens of sites, created to encourage and facilitate intercultural and international dialogue among students, also exist (Talleyrand & Kitsantas, 2003). Many of these sites, including *International Kids' Space*, connect students around the world with pen pal programs and various interactive features—an excellent opportunity for multicultural pedagogy (Cushner, McClelland, & Safford, 2003). Others provide outlets for specific populations of students to interact and find support. For example, *Youth! Be Yourself* hosts e-mail discussion outlets in which gay, lesbian, bisexual, transgender youth, and heterosexual allies share experiences regarding schools, parents, coming out, and related issues. This and similar resources can be particularly powerful for students from oppressed groups who have not found a community of support within their schools or classrooms. While written pen pal programs have been in place for generations, these sites, by connecting students who would otherwise have no opportunity to interact and learn from each other, facilitate more immediate—sometimes even real time—exchanges.

Several Web sites are virtual portals for teachers who want to forge international or intercultural relationships with other teachers in order to arrange interaction among their students. *Intercultural E-mail Classroom Connections* has been among the most popular and successful of these, helping facilitate hundreds of pen pal and project exchanges across national and cultural boundaries.

Each of these types of interactive opportunities can contribute to a multicultural teaching approach by actively engaging students in their own learning, encouraging the exchange of critical questions and thought, and expanding students' understandings of various issues by supplementing textbook learning with first-person international and intercultural perspectives and ideas. But again, it is up to teachers, the facilitators of learning, to promote a learning context in which students understand the significance of these opportunities and take full advantage of them.

Inclusive Teaching and Learning

Inclusivity is another fundamental principle of multicultural teaching and learning. Many educators understand inclusive teaching to be the incorporation into the curriculum of diverse voices and perspectives that represent the students in the classroom. These educators implement inclusive teaching by seeking out materials and curricular resources that are representative of their students' experiences. Multicultural education takes this brand of *representational* inclusion a step further. If education is to be truly student centered, then the experiences, perspectives, voices, and ideas of the students must be brought to the fore in the learning experience. In the context of this *critical* inclusion, students as well as teachers are given opportunities to share their voices and to learn from one another's experiences.

The Internet can help facilitate critical inclusivity through forums that engage teachers and students in virtual global communities with a diversity of peers. Web sites like *Cyberkids* and *KidsCom* include sections created specifically to engage a cross section of student voices through problem-solving and interactive activities. These sites do not simply facilitate discussion and the exchange of ideas. They include students' voices in one another's learning process by sponsoring an exchange of creative writing, art, and dialogue on various learning topics.

Other Web sites are designed to publish history essays, news, and current events stories from the perspectives of students for consumption by other students. *KidPub* is an international, intercultural online repository of more than forty thousand stories written by kids for kids. Students can visit these sites to learn from and with their peers—a strategy that can often enhance the perceived relevance of a lesson or unit, a key characteristic of multicultural curriculum (Grant & Sleeter, 1998). But these sites also turn a student of poetry into a poet and a student of current events into a contributor to news media by providing a platform through which students can share their work. Again, the Internet, unlike any other educational medium, provides opportunities to broaden the extent to which the student becomes the teacher, the expert, and a central voice on relevant issues—a crucial aspect of multicultural teaching and learning (Tetreault, 2001; Wiburg, 2003).

Similar opportunities to share and publish writing exist for educators. *Voices of Women* publishes the writing of women on a variety of topics, encouraging them to learn from one another through "sharing their stories." *Voices!*, the *Multicultural Pavilion's* electronic poetry journal, is a growing collection of poetry and prose about diversity and identity issues written by and for educators. Other online journals, such as the *Electronic Magazine of Multicultural Education (EMME)*, publish educators' articles about multicultural teaching practice.

The key to inclusive teaching and learning with the Internet, like that for interactive teaching and learning, is to take full advantage of the Internet's capability to connect people with people. Find ways to engage students in the give-and-take of learning, in the process of sharing, and in doing so, in the discovery of their own voices. Again, this is most effectively accomplished in an educational context in which the principle of critical inclusivity is already established. If we have not helped construct such a learning environment, we cannot reasonably expect our students to feel confident sharing their voices on cue. But if used within the context of a critically inclusive classroom, the Internet provides wonderfully diverse, international, and engaging opportunities to bring a diversity of student voices to the fore in the learning process.

Collaborative Teaching and Learning

Collaborative and interdisciplinary teaching and learning have been introduced, attempted, and reintroduced for decades. It is not uncommon for a group of teachers from a particular school to combine efforts in an attempt to connect lessons from subject to subject. For many teachers who struggle with time constraints and burnout, resource sharing and collaborative planning become vital aspects of day-to-day teaching operations. For others they become avenues for modeling constructive and cooperative bridge building across cultures, the sort of cooperative spirit we hope to build in our students (Cushner, McLelland, & Safford, 2003). Collaborative teaching also helps us demonstrate the interconnectedness of subjects we teach—relationships often lost in highly structured, disconnected curricula (Brooks & Brooks, 1999).

The Internet has the potential to expand the breadth and depth of collaborative opportunities for educators (Fiske, 2000; Shcrum & Bracey, 2003; Sleeter & Tettegah, 2002; Trewern & Lai, 2001). One's network of collaborative partners is no longer constrained to those educators and activists in one's immediate department, school or community. Electronic mail, in and of itself, infinitely expands my access to colleagues, not only in the United States, but from around the world. Through my Web site, the *Multicultural Pavilion*, I receive correspondence from every continent—electronic mail from teachers who are similarly interested in equity and social justice in education. Without access to these technologies, the ease of this communication would disappear and the ongoing dialogues among colleagues would slow considerably. (Again, the convenience I experience because of my access to this technology gives me pause to consider that most of the world's teachers do not have access to computers or the Internet. As a multicultural educator, I must always think critically about such discrepancies, as discussed in Chapter 3.)

Many of the online collaborative relationships among educators are initially developed through interactive discussion forums such as e-mail discussion groups, Web-based discussion boards, and chat rooms. Such forums provide educators and others opportunities to interact and dialogue interculturally on a variety of education-related topics. Many, such as the *MCPAVIL-ION* e-mail discussion forum, focus specifically on multicultural education. While most educators use these forums solely for dialogue or to share information about new materials and resources, others use them to build coalitions or to collaborate on the development of new resources. (These forums are discussed in more detail in Chapters 6 and 7.)

A plethora of Web sites facilitate collaborative relationship building and resource sharing. *Nicknacks Telecollaborate Site* and *PedagoNet* (see Figure 4.2) are global collaboration sites through which educators share lesson plans and effective curriculum transformation projects or download or print these resources for their own use. *Nicknacks* also includes discussion forums as well as a service that connects individual educators who are looking for similar collaborative or interactive opportunities. Dozens of prominent education sites function as portals for the exchange of lesson plans; most popular sites for teachers have a searchable database of such resources. While these Web sites obviously expand my instructional resource base, they also introduce opportunities for me to learn from colleagues, to grow as an educator by considering my colleagues' approaches to teaching and learning.

Other Internet technologies enable teachers to connect their students in real time to those in another city, state, or country. Stephen Zsiray, Jr., Zan Burningham, and Lori McGivern describe one such project that connected kids in Utah and New York:

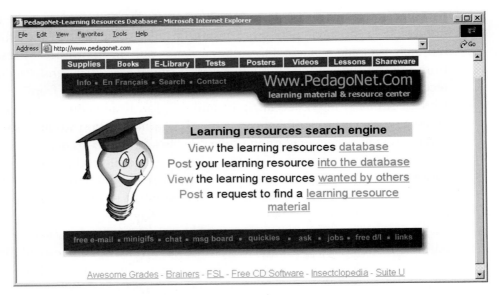

Figure 4.2   Pedago Net
http://www.pedagonet.com

> *Capital punishment is a hot topic in the United States, with cases being heard by the U.S. Supreme Court and some prominent executions during the past few years. Why not help students connect to discuss and debate this issue as a means of understanding the U.S. Constitution and the Bill of Rights? The project we came up with illustrates successful use of technology to bridge distance; build a teacher and student partnership; and enhance the study of the death penalty using discussion, writing, and artistic expression. (2003, p. 42)*

This collaborative team facilitated a host of online discussions and exchanges among students, employing videoconferencing technology. The students, though a couple thousand miles apart, could hear one another, see one another, and experience the sort of collaborative learning that would have been impossible just a few years earlier.

Student Engagement

An active learning pedagogy dedicated to student engagement abandons educational approaches that rely solely on the transmission of knowledge from teacher to student through lecture. In an active learning environment, students are encouraged to learn by doing, exploring, examining, and experiencing. They actively engage in the learning experience as opposed to scrambling to take notes as the teacher imparts a string of facts and figures most likely unrelated and inconsequential to the students' lives and experiences.

Student engagement can be achieved in a variety of ways, and in fact must be achieved in a variety of ways in order to engage a variety of learning styles. Students learn about poetry by writing poems. They learn math skills by working in teams to develop and solve relevant problems they find in their daily lives. They learn about gravity by formulating and conducting science experiments. These and other active learning experiences take more than pencil speed and memorization skills. They call for, and result in, self-motivation, creative thinking, and confidence. And most important to the multicultural education framework, these activities engage students in their own learning process instead of alienating them from that process through a one-way transmission of information (Cunningham & Billingsley, 2003; Rivera & Poplin, 1995).

Two dimensions of Internet media make it a valuable resource for the creation and facilitation of active educational teaching and learning opportunities for students. The multimedia nature of the World Wide Web supports the use of a large range of media within a single Web site including photography, graphic art, music, sound effects, animation, video, and text. Students who learn better through, or are more intrigued by, text and still pictures can choose to focus on the sections of a particular Web project that contain those elements. Those who prefer sound and animation, or any other combination of effects, can spend their time at those sections of the site. In a multimedia environment, students have the opportunity to learn about a particular topic in a variety of ways using a variety of senses. Many sites, including *A Cybrary of the Holocaust*, take full advantage of the multimedia nature of the Web. Combining text documents, photographs, discussion forums, and other resources, Alliance for a Better Earth, the site's sponsor, caters to a diversity of learning styles and attracts a wide array of potential users to its site.

The second dimension of Internet media that helps make it a potentially contributive tool for student engagement is the hypernavigability of the Web. To be more specific, it is its hypernavigability that makes the Web what it is: a virtual "Web" of hypertext pages that allow users to jump from place to place through cyberspace. With a simple mouse click, a student can take a virtual trip from her or his own classroom to Antarctica, a rain forest, outer space, or almost any other worldly or non-worldly place. Or she or he can visit *Exploratorium* and participate in an array of science learning activities. What is important in either case is the employment of student choice and creative thinking in the learning process.

Paul Hamill (2002) describes specific ways in which student choice and critical thinking are enhanced through student projects in the humanities programs at Ithaca College:

> Faculty now take students on virtual tours of nineteenth-century Paris, Japanese temple complexes, and even fourteenth-century Chartres as pilgrims would have encountered it. A Web site on medieval literature offers the text of Sir Gawain and the Green Knight as a digital palimpsest, bejeweled with illustrations of medieval objects and costumes, with links to bibliographies and glossaries. Another course asks students to design, curate, and present to peers a virtual gallery, whose exhibits are drawn from thousands of available digital images. In a writing course, students compare their draft theater and cinema reviews with an archive of previous students' reviews and professional examples, eventually "publishing" for peers online. An English course makes little-known eighteenth century women's and servants' narratives available to students, whose annotations and commentaries will benefit successor classes... What these courses offer students is deep, complex, and multifaceted. Students "own" their work as they rarely could in traditional modes of instruction, achieving explorations that our library holdings could not have supported. (p. 50)

His observations are supported by a decade of studies that show that technology-rich classrooms tend to be more student centered and engaging than classrooms in which technology is sparingly used (Cifuentes, 1997; Ertmer, Ross, & Gopalakrishanar, 2000; Hancock & Betts, 1994; Norum, Grabinger, & Duffield, 1999).

But again, as with the aforementioned principles of multicultural education, if I fail to incorporate the technology in multicultural-minded ways, it can just as quickly become a tool for the reconstitution of traditional forms on unengaging, uncollaborative, and exclusive teaching and learning (Gay, 1995). I must dedicate to empowering my students to take advantage of the full potentials of the Web, whether allowing them to find their way around a particular educational site or facilitating their development of research questions and methods for answering those questions. In fact, if I develop this consciousness in them through my day-to-day construction of teaching and learning, they will likely recognize these potentials of the Internet with greater scope than I do—many already seem to have surpassed my understanding of the Internet and its powers. The question, even for veteran multicultural educators, is whether we are willing to empower our students to take control of their learning. If we are, the Internet will prove to be a contributive educational tool.

Personal and Professional Development

Too often, a conversation about multicultural education becomes so tightly focused on the transformation of curriculum and pedagogy that too little attention and energy are spent on the most important transformation of all: the transformation of self. As I mentioned earlier, the most important first step toward actualizing multicultural education is initiating (and continually engaging in) a process of examining our own perspectives, prejudices, and biases, and how these are informing our teaching practice and thus affecting our students' learning. Though individual teachers find different but equally effective ways to engage in this process, an important early step for all involved is to develop a diverse, supportive cohort of colleagues with whom to share ideas and experiences, dialogue about specific issues, and collaboratively challenge each other to grow as educators and people. This can be a challenging task, especially for people who have been unable to find a supportive cohort within their own school's walls.

The Internet's interactive nature and relatively wide use are resulting in new opportunities for educators to find support, dialogue, professional development, and even mentoring, whether or not it is readily available in one's school. Discussion forums, like many of those previously mentioned, are becoming communities of support in themselves, sometimes facilitating relationship building among hundreds of teachers from around the world. Participants not only share resources and ideas, but also challenge each other and work together toward the examination and elimination of personal prejudices.

Once again, this illustrates that while the Internet can be a powerful tool even when viewed and experienced simply as a compendium of electronically presented print resources, its most important educational and multicultural contributions are those that connect people with people. In that single potentiality, it transcends the capabilities of many other educational media, making it one of the most potentially contributive, multicultural complements to effective, transformative, multicultural education.

With these pedagogical understandings in place, we can begin to think more practically about the ways in which the Internet can support multicultural curriculum transformation.

MORE WEB SITES

INTERACTIVE TEACHING AND LEARNING

Ask Dr. Math

http://mathforum.org/dr.math/

The *Math Forum Project* hosts this interactive feature encouraging teachers and students to send questions about math or math problems to its expert panel of mathematicians. The site includes a list of frequently asked questions and an archive of previous questions and answers.

Ask an Expert

http://www.askanexpert.com/

Pitsco Innovative Education has recruited the most complete and diverse collection of content area experts on the World Wide Web. The site allows teachers or students to direct questions regarding virtually any topic to an expert in the respective field.

Chabad-Lubavitch in Cyberspace: Ask Your Question

http://www.chabad.org/question.htm

This Web site, hosted by the educational wing of the Lubavitch movement, devotes an entire section to encouraging users to send questions on Judaism. When I wrote in, I received a reply in less than one week.

Eyewitness: A North Korean Remembers

http://www.kimsoft.com/korea/eyewit.htm

This is the online autobiography of Kim Young Sik, a North Korean participant in the Korean War. Read his stories and e-mail him questions and comments.

iEARN

http://www.igc.apc.org/iearn/

The *International Education and Resource Network* connects young people around the world to work collaboratively on social and global issues. The site includes a section for teachers and descriptions of current projects.

Intercultural E-mail Classroom Connections

http://www.iecc.org

The IECC (Intercultural E-Mail Classroom Connections) mailing lists are provided by St. Olaf College as a free service to help teachers and classes link with partners in other countries and cultures for e-mail classroom pen pal and project exchanges.

International Kids' Space

http://www.kids-space.org/

Kids' Space is an interactive site where kids can share their stories, poetry, and art with peers around the world.

Meet Matthew

http://www.ozemail.com.au/~ctech/matt.htm

Matthew Slater, an 8-year-old Australian student, created this page to help educate other students about his disability, cerebral palsy. He invites visitors to e-mail him with questions and comments.

Multicultural Community Forums

http://www.edchange.org/multicultural/pavboard/pavboard.html

The *Multicultural Pavilion*'s discussion forums host ongoing dialogues about multicultural education theory and practice.

NASA Quest: Meet NASA People

http://quest.nasa.gov/services/people.html

NASA gives students and teachers opportunities to interact with a variety of folks under several programs, including "Space Team Online," "Women of NASA," and "Space Scientists Online."

Sidney Finkel's Page

http://members.aol.com/ghetto1942/

This Holocaust survivor tells his story and invites discourse from his site's visitors.

YOUTH! Be Yourself

http://www.youth-guard.org/youth/

The Youth lists establish an outlet for gay, lesbian, bisexual, transgender, questioning, and straight supportive youth ages 25 and under to talk with one another concerning such issues as coming out, schools, parents, friends, relationships, and other gay-related and non-gay-related youth issues.

INCLUSIVE TEACHING AND LEARNING

Band-Aides and Blackboards

http://www.faculty.fairfield.edu/fleitas/contents.html

Joan Fleitas is using the Web to collect and share the educational experiences and stories of students with chronic illnesses. This site educates other students, as well as teachers and parents, on chronic illness and related experiences.

Cyberkids Connection

http://www.cyberkids.com/

According to this site, "*Cyberkids Connection* is a virtual place for kids to share their thoughts and ideas with each other. *Cyberkids* readers from all over the world are forming a global community which we hope will improve communication and understanding among all the world's kids."

Electronic Magazine of Multicultural Education

http://www.eastern.edu/publications/emme

EMME, published twice per year, includes articles and essays about promising practices and prevailing theories and philosophies related to multicultural education.

Flat Stanley Project

http://www.enoreo.on.ca/flatstanley/

Flat Stanley connects teachers and students in an international, interactive activity by facilitating the exchange of writing and cultural learning through a unique educational process.

International Gallery of Children's Art

http://www.papaink.org/gallery/home/index.html

PapaInk, a nonprofit organization dedicated to youth art, exhibits its archives of art by children around the world. Exhibit your students' work!

KIDLINK

http://www.kidlink.org

This site facilitates global dialogue among grade school children; it also offers resources to encourage parent/teacher collaborations.

KidPub

http://www.kidpub.org/kidpub/

Children can add their writing to this collection of over thirty-six thousand stories submitted by young writers around the world. *KidPub* also includes a twenty-five-thousand-member pen pal exchange.

Kids Philosophy Slam

http://www.philosophyslam.org/

Based in Minnesota, this online program gives students a voice by hosting and posting "slam" events. Students "sound off" on contemporary philosophical and social issues such as the war in Iraq.

KidsCom

http://www.kidscom.com

KidsCom is an educational, interactive Web site for kids with plenty to keep them busy learning. Kids can "go around the world" and learn about different cultures, share their experiences and stories through different interactive forums, or play games (mostly educational) online.

New Mobility's Interactive Café

http://www.newmobility.com/

Hosting over a million visitors per month, *Interactive Café* is "the largest community on the web for disability news, resources and culture." It includes an online magazine, a message board, chat rooms, links, a jobline, and a bookstore.

Voices! Multicultural Poetry Journal

http://www.edchange.org/multicultural/voices.html

Part of the *Multicultural Pavilion*, this site publishes poetry and other creative writing about multicultural issues, identity, and teaching, written by and for educators. Submit your writing or learn from the experiences and voices of others.

Voices of Women Journal and Resource Guide

http://www.voiceofwomen.com/

Voices of Women is an online collection of writing by women about, and for, women. Users are encouraged to contribute to the project by sharing their stories, information, and resources.

COLLABORATIVE TEACHING AND LEARNING

Active Learning Principles for Schools

http://learnweb.harvard.edu/alps/

The Harvard Graduate School of Education hosts this virtual community of educators working toward the improvement of schools. It includes several tools for helping educators reflect on their teaching practice, then connect with other educators engaging in the same process.

ATLAS Communities

http://www.atlascommunities.org/

Through electronic newsletters and online chats, *ATLAS* is connecting teachers at all levels who are determined to work together to forge new learning atmospheres and greater understanding of student needs among educators and academics.

Collaborative Lesson Archive

http://faldo.atmos.uiuc.edu/CLA/

Sponsored by the University of Illinois, this is an archive of lesson plans ranging across all subjects and age groups. Search for a lesson on a particular topic or for a specific age group, or submit one of your own.

The Creative Connections Project

http://www.ccproject.org/

CCP links teachers and students around the world for collaborative learning experiences.

The Global Schoolhouse

http://www.gsn.org/

Global Schoolhouse hosts several collaborative teaching opportunities to engage students in the active exchange of information and knowledge. Current projects include "Field Trips," in which students exchange information about trips they have taken and "Online Expeditions" in which students take virtual trips to destinations around the world.

Multicultural Passport

http://jeffcoweb.jeffco.k12.co.us/passport/index.html

Compiled and created collaboratively by teachers from Jefferson County, Colorado, *Passport* is a compendium of multicultural lesson plans and ideas arranged by subject area, region, and identity dimension.

Nicknacks Telecollaborate Site

http://telecollaborate.net/

This site facilitates educational collaboration among teachers in the "global" classroom by sponsoring a lesson plan exchange, hosting discussion forums, and connecting educators who are looking for collaborative opportunities.

Pedagonet

http://www.pedagonet.com

This site includes a database of lesson plans from which to pull or to which to contribute resources as well as a forum for requesting plans and resources on a specified topic.

Tapped In

http://www.tappedin.sri.com/

This community of over seven thousand K-12 teachers works collaboratively on a wide range of projects. They work together toward professional development and develop collaborative programs between their students.

Teachers Helping Teachers

http://www.pacificnet.net/~mandel/

Scott Mandel hosts this site connecting educators through shared resources including book reviews, a chat line, and lesson plans.

STUDENT ENGAGEMENT

Bats

http://www.cccoe.k12.ca.us/bats/welcome.html

This thematic unit was designed by a team of educational technology experts from the Contra Costa County Office of Education and the Oakland Unified School District. It combines literature, art, text, and photographs to present an interdisciplinary look at bats.

Cybrary of the Holocaust

http://remember.org/

This online multimedia library of resources on the Holocaust includes photographs, a teacher's guide, poetry, and myriad other diverse learning experiences for both teachers and students.

Educational Web Adventures

http://www.eduweb.com/adventure.html

EduWeb has developed a series of online learning adventures to support the idea that active learning is based on adventure and discovery. All of these multimedia adventures are organized into categories, including "Art and Art History," "Science and Nature," and "History and Geography."

Exploratorium

http://www.exploratorium.edu/

This online museum of "science, art, and human perception" includes hundreds of interactive multimedia exhibits. Students can step through activities that cover the science behind various sports, the solar cycle, robots, and seemingly everything else.

Frogland

http://allaboutfrogs.org/

This site combines a host of active learning opportunities for students to learn about frogs. The multimedia resources on *Frogland* include a virtual dissection kit, audio clips of frog sounds, and a collection of photographs.

FunBrain.com

http://www.funbrain.com/

FunBrain combines a plethora of active learning opportunities for K-8 students, including games, puzzles, and fun quizzes. The site incorporates audio and visual effects to actively engage students in learning about a wide range of topics.

GLOBE

http://www.globe.gov/

The *GLOBE* (Global Learning and Observations to Benefit the Environment) program consists of a worldwide network of students and teachers from more than eight thousand schools in more than eighty-five countries who work with scientists to learn more about environmental issues. Participants are asked to research, observe, and report on environmental conditions near their schools. That information is then shared with the rest of the network via the Web.

The Greatest Places

http://www.sci.mus.mn.us/greatestplaces/

The Greatest Places is an impressive collection of tours and information about the Amazon, Greenland, Iguazu, Madagascar, Namib, Okavango, and Tibet. Tours include various text features and photographs as well as discussion forums.

The Heart: An Online Exploration

http://sln.fi.edu/biosci/heart.html

The Franklin Institute Science Museum developed this "tour" of the heart that includes stops at all related parts of the body's machinery. A textual history of heart science, along with relevant learning activities, is also included.

Life from Antarctica 2

http://quest.arc.nasa.gov/antarctica2/

Students can take part in a virtual expedition to Antarctica through the text, film, graphics, and photography of this multimedia site. A discussion forum and teacher resources are also provided.

The Odyssey

http://www.worldtrek.org/odyssey/index.html

Viant sponsors this worldwide trek, guiding students and teachers around the world from the comfort of their own classrooms. The trek is broken into stages, taking participants through India, China, the Middle East, Africa, Latin America, and Mexico.

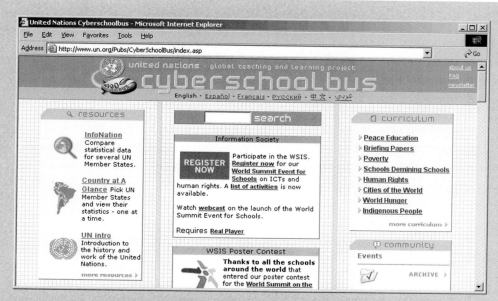

Figure 4.3   United Nations Cyber School Bus
http://www.un.org/Pubs/CyberSchoolBus/index.asp

United Nations Cyber School Bus (see Figure 4.3)

http://www.un.org/Pubs/CyberSchoolBus/

The United Nations hosts this colorful multimedia virtual tour page. The site also includes lessons and materials on global issues, human rights, the environment, and poverty.

United States Holocaust Memorial Museum Online Exhibitions

http://www.ushmm.org/exhibits/exhibit.htm

The United States Holocaust Memorial Museum in Washington, D.C., remains one of the most popular and powerful museums in the country. This collection of multimedia online exhibits includes "The Holocaust in Greece," "Life Reborn: Jewish Displaced Persons, 1945–1951," "Hidden History of the Kovno Ghetto," and "The Nazi Olympics: Berlin 1936."

Virtual Creatures

http://k-2.stanford.edu/

The National Science Foundation funds this new project from Stanford University. Through three-dimensional images, online adventures, and graphic-aided visualizations, students can literally examine creatures inside and out.

Virtual Field Trips Site

http://www.field-trips.org/vft/index.htm

This site serves as a "jumping off point" for many virtual fieldtrips to areas and events of geographic and scientific interest including deserts, volcanoes, hurricanes, and oceans.

Willoughby Wanderings

http://schoolcentral.com/willoughby/

Educators at Willoughby Elementary School created this set of interactive educational math resources. The site includes brainteasers, math drills, and tutorials.

For more Web sites related to this chapter, please visit the Multicultural Education Supersite *at*

http://www.mhhe.com/socscience/education/multi/sites/chapter4.html.

References

Arvedson, P. (2003). Teaching teachers to use online information. *Academic Exchange Quarterly, 7* (1), 57-60.

Brooks, J. & Brooks, M. (1999). *In search of understanding: The case for constructivist classrooms.* Alexandria, VA: Association for Supervision and Curriculum Development.

Cifuentes, L. (1997). From sages to guides: A professional development study. *Journal of Technology and Teacher Education, 5* (1), 67-77.

Cunningham, C., & Billingsley, M. (2003). *Curriculum webs: A practical guide to weaving the web into teaching and learning.* Boston: Allyn & Bacon.

Cushner, K., McClelland, A., & Safford, P. (2003). *Human diversity in education: An integrative approach.* Boston, MA: McGraw-Hill.

Ertmer, P., Ross, E., & Gopalakrishanan, S. (2000). Technology-using teachers: How powerful visions and student-centered beliefs fuel exemplary practice. In J. Willis, B. Robin, & D. Willis (Eds.), *Technology and teacher education annual* (pp. 1519-1524). Charlottesville, VA: Association for the Advancement of Computing in Education.

Fiske, S. (2000). A new culture of teaching for the 21ˢᵗ century. In D. Gordon (Ed.), *The digital classroom: How technology is changing the way we teach and learn.* Cambridge, MA: Harvard Educational Letter.

Fulton, K., & Sibley, R. (2003). Barriers to equity. In G. Solomon, N. Allen, & P. Resta (Eds.), *Toward dgital equity: Bridging the divide in education* (pp. 14-24). Boston: Allyn & Bacon.

Gay, G. (1995). Mirror images on common issues: Parallels between multicultural education and critical pedagogy. In C. Sleeter & P. McLaren (Eds.), *Multicultural education, critical pedagogy, and the politics of difference* (pp. 155-189). Albany, NY: State University of New York Press.

Goddard, M. (2002). What do we do with these computers?: Reflections on technology in the classroom. *Journal of Research on Technology in Education, 35* (1), 19-26.

Gorski, P. (1999). The multiculturality of the world wide web. *Multicultural Perspectives, 1* (3), 44-46.

Grant, C., & Sleeter, C. (1998). *Turning on learning: Five approaches for multicultural teaching plans for race, class, gender, and disability.* Columbus, OH: Merrill.

Hancock, V., & Betts, F. (1994). From the lagging to the leading edge. *Educational Leadership, 51* (7), 24-29.

Hamill, P. (2002). Humanists among their machines. *Liberal Education, 88* (4), 48-53.

Kleiman, G. (2000). Myths and realities about technology in K-12 schools. In D. Gordon (Ed.), *The digital classroom: How technology is changing the way we teach and learn* (pp. 7-15). Cambridge, MA: The Harvard Education Letter.

Lai, K. (2001). Professional development: Too little, too generic? In K. Lai (Ed.), *E-learning: Teaching and professional development with the Internet* (pp. 7-19). Dunedin, New Zealand: University of Otago Press.

Livingstone, S. (2003). Children's use of the internet: Reflections on the emerging research agenda. *New Media and Society, 5* (2), 147-166.

Meyer, K. (2003). The web's impact on student learning: A review of recent research reveals three areas that can enlighten current online learning practices. *Technological Horizons in Education Journal, 30* (10), 14-19.

Nieto, S. (2001). School reform and student learning: A Multicultural Perspective. In J. Banks & C. Banks (Eds.), *Multicultural education: Issues and perspectives* (pp. 381-401). New York: John Wiley & Sons.

Norum, K., Grabinger, R., & Duffield, J. (1999). Healing the universe is an inside job: Teachers' views on integrating technology. *Journal of Technology and Teacher Education, 7* (3), 187-203.

Rivera, J., & Poplin, M. (1995). Multicultural, critical, feminine, and constructive pedagogies seen through the eyes of youth: A call for the revisioning of these and beyond: Toward a pedagogy for the next century. In C. Sleeter & P. McLaren (Eds.), *Multicultural education, critical pedagogy, and the politics of difference* (pp. 221-244). Albany, NY: State University of New York Press.

Schrum, L., & Bracey, B. (2003). Refocusing curricula. In G. Solomon, N. Allen, & P. Resta (Eds.), *Toward digital equity: Bridging the divide in education* (pp. 129-143). Boston: Allyn & Bacon.

Sleeter, C., & Tettegah, S. (2002). Technology as a tool in multicultural teaching. *Multicultural Education, 10* (2), 3-9.

Sprague, D. (1995). ITS changing teachers' paradigms. In J. Willis, B. Robin, & D. Willis (Eds.), *Technology and teacher education annual* (pp. 273-277). Charlottesville, VA: Association for the Advancement of Computing in Education.

Talleyrand, R., & Kitsantas, A. (2003). Multicultural pedagogy and Web-based technologies. *Academic Exchange Quarterly, 7* (1), 23-28.

Tetreault, M. (2001). Classrooms for diversity: Rethinking curriculum and pedagogy. In J. Banks & C. Banks (Eds.), *Multicultural education: Issues and perspectives* (pp. 152-173). New York: John Wiley & Sons.

Trewern, A., & Lai, K. (2001). Online learning: An alternative way of providing professional development for teachers. In K. Lai (Ed.), *E-learning: Teaching and professional development with the Internet* (pp. 37-55). Dunedin, New Zealand: University of Otago Press.

Wang, Y. (2002). When technology meets beliefs: Preservice teachers' perception of the teacher's role in the classroom with computers. *Journal of Research on Technology in Education, 35* (1), 150-161.

Weasenforth, D., Biesenbach-Lucas, S., & Meloni, C. (2002). Realizing constructivist objectives through collaborative technologies: Threaded discussions. *Language, Learning and Technology, 6* (3), 1-27.

Weis, T., Benmayor, R., O'Leary, C., & Eynon, B. (2002). Digital technologies and pedagogies. *Social Justice, 29* (4), 153-167.

Wiburg, K. (2003). Factors of the divide. In G. Solomon, N. Allen, & P. Resta (Eds.), *Toward digital equity: Bridging the divide in education* (pp. 25-40). Boston: Allyn & Bacon.

Zhirsay, S., Burningham, Z., & McGivern, L. (2003). Connecting curriculum across the continent: Students on opposite sides of the United States use technology to connect and debate a controversial topic: The death penalty. *Learning and Leading with Technology, 30* (6), 42-44.

CHAPTER 5

Web Integration and Multicultural Curriculum Transformation

Curriculum transformation is an essential dimension of the holistic reexamination of schools and schooling that constitutes multicultural education. As discussed briefly in Chapter 2, a multicultural approach to curriculum transformation is based on a dedication to providing accurate and complete understandings of all covered topics and subjects. This chapter examines how teachers can complement these efforts through the integration of Web resources at various stages in the transformation process.

Multicultural Curriculum Transformation

The accuracy and completeness of a multicultural curriculum is achieved, in part, through the inclusion of diverse perspectives and sources, including those representing traditionally unheard or underrepresented individuals or groups (Davidman & Davidman, 1997; Grant & Sleeter, 1998; Tetreault, 2001). For example, instead of relying on textbooks and other sources written from a purely European perspective to learn about the lives and experiences of Native Americans, students in a multicultural education classroom have access to first-person sources and other resources that relate history from the perspective of Native Americans. In a multicultural curriculum, teachers and students challenge notions of a central voice or perspective on any topic and critique the tendency to center the perspective of middle- and upper-class, heterosexual, white men.

The "transformation" in multicultural curriculum transformation refers to the extent to which current curricular policies and structures must change in order to establish a curriculum free from a blatant reliance on Eurocentric and malecentric perspectives, voices, and worldviews. An often-cited illustration of the deepness of this problem is a "fact" that establishes the foundation for many American history textbooks and classes: "Christopher Columbus discovered America." This statement begins the story of U.S. history from a perspective not shared by most Native American historians, or by other historians who recognize how it immediately elevates the status of European explorers over that of the people who already occupied the land those explorers supposedly "discovered." Examples also can be cited readily from Language Arts classrooms, where literature textbooks have made strides in including the work of women and some U.S. people of color, but are often still limited to conceptualizing "classic literature" in a way that excludes that from entire continents such as South America, Asia, and Africa. Math and science curricula are not free from the need for transformation, either. Recent studies show only slight improvements in the malecentric language and illustrations in these textbooks. These examples, coupled with the fact that many teachers and students, socialized in a society in which mainstream information sources have always centered people in power at the expense of other people, do not recognize the need for change, illustrate how deeply entrenched inequitable curricula remain.

Ultimately, multicultural curriculum transformation will accomplish several critical educational and social equity tasks, improving teaching and learning for all students. First, in a multicultural curriculum, a diversity of voices, experiences, and perspectives are woven seamlessly into current frameworks of knowledge, providing fuller understandings of all subjects (Grant & Sleeter, 1998). Presented with a wider array of resources, students will develop greater critical thinking skills that can then be applied to future learning both inside and outside the classroom. They will also develop a fuller understanding of the world around them—one not limited by a single conception of people, places, and events.

Second, because a multicultural curriculum directly and honestly addresses social justice issues including racism, sexism, classism, and heterosexism, students develop deeper awareness and consciousness about the world around them and their roles as agents of social change. Schools who, through mission statements and other official documents, claim to prepare students to actively participate in a democracy or to be active members of society begin to fulfill that promise by initiating discourse about the power and privilege dynamics that define contemporary society. Students, in turn, build critical awareness, but they also learn how to negotiate difference and understand their roles in larger society more thoughtfully (Davidman & Davidman, 1997; Grant & Sleeter, 1998; Weis, et al., 2002).

In addition, multicultural curricula are structured to be relevant in the lives of contemporary students. Research indicates that students learn much more effectively when they construe that concepts in a lesson are relevant to their lives outside of school. Because multicultural curricula center students, they provide constant points of relevance and meaning to students' everyday experiences.

Some argue that multicultural curriculum transformation is anti-white and anti-male, or that it is purely a political movement that caters to the interests of students of color. Others suggest that it is an attempt to improve the self-esteem of girls and people of color. To the extent that this encompasses a greater inclusion of historically unheard or underrepresented voices and perspectives, and to the extent that this will lead some students to learn about the world in such a way that they feel more personally connected to the educational process, increased self-esteem for some students is a likely and important outcome of a multicultural curriculum. Still, those posing these arguments fail to take into account the massive injustice that traditional, Eurocentic, and malecentric curricula represent in the learning process of all white students and male students, as well as female students and students of color. Multicultural curriculum transformation is not simply an attempt to stroke the self-esteem of certain groups of students. It is a movement to reexamine, reassess, and ultimately transform the curriculum so that it provides all students with more accurate and complete understandings of all subjects as well as a critical social consciousness (Nieto, 2001).

The Internet, by expanding teachers' collaborative opportunities and access to an enormous set of diverse resources and materials, can play an important role in these curriculum transformation efforts (Sleeter & Tettegah, 2002). But the use of these technologies is not analogous to equitable or effective curriculum (Livingstone, 2003; Schrum & Bracey, 2003). If not used in multiculturally progressive ways, they will simply reproduce whatever curricular structure is already in place in a given classroom context (Munoz, 2002).

Steps Toward Web Integration for Curriculum Transformation

Unfortunately, as teachers and administrators attempting to effect change have come up against increasingly constraining barriers, multicultural curriculum efforts have been slow to materialize into large-scale transformation. As state and federal standards of learning and high-stakes tests become more and more strongly identified as primary measures of achievement, not only for students, but also for teachers, administrators, schools, and school districts, teachers feel less and less empowered to employ creative means for making their curricula more inclusive, relevant, and accessible to all students. Without strong institutional support or multicultural curriculum development training, most teachers find the idea of transformation daunting. Add to this the continually looming pressures of the next round of test scores, and the seemingly simple, early-stage curriculum transformation task of adding new information to the current curriculum can be a formidable challenge for teachers, even with the new educational opportunities presented by the Internet and other electronic educational media.

Regardless of these and other challenges, most teachers dedicated to the ideals and principles of multicultural education find some way—some entry point—to begin working toward multicultural curriculum transformation. As some of us move toward a fully transformative curricular model and others start with more manageable, small-scale curricular changes, a series of stages or steps toward multicultural curriculum transformation can be identified. The role of the Internet in multicultural curriculum transformation can best be understood in the context of these steps. And, when combined with the pedagogical notions (active, interactive, inclusive, and collaborative teaching and learning) described in Chapter 4, the existence of countless Web resources may make the process easier and more fruitful.

The following steps toward multicultural curriculum transformation, though based primarily on my personal experience, also were inspired, in part, by similar models by James Banks (1993) and Peggy McIntosh (2000). A brief description of each step is followed by a discussion on how the Internet can contribute to a teacher's progress along the curriculum transformation continuum toward the ultimate goal—social action and awareness.

Step One: Recognizing and Naming the Curriculum of the Mainstream

The curriculum of the mainstream is Eurocentric and malecentric. It fully ignores the experiences, voices, contributions, and perspectives of members of non-dominant groups in all subject areas. All educational materials including textbooks, films, and other teaching and learning tools present information in a purely Eurocentric, malecentric format. This stage is harmful both for students who identify with mainstream culture and for those from non-dominant groups. While the impact imparted by this brand of curriculum to the latter is easily identified—lack of connection points and inability to see oneself reflected in the curriculum, continual curricular socialization away from one's heritage and historic self, a lack of relevance to one's own existence, and general invalidation (Nieto, 2001)—it also has negative consequences for the former. According to Banks (1993) it

> reinforces their false sense of superiority, gives them a misleading conception of their relationship with other racial and ethnic groups, and denies them the opportunity to benefit from the knowledge, perspectives, and frames of reference that can be gained from studying and experiencing other cultures and groups. (p. 195)

Moreover, the curriculum of the mainstream is incomplete and dishonest, failing to provide all students an understanding of the complexity of the world around them. In doing so, it inhibits critical thinking and reaffirms the status quo by centering the voices and experiences of those who continue to enjoy power and privilege in and out of the school system, including white people, men, the wealthy, heterosexual people, and Christians. For instance, returning to a previous example, if I study the story of Christopher Columbus from a purely Eurocentric perspective, I cannot possibly develop a significant understanding of the full impact he had on the world, much less the experiences of the rest of the people in that world.

Just as the Internet can help teachers move along the multicultural curriculum transformation continuum, it can help other teachers maintain and reinforce the curriculum of the mainstream. If I browse the Web looking for sources that merely support the textbook's perspective or that include the sort of malecentric images and language for which science texts have long been criticized, or if I do not encourage my students to seek out sources that offer different and equally valid perspectives, I have failed to move beyond the curriculum of the mainstream, despite my attempts to incorporate Internet technology. We are reminded once again that the Internet, in and of itself, is not the solution. Instead, it is a tool that can only be as progressive as the person employing it.

Step Two: Heroes and Holidays

Teachers at the heroes and holidays stage "celebrate" differences by adding information or resources about famous people and cultural artifacts from various groups into the mainstream curriculum. Bulletin boards frame posters of Martin Luther King, Jr., or Amelia Earhart, and teachers plan special celebrations for Black History Month or Women's History Month. Students learn about "other cultures" from a surface orientation: costumes, food, music, and other tangible cultural items.

The primary strength of this stage is that it reflects some effort on the teacher's part to diversify the curriculum by providing materials and knowledge outside the mainstream culture. Another benefit is that the heroes and holidays approach is fairly easy to implement with minimal requirements on the teacher's part for acquiring new knowledge or reorganizing the existing curriculum.

But what may seem like strengths of the heroes and holidays step are better described as symptoms of the weaknesses of the approach. By focusing celebratory attention on non-dominant groups outside the context of the rest of the curriculum, the teacher further defines these groups as "the other" or lesser than those represented by mainstream culture. When we start to talk about "other cultures," we must ask ourselves, "Other than what?" The designation of "the other" assumes a central perspective or way of being. In addition, curricula at this stage fail to address the real experiences of non-dominant groups, instead focusing on the accomplishments of a few heroic characters. Students may learn to consider the struggles of non-dominant groups as "extra" information instead of important knowledge in their overall understanding of the world. And they are still left with little understanding of the overall experiences and contributions of people of color, women, and other historically oppressed groups of people. Another weakness of this approach is that special celebrations such as Black History Month are often used to justify the exclusion of real inclusion from the mainstream curriculum. As a result, it trivializes the overall experiences, contributions, struggles, and voices of non-dominant groups, again reestablishing the white, male, heterosexual, upper-middle-class, Christian centrality of the curriculum.

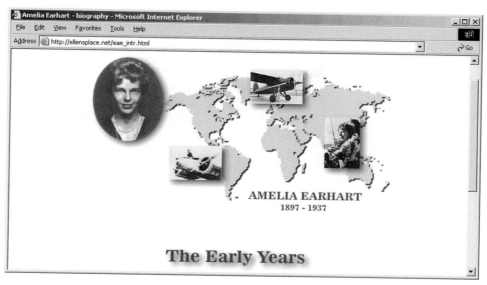

Figure 5.1   Amelia Earhart — Biography
http://ellensplace.net/eae_intr.html

With these weaknesses in mind, teachers who, with little support, are trying to break the cycle of a mainstream curriculum may find the heroes and holidays step a necessary point of departure. They might integrate resources by or about famous African American, Asian American, Latina(o), or Native American people, or by or about white women, into the existing curricular structure. The Web can be a contributive tool in this process, as it provides access to sites like *Malcolm X: A Research Site, Amelia Earhart—Biography* (see Figure 5.1), and others that highlight famous historical figures. Although a better scenario would involve weaving these resources directly into the curriculum instead of separating them as celebrations or monthly acknowledgments, they can be used at this step toward multicultural curriculum transformation to complement textbooks and other traditional educational media that fail to include information about people from historically underrepresented groups.

Step Three: Integration

At the integration step, teachers move beyond heroes and holidays, introducing substantial materials and knowledge about non-dominant groups to the existing curriculum. For example, the teacher might add books by people of color or by women to her or his collection. She or he might include a unit that covers the role of women in World War II. A music teacher decides to add slave hymns or songs from Africa to her or his repertoire. At the school level, a course on African American history might be added to the overall curriculum. In all cases, the roles of individuals from non-dominant groups are explored within the context of specific events, subjects, and topics. The major strength of the integration stage is that it transcends special celebrations to deal with real issues and concepts, more closely tying diverse perspectives and understandings into the rest of the curriculum.

Still, important and severe weaknesses remain. New materials and units incorporating underrepresented voices and perspectives become secondary sources of knowledge as textbooks and the meat of the curriculum are still based on a Eurocentric and malecentric orientation (Banks, 1993). Many textbook authors reach this step by incorporating the well-recognized shaded boxes, highlighting who we are led to believe are the one or two women or the one or two African Americans who contributed to the subject at hand. In addition, at the integration step, all content is delivered from a Eurocentric, malecentric perspective. For example, while a teacher includes a Native American perspective in an overall understanding of the European "settlement" of North America (starting, of course, with the faulty assumption that there is a singular Native American perspective), this content is presented in relation to the European experience. Some of the information changes, but the focal point remains the same. Despite these weaknesses, the integration step is a step toward progress for those attempting to push beyond a heroes and holidays curricular orientation and toward a fuller multicultural curriculum.

A popular genre of educational Web sites consists of those that explore particular subjects or topics from the perspectives and through the voices of people whose contributions to the respective field or event are underrepresented or completely ignored by mainstream curricular materials. The *Disability Social History Project* draws from the voices of people with disabilities to offer a largely untold angle of U.S. history. *First Nations Histories* presents historical information from the perspectives of an almost exhaustive list of North American First Nations tribes. *Women Come to the Front* highlights the experiences of women journalists and photographers during World War II. These and similar sites can enhance the efficacy of current classroom materials by adding separate but new dimensions of understanding to those accessible through textbooks or other media of limited scope.

As educators push through the integration step, working to incorporate diverse perspectives and critical thought more deeply and broadly into the curriculum, we approach the first truly transformative step toward curriculum reform: structural reform.

Step Four: Structural Reform

New materials, perspectives, and voices are woven seamlessly together with current frameworks of knowledge to provide new, more complete, and accurate levels of understanding. Teachers dedicate themselves to continually expanding their knowledge base through the exploration of various sources from various perspectives and share that knowledge with their students. Students learn to view events, concepts, and facts through various and equally valid and valued lenses. "American History" includes African American History, Women's History, Asian American History, Latino American History, Native American History, History of People with Disabilities, Lesbian, Gay, and Bisexual History, and all other previously differentiated fields of knowledge. The contributions, roles, voices, and perspectives of all groups are considered in all subject areas without the use of special topics or events.

When textbook producers reach this step of curriculum transformation, the immediate need to seek out a more representational cross section of complements to books currently in use will ease. History books will seamlessly integrate a diversity of voices and perspectives. But until this happens, it remains the responsibility of individual teachers and curriculum designers to expand their own sense of accuracy and completeness in curriculum through diverse and divergent sources. When a dedication to this principle has been achieved, the Internet can be an important tool in the transformation process.

The structural reform step is the first truly transformative step in the multicultural curriculum transformation process in that it completely abandons the Eurocentric, malecentric, anybody-centric curricular model instead of affecting smaller changes by building around it. Teachers who have reached this step can incorporate educational Web sites that serve as, or house, first-person sources or documents, not as additional or alternative resources, but as primary resources for teaching and learning. Sites like *The Holocaust: A Tragic Legacy* and *The Louisiana Holocaust Survivor's Homepage* cease to be supplements to a central textbook's information on World War II. Instead, they become two among many contributing perspectives, woven fully together to form a more complete, accurate, holistic understanding of the people and events that define that era in history. The poetry and prose of sites like *My China* become an integral part of the literary canon as opposed to a special, separate literature topic. In addition, sites like the *Fourth World Documentation Project* and *Civil War Women*, both collections of primary and first-person documents, can play an important role in the structural reform stage as teachers rethink the value of single-perspective textbooks. These resources are not supplements. Rather, they are primary learning resources.

As a group, these and similar Web sites can provide a valuable start in the amassment of diverse resources. It then becomes the pedagogical responsibility of the individual teacher to employ them in a way that presents a multidimensional, holistic picture of the given topic of study.

Step Five: Social Action and Awareness

Building upon the reconceptualizations of the structural reform step, important social issues, including classism, ableism, racism, sexism, and heterosexism, are directly addressed in the social action and awareness curriculum. Additionally, the voices, ideas, and perspectives of the students regarding these and other topics are brought to the fore in the learning experience, the students themselves becoming the central multicultural classroom resources.

At this step, the textbook is viewed as a single perspective among many and the relevance of its limitations, along with those of other educational media including Web sites, are explored and discussed. Who wrote this book? Why? Who developed this Web site? Who funded its creation? Whose voices are being heard and whose are being excluded? Teachers who have reached the social action and awareness step of curriculum transformation consider these questions and discuss them with their students. Students emerge with a new level of critical and social awareness.

Additionally, at this step, the Web is seen not just as an informational medium, but also as a tool for the generation of knowledge and learning opportunities. Interactive and dialogue-facilitating sites (see Chapters 4 and 7) allow students and teachers to engage in discussion and story-sharing across borders and boundaries. Digital technologies allow students to build and tell their stories through contemporary audiovisual media (Weis, et al., 2002).

Teachers who have reached this step might also consider working with their students to create original Web sites through which to share their own stories and perspectives with others who have Internet access around the world. For example, students from South Kingstown High School learned by doing and engaged in their own learning experience by interviewing women who participated in World War II, then creating a Web site creatively titled *What Did You Do in the War, Grandma?* to make those interviews available to others. These projects empower students to participate in, as opposed to simply observing, the sociocultural and sociopolitical discourses in contemporary society, helping prepare them to be active and engaged citizens (Pittman, 2003).

Though most teachers—even those with a strong dedication to the ideals and principles of multicultural education—remain at an early step in the process of curriculum transformation, each of these steps represents positive movement toward the realization of a fully transformed classroom. The Internet should never be seen as the multicultural savior or *the way* to move teachers from one step to the next. However, combined with the pedagogical approaches discussed in Chapter 4 and the strategies for implementation described in the following chapters, the Internet and its endless kingdom of resources, materials, and interactive opportunities can be one of many solidly contributive tools for a multicultural approach toward transforming curricula.

MORE WEB SITES

CURRICULUM TRANSFORMATION

Advice for Effective Curriculum Transformation

http://www.diversityweb.org/Digest/W97/advice.html

This article was published in *Diversity Digest*, the print and online journal of *DiversityWeb*. It provides useful starting points and steps for transforming higher education curricula at an institutional level.

Curriculum Guidelines for Multicultural Education

http://www.muskegon-isd.k12.mi.us/multicultural/curriculum.htm

Prepared by the National Council for the Social Studies, this position statement lays out clear guidelines for the development and implementation of multicultural curricula. Though it is specific to social studies, the piece does a good job of framing the need for, and an approach for, an overall transformation of the curriculum.

Equity Checklist for Standards Based Classrooms

http://www.terc.edu/wge/checklist.html

Christina Perez shares a reflective checklist of concerns and considerations for equity in math classrooms.

Multicultural Supersite: Curriculum Transformation

http://www.mhhe.com/socscience/education/multi/curriculum.html

McGraw-Hill's *Multicultural Supersite* includes this collection of informational resources that help teachers and teacher educators develop theoretically and pragmatically sound conceptualizations for multicultural curriculum transformation. Among the resources available on the site are a "Q&A" through which the site author answers users' questions about multicultural curriculum and an article on steps for transforming curriculum.

National Center for Curriculum Transformation Resources on Women

http://pages.towson.edu/ncctrw/

Though the Center itself is primarily a research and consulting group, its site includes some useful resources such as a statement on "What Is Curriculum Transformation?" and short descriptions of some curriculum transformation projects in secondary schools.

HEROES AND HOLIDAYS

Amelia Earhart — Biography

http://www.ellensplace.net/eae_intr.html

This graphic-heavy biographical site focuses on three aspects of Earhart's life: "The Early Years," "The Celebrity," and "The Last Flight." The creator of the site, identified simply as "Ellen," has also developed sites highlighting the lives of Marilyn Monroe, Georgia O'Keeffe, and Gertrude Stein.

A Celebration of Women Writers

http://digital.library.upenn.edu/women/

This site was created in conjunction with the *Online Books Page* to celebrate the contributions and voices of women in American literature. Full texts and biographies of women writers from around the world are included in this index.

Cesár E. Chávez

http://www.colapublib.org/chavez/index.html

The County of Los Angeles Board of Supervisors and Public Library collaboratively sponsor this set of resources, including curriculum plans, about the great labor leader.

Chief Sitting Bull

http://www.pbs.org/weta/thewest/people/s_z/sittingbull.htm

Sitting Bull is introduced through PBS's biography and links.

Elizabeth Cady Stanton

http://www.nps.gov/wori/ecs.htm

The National Park Service provides a biography of this activist for women's rights. It includes an exceptional collection of photographs as well.

John Brown Homepage

http://www.iath.virginia.edu/jbrown/master.html

The University of Virginia's Institute for Advanced Technology in the Humanities hosts a site about the white abolitionist who raided the federal armory in Harpers Ferry.

Malcolm X: A Research Site

http://www.brothermalcolm.net

The life of Malcolm X is explored and celebrated through a detailed timeline, a bibliography of his works and speeches, information about his family, and a list of links to other Malcolm X Web sites.

Martin Luther King, Jr.

http://www.seattletimes.com/mlk/

The Seattle Times hosts this tribute site that combines biographical information with ideas for celebrating Martin Luther King, Jr. Day and a small selection of teacher resources.

The Martin Luther King, Jr. Papers Project

http://www.stanford.edu/group/King/

Stanford University offers a large collection of King's speeches, papers, autobiographical writings, and sermons.

Nelson Rolihlahla Mandela

http://www.anc.org.za/people/mandela.html

This collection of biographical information, photographs, and other documents introduces the onetime political prisoner who became the president of South Africa.

Spectrum Biology: Harriet Tubman

http://www.incwell.com/Biographies/Tubman.html

Researcher Rachel Sahlman and artist Dick Strandberg collaborated on this biographical Web site about Harriet Tubman, the escaped former slave who helped run the Underground Railroad.

Susan B. Anthony

http://womenshistory.about.com/library/bio/blanthony.htm

About.com section editor Jone Johnson Lewis compiled this selection of resources about the U.S. suffragist. The site contains wonderful photographs, quotations, and a vetted list of links to related sites.

Thurgood Marshall: American Revolutionary

http://www.thurgoodmarshall.com/home.htm

Juan Williams's book of the same name provides most of the content for this site about the first African American Supreme Court justice. The site includes speeches, articles, interviews, and photographs.

Tipu Sultan

http://home.btconnect.com/tipusultan/

This site commemorates the life of the first Indian leader to fight for freedom from the English. The site includes a biography, a picture gallery, and a discussion forum.

INTEGRATION

African American Women: On-line Archival Collections

http://scriptorium.lib.duke.edu/collections/african-american-women.html

Duke University hosts a collection of original documents including letters to and from slaves, photographs, and other scanned materials.

Asian-Nation

http://www.asian-nation.org/index.shtml

This portal of historical and cultural information about Asian Americans includes news articles, discussion forums, and an exploration of many contemporary issues.

Children of the Camps: Internment History

http://www.children-of-the-camps.org/history/index.html

Based on the film documentary of the same name, *Children of the Camps* provides a photographic and narrative history of the experiences of the young people who comprised most of the 120,000 Japanese Americans interned after Pearl Harbor. The site also includes copies of important documents like Executive Order 9066, which permitted the internment for the sake of "national defense."

A Deeper Shade of History

http://www.seditionists.org/black/bhist.html

This site serves as a clearinghouse for Black History resources in a way that is not limited to Black History Month or special celebrations. The site includes a "This Week in Black History" feature.

Disability Social History Project

http://www.disabilityhistory.org/

This site represents a movement by people with disabilities to reclaim their history and to highlight the contributions of people from the disabilities community in the history of the world. Resources include a timeline and an index of related sites.

First Nations Histories

http://www.tolatsga.org/Compacts.html

This site provides an examination of history by and about First Nations peoples, challenging Eurocentric perspectives on an important thread of American history.

Letters from an Iowa Soldier in the Civil War

http://www.civilwarletters.com/home.html

Bill Proudfoot offers a collection of letters written by Private Newton Robert Scott, Union clerk in Iowa during the Civil War. Fifteen letters are included in their entirety. The site also includes related links.

Transsexual, Transgender, and Intersex History

http://www.transhistory.org/

This site provides historical information by and about people whose gender identities do not fit neatly into the male/female dyad.

Women Come to the Front

http://lcweb.loc.gov/exhibits/wcf/wcf0001.html

The Library of Congress hosts this collection of exhibitions about women journalists and photographers who covered World War II.

STRUCTURAL REFORM

Been Here So Long

http://newdeal.feri.org/asn/

The fruits of a 1930s project to document slave narratives are the basis of this Web site, hosted by the New Deal Network and built around seventeen such narratives. The site also includes background on the original project.

Civil War Women

http://scriptorium.lib.duke.edu/women/cwdocs.html

Duke University houses an index highlighting primary sources about the role of women in the Civil War. Resources include diaries, letters, documents, photographs, and prints.

Fourth World Documentation Project

http://www.cwis.org/fwdp/fwdp.html

The Center for World Indigenous Studies presents the online community with access to Fourth World documents and resources. This project is an online library of those documents and resources, all of which represent Indigenous People's struggles to be rightfully recognized in the international community. The project archives are divided into categories including "Tribal and Inter-Tribal Resolutions and Papers," "Internationally Focused Documents," "United Nations Documents," and "Treaties, Agreements, and Other Constructive Arrangements."

Louisiana Holocaust Survivors Homepage

http://www.tulane.edu/~so-inst/laholsur.html

Five Holocaust survivors offer their stories, memories, and experiences. This site can be a perfect supplement to textbook information on the Holocaust.

Mountain Voices

http://www.mountainvoices.org/

This site is a portal of the voices and stories of over three hundred people who live in mountainous regions around the world. Interviewees from Pakistan, Kenya, Poland, Ethiopia, Peru, and other nations share struggles and triumphs with culture, change, and reform.

My China: Chinese Culture

http://www.wku.edu/~yuanh/China/proverb.html

Haiwang Yuan compiled and translated this collection of Chinese stories and proverbs and included them among the many resources of his *My China* site.

The Papers of Elizabeth Cady Stanton and Susan B. Anthony

http://adh.csd.sc.edu/sa/sa-table.html

Ann D. Gordon, Ann Pfau, Kimberly Banks, and Tamara Gaskell Miller compiled this collection of the early collaborative works of Stanton and Anthony, pioneers in the women's suffrage movement.

SOCIAL ACTION AND AWARENESS

The Dakota Conflict of 1862

http://www.isd77.k12.mn.us/schools/dakota/conflict/history.htm

Twenty-three 13- and 14-year-old students from Dakota Meadows Middle School collaborated on this Web site about a little-known battle between Native Americans and white settlers in Minnesota during, but not directly related to, the Civil War.

Human Rights Education Library

http://www.hrea.org/erc/Library/

Human Rights Education Associates (HREA) sponsors an extensive collection of curricular and teaching resources on local and global human rights concerns.

A More Perfect Union

http://americanhistory.si.edu/perfectunion/non-flash/index.html

Combining text and image media, *A More Perfect Union* encourages critical thinking about the relationship between human rights and the power of the state through an examination of Japanese American internment during World War II.

Never Again

http://www.africana.com/slavery/

Eric Ensey, a fifth-grade teacher, engaged his students in an in-depth examination of African slavery when they collaboratively decided that the three pages their textbook dedicated to the topic were inadequate. This Web site is the result of their work to learn more and share their findings.

Students Against Landmines

http://www.occdsb.on.ca/~sel/mine/

Over one hundred students from St. Elizabeth Catholic School in Ottawa, Ontario, Canada, contributed to the development of this site through which they lobby for the clearing of landmines from schoolyards in Afghanistan and Mozambique. The site also highlights similar work by students around the world.

What Did You Do in the War, Grandma?

http://www.stg.brown.edu/projects/WWII_Women/tocCS.html

Students in the Honors English Program at South Kingstown High School created this site, built primarily around interviews they conducted with women who served in the armed forces during World War II.

For more Web sites related to this chapter, please visit the Multicultural Education Supersite *at*

http://www.mhhe.com/socscience/education/multi/sites/chapter5.html.

References

Banks, J. (1993). Multicultural education: Characteristics and goals. In J. Banks & C. Banks (Eds.), *Multicultural education: Issues and perspectives* (pp. 3-30). Boston: Allyn & Bacon.

Davidman, L., & Davidman, P. (1997). *Teaching with a multicultural perspective: A practical guide.* New York: Longman.

Grant, C., & Sleeter, C. (1998). *Turning on learning: Five approaches for multicultural teaching plans for race, class, gender, and disability.* Columbus, OH: Merrill.

Livingstone, S. (2003). Children's use of the internet: Reflections on the emerging research agenda. *New Media and Society, 5* (2), 147-166.

McIntosh, P. (2000). Interactive phases of personal and curricular re-vision with regard to race. In P. Gorski & G. Shin (Eds.), *Multicultural resource series: Professional development for educators* (pp. 41-61). Washington, DC: National Education Association.

Munoz, J. (2002). [Dis]integrating multiculturalism with technology. *Multicultural Education, 10* (2), 19-24.

Nieto, S. (2001). School reform and student learning: A multicultural perspective. In J. Banks & C. Banks (Eds.), *Multicultural education: Issues and perspectives* (pp. 381-401). New York: John Wiley & Sons.

Pittman, J. (2003). Empowering individuals, schools, and communities. In G. Solomon, N. Allen, & P. Resta (Eds.), *Toward digital equity: Bridging the divide in education* (pp. 41-56). Boston: Allyn & Bacon.

Schrum, L., & Bracey, B. (2003). Refocusing curricula. In G. Solomon, N. Allen, & P. Resta (Eds.), *Toward digital equity: Bridging the divide in education* (pp. 129-143). Boston: Allyn & Bacon.

Sleeter, C. & Tettegah, C. (2002). Technology as a tool in multicultural teaching. *Multicultural Education, 10* (2), 3-9.

Tetreault, M. (2001). Classrooms for diversity: Rethinking curriculum and pedagogy. In J. Banks & C. Banks (Eds.), *Multicultural education: Issues and perspectives* (pp. 152-173). New York: John Wiley & Sons.

Weis, T., Benmayor, R., O'Leary, C., & Eynon, B. (2002). Digital technologies and pedagogies. *Social Justice, 29* (4), 153-167.

CHAPTER 6

Bridges and Dialogues: Online Networking for Educators

*I*ntercultural networking is an important component of developing, honing, and instituting multicultural teaching practices for two primary reasons. First, a teacher's personal and professional development in multicultural education relies, in part, on making connections with culturally diverse colleagues. These groups of educators can challenge each other to examine assumptions, prejudices, and biases, and how these may be informing their teaching and their students' learning. Second, intercultural networking expands and diversifies a teacher's resource base beyond what can be found within the walls of her or his classroom, school, or district. Because most teachers have not been prepared to develop or use methods and resources consistent with a multicultural education paradigm, this expansion of access to tools and ideas is crucial to pedagogical and curricular reforms like those discussed in Chapters 4 and 5.

The Internet, initially conceived and designed to enable exchanges among colleagues in the sciences, can help facilitate this networking process. Access to the Internet expands our material resource bases to a previously unimaginable extent. But more important, the Internet and its interactivity provide virtually boundless opportunities for cross-cultural communication, interpersonal bridge building, and intercultural resource sharing. Through Web- and e-mail-based discussion forums like bulletin boards, chat rooms, and listservs, educators can share ideas and resources or even collaborate in the creation of new ideas and resources across national and cultural boundaries.

This chapter highlights three types of interactive forums that, when used thoughtfully and collaboratively, will help teachers at all levels expand their resource bases and opportunities for personal and professional intercultural development. It concurrently provides a starting point for online networking by highlighting several existing online forums developed for the purpose of building connections among educators.

I have employed aliases for all individuals referred to by name in this chapter.

Bulletin Board Threaded Discussions

Robert, a recent visitor to the *Teachers.net* Web site, initiated a dialogue about "middle students" on the site's bulletin board threaded discussion forum:

> So much time and energy are given to [gifted and special needs] groups that I now see the middle students getting the short end of the stick. Who has the largest classes, the largest number of disruptive students, the smallest amount of resources, the least attention of the administration, and the least positive motiva-tion? ...It is the "average" student.

He continued by sharing the frustrations he experiences trying to teach "gift-ed students" who are routinely taken from his classroom at least one full day of every week. He struggles to structure his class so that such students do not fall behind the regular curriculum:

> The result of that policy is that the middle students lose 20% of their educational time. Additionally, teachers are held responsible for objectives of the school system, even for the gifted students. How can a teacher be held responsible for meeting all the objectives for a student who is absent from their class for a full fifth of the year? In essence, the teachers are also stripped of the opportunity to cover the objectives for all students in their classes for 20% of the school year.

The *Teachers.net* bulletin board provides educators a forum through which to share concerns, ideas, and resources with one another as well as parents, activists, and others interested in, or knowledgeable about, education. In fact, while the bulletin board plays a valuable educational role by simply giving Robert a forum through which to share his concerns, perspectives, and frustrations with an audience extending beyond the walls of his school, its real worth to education is in the subsequent potential for dialogue and problem solving among him and hundreds of other interested and experienced individuals. In this particular case, seven different individuals responded to Robert's concerns, each bringing a different but equally valuable set of cultural lenses and perspectives.

Jennifer, a mother of two elementary-aged students, agreed with Robert's assessment, adding:

> *It is amazing to me how many more opportunities are offered to the "gifted" children in our county. I didn't realize it until I had a "gifted" child... I am grateful that my "gifted" child has been given opportunities such as more field trips, smaller classes, and excellent teachers. But my heart aches for my "average" child who deserves these things also!*

Later the same day, Joe, a teacher with twenty years of experience teaching "gifted, regular, and now special education" students, empathized with Robert and Jennifer: "Isn't it a shame our educational system is so complex, complicated, and administratively heavy, yet so inefficient to the majority of our students." He challenged all of the participants in the conversation to "come up with some answers."

Joe's prodding encouraged Terry, who self-identified as neither a parent nor a teacher, but an activist interested in multiculturalism, inclusion, and equal opportunity for all students, to scan the Web for articles on related topics and events. He posted a message providing links to several such articles. While dozens of other teachers, administrators, parents, and other interested individuals started new discussions including how to teach the Holocaust, prayer in schools, and strategies for broaching diversity issues in the elementary classroom, this small group of people engaged in an active, lively dialogue, working together toward greater understandings of both the individual and institutional dynamics involved.

The forum at *Teachers.net* that has allowed Robert, Jennifer, Joe, Terry, and others to engage in a discussion on "the average student" is a bulletin board (also commonly referred to as a "discussion board"). Thousands of these forums exist covering virtually every imaginable topic, educational and otherwise. Many, like the one at *Teachers.net*, focus specifically on education and teaching practice. Others, like *Café UTNE*, cover a wide array of issues, including education, race, and culture.

Bulletin boards are accessible via the World Wide Web and a Web browser such as Netscape or Internet Explorer and usually do not require additional software. Users can post a question, resource, or comment onto a bulletin board, and it immediately becomes accessible to other users who can then read it, respond to it, or ignore it altogether at their leisure. Usually, bulletin boards use a "threaded" format, so that all responses to a particular post are automatically placed directly under that post, forming a clear distinction between various strands of the conversation. The primary advantage of bulletin boards compared with listservs and chat rooms is that they are the easiest to use among the three for novice Internet users. The disadvantage is that, unlike e-mail discussion groups (in which users automatically receive each post) and chat rooms (in which discussions happen in real time), the poster of a message to a bulletin board is at the mercy of whoever happens upon the forum. Less consistency exists in terms of who participates in these than the other two types of discussion forums.

Many existing bulletin boards focus on multicultural education and related topics.

Chat Rooms

Chat rooms, like bulletin boards, require access to the World Wide Web. However, they differ from bulletin boards in that the dialogues in chat rooms happen in real time. That is, users, possibly from all over the world, congregate to a particular Web site via the Internet. When one user enters a comment or question, it appears instantaneously on other participants' computer screens. Those participants can respond to the comment or question or post an altogether different thought. Among the three forms of online forums described here, chat rooms represent the closest approximation to face-to-face interaction.

Several different types of chat rooms currently exist. Open chat rooms constantly remain active. Users can enter an open chat room at any time of the day or night and interact with whomever else has chosen to enter the chat room at that time. For example, *Dave's ESL Café Chat Central* remains open and active at all times. Although most social chat rooms attract enough visitors to consistently maintain a discussion, most educational chat rooms, *Dave's ESL Café* notwithstanding, must use a different approach.

Some chat rooms open only for specific dialogue events based around tightly defined topics. Chat events often include a high-profile or "expert" participant who either fields questions from other users or moderates the session, attempting to keep the conversation focused on the predetermined topic. For example, *PBS TeacherLine*, a site for teachers sponsored by the Public Broadcasting System, recently hosted a chat on "Gender Equity in Mathematics" for P-12 educators. Sundra Flansburg, Senior Project Director of the Gender and Diversities Institute at the Education Development Center, Inc., was the guest moderator. Many of these sites offer archives of previous chats. You can browse these archives to gain a clearer picture of the discussion format and participant expectations.

An advantage of chat forums is that they provide the closest approximation of live interaction and are often skillfully moderated, allowing close attention to very specific problems and solutions. As in the case of *TeacherLine*, they may also give you the opportunity to directly interact with one of the top people in the field of multicultural education. The primary disadvantage of chat room dialogues is that they are usually limited to a given amount of time, necessarily constraining the participation of each individual. Another possible challenge emerges when chat forums are not skillfully moderated, resulting in a lack of organization and conversational flow as an avalanche of unrelated posts tumble down users' screens.

E-mail Discussion Groups

Whereas bulletin boards and chat rooms rely on users coming to a single site, e-mail discussion groups (also known as "mailing lists" or "listservs") essentially deliver the conversation to participants via electronic mail. When you "subscribe" to a listserv, your e-mail address is added to an electronic list of addresses (hence the term "mailing list"). Then, when somebody sends a message to an e-mail address that has been designated for that list, the message is automatically distributed to every member's individual e-mail address.

For example, as a member of *MCPAVILION*, the official listserv of the *Multicultural Pavilion*, I can send a single message to the list address, and that message will automatically be distributed to the hundreds of other members. They, in turn, can respond to my personal e-mail address (in which case the rest of the list members will not receive a copy of the response) or respond to the list address (in which case the rest of the list will receive a copy), initiating a public dialogue.

A recent exchange involving several members of *MCPAVILION* began when one member posted a message asking how we can balance the need for multicultural awareness for preservice teachers with the concurrent need to equip teachers-to-be with the practical skills and competencies needed to teach a diverse student population. Several different conversations emerged from this single post as list members with different experiences, perspectives, under-standings, areas of expertise, biases, and backgrounds responded. One conver-sational strand focused on the challenge of balancing both areas of preservice preparation with the growing focus on learning standards and standardized tests. Another strand touched off an examination and critique of Eurocentrism in history and literature curricula. Yet another strand centered on the respon-sibility of individual teachers to seek professional development opportunities that will challenge them to rethink the limitations of their own perspectives and approaches to teaching and learning. Each new message gave rise to a fresh set of questions and varying paths of discovery for all participants.

The greatest advantage of e-mail forums is that, among all existing Internet-based discussion formats, *MCPAVILION, NAME-MCE,* and other listservs have proven the most conducive to the engagement of educators, researchers, theorists, parents, activists, students, and all other stakeholder groups in a single, ongoing dialogue about multicultural education. Listservs allow for some of the most active and effective contemporary avenues for bridging the gap between theory and practice in multicultural education because they are accessible and open to a wonderfully broad base of preservice, K-12, and postsecondary educators; grade school, college, and graduate stu-dents; education researchers, theorists, and philosophers; and parents, activists, and community members.

Several Web sites help educators find relevant educational and scholarly listservs. Some, such as the *Directory of Scholarly and Professional E-Conferences* cover a wide array of subject and interest areas. Others maintain a tighter focus. For example, *StudentAffairs.com,* a site for student affairs professionals, offers a searchable index of listservs related to student experience and learning.

Disadvantages of listservs include the potential for a flooded mailbox and the tendency for a few outspoken and extreme voices to control the conversa-tion and intimidate, or even silence, other users. An effective facilitator or moderator can often minimize the latter concern.

Several new multicultural- and diversity-related listservs have emerged over the past five years. Many are listed next along with subscription informa-tion. In addition, you can read about some of the most popular multicultural education listservs in Chapter 7.

Whether through educational chat rooms, bulletin boards, or e-mail discussion groups, the Internet provides educators with valuable opportunities to network interculturally. Your participation in these forums will help expand your resource base and enhance your personal and professional multicultural development. They will give you access to people, perspectives, ideas, and resources from other educators, parents, activists, students, and people generally interested in education across social, cultural, and national boundaries. Whether these forums contribute something as complicated as shrinking the gap between multicultural education theory and practice or something as simple as the exchange of resources and lesson plans, they facilitate interactions that would likely have not occurred otherwise. And where dialogue begins, the possibility of progress emerges.

MORE DIALOGUE FORUMS

BULLETIN BOARD THREADED DISCUSSIONS

Café Progressive Editorials

http://www.cafeprogressive.com/cpinteractivism.html

Users post thoughts, research, ideas, and resources on education, politics, and community on these discussion boards. Editorials are divided into subsections including "Race & Gender," "Class & Economics," "Institutions & Politics," and "Education." Most users are social activists.

Café UTNE Conversations

http://cafe.utne.com/cafe/cafelist3.html

This site hosts several different discussion forums on a variety of cultural topics. One of these forums, "Education," focuses on school reform. Other forums include "Globe," "History," "Stonewall" (gay, lesbian, and bisexual issues), and "Culture."

Cultural Debates Online

http://www.teachtsp2.com/cdonline/

Tom Snyder Productions hosts a set of dialogue forums about a variety of cultural issues. Several types of forums exist alongside multimedia presentations that help spark the discussions. A "Teacher Information" section helps educators find ways to effectively weave this resource into a curriculum.

Economic Justice Discussion Room

http://www.progress.org/progs/wwwboard/

Part of the *Economic Justice Network*, this very active forum covers social class, capitalism, socialism, and global economy. Current discussion strands focus on NATO, Yugoslavia, and India. Usership includes activists, researchers, and educators.

History Channel Discussions

http://www.historychannel.com/discuss/

The History Channel hosts hundreds of discussion boards on a wide range of topics. Some include "International Personalities," "The Holocaust," "Veteran's Forum," and "Underground Railroad." Though most users are not educators, these boards provide an opportunity for teachers and students to interact with historians and people in other related fields.

Lycos Message Boards: Education

http://boards.lycos.com/

Among its many bulletin board offerings, *Lycos* includes several on education. The most active of these is "Teaching Methods, Issues & Resources." Current topics range from discrimination in schools to adult literacy. Most participants are K-12 educators, with parents, postsecondary educators, and activists occasionally chiming in.

Multicultural Pavilion Community Forums

http://www.edchange.org/multicultural/pavboard/pavboard.html

Part of the *Multicultural Pavilion*, this is an open discussion on multicultural issues and education. Users can respond to the posts of others or start a new discussion strand, so topics change constantly. Some recent discussions have focused on the philosophy behind multicultural education, the nature of Eurocentrism, and an examination of alternative views on Columbus, Jefferson, and other historical figures. Participants include K-12 and college-level educators and preservice teachers.

Parent Soup Boards: Education

http://www.ivillage.com/boards/?arrivalSA=1&arrival_freqCap=2

Through a subsection called "Education Central," *Parent Soup* hosts several education-related discussion boards. Parents and teachers interact and maintain dialogues within the boards on topics including Montessori learning, home schooling, and special education. A separate board titled "Hot Education Topics" delves into current events in public and private schools.

People in Action Message Board

http://peopleinaction.info/board/1/1.html

People in Action for a Better World, a Web site that covers a wide array of social issues, hosts this discussion board. Participants include educators and activists around the world. Recent conversation strands have included "Women and Spirituality," and "Assimilation."

Teacher Focus

http://www.teacherfocus.com/phpBB2/

This collection of threaded discussions facilitates dialogues for educators of all types. Topics include "The New Teacher," "Educational Technology," and "Special Education."

Teachers.Net Chatboard

http://www.teachers.net/chatboard/

Teachers.Net is one of the top teacher-related Web sites available. It includes this discussion forum "as an online tool for teachers everywhere." Because of a high level of participation (usually over one hundred posts per day), discussion topics are varied and responsive to day-to-day educational happenings. Current discussion strands include the Ten Commandments in schools, ability grouping, parental participation, and multiple intelligences.

The Teachers' Place

http://www.unicef.org/voy/research/reshome.html

The Teachers' Place provides a series of forums for teachers to exchange ideas and resources related to human rights education. The site also contains strategies for beginning the process of dealing with human rights in the classroom.

TeachNet.org Bulletin Boards

http://teachersnetwork.org/bb/Topic_List.cfm?boardID=7

TeachNet hosts a series of very active, topically distinct discussion board sites for teachers. These include "Learning Styles," "Equality of Education," and "The Authentic Assessment Debate."

UNICEF Voices of Youth

http://www.unicef.org/voy/

UNICEF hosts a set of dialogues for students discussing human rights issues. Current discussions address gender inequality, children's rights, and AIDS.

ProTeacher Community

http://proteacher.net/

A feature of *Proteacher*, this discussion board was created for new teachers to share their joys, frustrations, concerns, and experiences. The moderator of the board has done an admirable job creating an online atmosphere of support, empathy, and the free flow of ideas.

Y? The National Forum on People's Differences

http://www.yforum.com/welcome1.html

Y?, created and maintained by Phillip Milano and Robin Dycus-Milano, is a unique and progressive series of forums. *Y?* challenges users to post their most uncomfortable—and discomforting—questions, working from the philosophy that stereotypes and assumptions can only be broken down when such forums exist and such questions are asked. Choose from categories including "Religion," "Sexual Orientation," "Gender," "Disabilities/Challenges," "Age," "Race/Ethnicity," and "Class."

Chat Rooms

Author Chats

http://www.authorchats.com/

The site hosts regularly scheduled chats featuring children's book authors. You can also use *Author Chats* to schedule a chat between your class and an author—a great opportunity to connect your students to somebody in the field.

Dave's ESL Café Chat Central

http://www.eslcafe.com/chat/chatpro.cgi

Dave Sperling hosts a chat room dedicated to bringing educators together to discuss the teaching and learning of English as a Second Language. There are usually at least six people in the chat room, but sometimes fifteen or twenty participants can be found there.

Homeschooling Chat

http://homeschooling.miningco.com/mpchat.htm

The home schooling section of *About.com*, hosted by Beverly Hernandez, runs chats on Thursday and Saturday nights for people interested in issues and concerns related to home schooling.

Illinois Early Learning Project Interactive Chat

http://www.illinoisearlylearning.org/chat.htm

IEL runs periodic chats on issues related to early childhood education, usually featuring a guest presenter. Recent topics have included "Autism," "Father/Male Involvement in Early Childhood," and "Supporting Children's Social Development."

PBS TeacherLine Community Center

http://teacherline.pbs.org/teacherline/calendar/calendar.cfm

The Public Broadcasting System's *TeacherLine* site features occasional Web chats for educators. Topics have included "Gender Equity in Mathematics," "Techno-Constructivism," and "Information Literacy."

Teachers.net Chatboard

http://teachers.net/chatboard/

One of the leading educational Web sites in the world, *Teachers.net* hosts dozens of open chat rooms with topics including "Politics," "Student Teachers," and "Classroom Management."

Washingtonpost.com Live Discussions

http://www.washingtonpost.com/wp-dyn/liveonline/?nav=hpleft1

The *Washington Post* offers several free live chat opportunities daily. These events are moderated by an expert participant. Topics of the discussions are often education related.

Y? Chat

http://www.yforum.com/welcome1.html

Through this chat forum, *Y? National Forum on People's Differences* encourages participants to "ask and answer questions about differences related to race, gender, sexual orientation, religion, age, etc." *Y? Chat* is moderated, so individuals relying on personal attacks can be "bumped out" of the discussion. But in general, "political correctness" takes a back seat to honest dialogue and challenging questions in this forum.

E-MAIL DISCUSSION GROUPS

Directory of Scholarly and Professional E-Conferences

http://www.kovacs.com/directory/

This award-winning site is a guide to scholarly e-mail-based discussion forums. Users can search the directory for keywords, browse the forums alphabetically, or scroll through categories including "Cross-Cultural Studies," "Economic Development," "Education," "Gender Studies," "Men's Studies," "Social Issues," and "Women's Studies." Each entry includes a description and contact/subscription information.

Gender-Related Electronic Forums

http://www-unix.umbc.edu/~korenman/wmst/forums1.html

Joan Korenman maintains an alphabetical directory of gender-focused listservs. Subcategories include "Education," "Activists Lists," "International," and "Women of Color." Each listserv description contains subscription information.

Student Affairs Listservs: Diversity Issues

http://www.studentaffairs.com/lists/divers.html

One of the many resources at *StudentAffairs.com* is this searchable directory of e-mail discussion groups, pertaining primarily to higher education. Users can also scroll through an index of the groups divided into categories including "Diversity Issues" and "Student Activism."

Individual Listservs

barrier-free: A group providing collaborative support among students with disabilities, parents, and teachers. For subscription information visit *http://barrier-free.arch.gatech.edu/Listserve/index.html*.

diversegrad-l: An e-mail group focused on multicultural and cross-cultural counseling. This forum is run out of American University and can be reached at *diversegrad-l@american.edu*.

dsshe-l: A list that shares information among providers of services for students with disabilities in higher education. DSSHE-L is a very active list of over eighty members with an average of 225 posts per week. Access DSSHE-L at *Listserv@listserv.acsu.buffalo.edu*.

heddvsty: A discussion group specific to diversity issues at colleges and universities. Estimate numbers of subscribers and weekly e-mails are unavailable. Subscribe to this listserv by writing to *Listserv@tamvm1.tamu.edu*.

mcpavilion: A discussion group of the *Multicultural Pavilion* linking teachers, teacher educators, activists and others interested in multicultural issues and education. To join this list, visit *http://www.edchange.org/multicultural/issues.html*. The list has 650 members and receives about twenty e-mails per week.

name-mce: The official listserv of the National Association for Multicultural Education. Over nine hundred people, mostly educators, are currently subscribed, with membership growing quickly. About twenty-five messages are distributed weekly. To subscribe, write to *listserv@listserv.umd.edu*.

ngltfcampus: A list hosted by the National Gay and Lesbian Task Force and designed to coordinate communication among individuals across the country involved or interested in the work of the NGLTF Campus Project. The list can be reached at *Ngltfcampus-request@nenet.org*. This listserv services about 150 people with an average of thirty e-mails per week.

CHAPTER 7

Forging Communities for Education Change through E-mail Discussion Groups

I recently participated in a dialogue on the role of multicultural education in math and science. I have previously participated in or facilitated dozens of similar discussions. But this particular dialogue was different and considerably more fruitful than any I had been privileged to experience before.

I could not see the other participants, but I knew there were nearly four hundred of them, diverse in race, gender, religion, age, nationality, ethnicity, sexual orientation, educational level, socioeconomic class, ability status, introverted- or extrovertedness, political affiliation, and every other identity dimension. We were school administrators, students, professors, activists, teachers, librarians, parents, day-care providers, corporate heads, researchers, writers, and combinations of these. Many were strong advocates for multicultural education, though we all clearly did not agree on its definition or what it looked like in practice. Some argued strongly against multicultural education and its ideals. Some were undecided.

The dialogue stretched across several days. As participants came and went, several varied strands of the conversation emerged until four or five different dialogues about multicultural education in the math and science classroom were happening concurrently. One strand focused on pedagogy. Another became a collaborative sharing of resources and suggested reading lists.

Several factors made this dialogue dynamically different from others in which I had participated: (1) the diversity of the participants, (2) the combinations of interests and perspectives informed by theory, philosophy, practical experience, and mixtures of these, (3) the flexibility of time and space, allowing participants to enter and exit the dialogue without disturbing its flow, and (4) the free emergence and expansion into several different strands of conversation on a single topic, with each participant maintaining the possibility of participating in every strand, any single strand, or no strand at all.

A single factor made the dialogue functionally different from others and set the context for its unique dynamics. It was taking place online via electronic mail, through *MCPAVILION*, an e-mail discussion group (also known as a "listserv" or a "mailing list").

This chapter explores e-mail discussion groups, including *MCPAVILION*, as collaborative forums for dialogues on multicultural education and other educational topics. Following a short examination of the nature of e-mail discussion group dialogues, several facilitators of current listservs offer descriptions of their forums along with a diversity of observations from their experiences facilitating and participating in them. The chapter closes with a short list of resources for finding and subscribing to e-mail discussion forums on multicultural education and related topics.

Opportunities and Challenges

As discussed in Chapter 6, e-mail discussion groups, along with other Internet dialogue media like bulletin boards, chat rooms, and newsgroups, illustrate one of the Internet's greatest potentials for education and education reform: opportunities for educators to interact, collaborate, exchange ideas, and engage in dialogue across cultural and national borders and boundaries. These forums are quickly becoming hotbeds, not only for trading resources, but also for professional development, interactive inquiry, and educational theory construction among all relevant constituencies. Several major educational projects and publications have been initiated through online discussions, many focused on progressive education reform. Over the past seven years, e-mail discussion groups have emerged as the most active and heavily used Internet-based medium for dialogue on multicultural education and related topics. Several such groups have been initiated by and for multicultural educators, researchers, counselors, practitioners, students, and activists, forming a variety of online communities dedicated to the development, examination, understanding, and practice of multicultural education.

E-mail discussion groups consist of communities of participants with e-mail access and an expressed interest in a specific topic. Participants send questions, comments, observations, or resources to a single address (sometimes called the "group address"), and their contribution is then automatically distributed to every other participant. Those participants, in turn, respond to that contribution, ignore it altogether, or post questions, comments, observations, or resources of their own.

The entire exchange happens via e-mail, giving these forums a host of distinctive characteristics. Because the conversations do not occur in real time, participants can engage at their leisure, carefully crafting responses or original posts. As a result, as in the previously described example, some dialogues can last several days or weeks (Haythornthwaite, 2002; Levin & Cervantes, 2002). In addition, unlike other Internet-based discussion forums such as bulletin boards, the content of e-mail discussions is distributed directly to participants who do not have to congregate at a particular Web site at a particular time in order to participate fully in the exchange. E-mail discussion forums provide an important alternative to more formalized and traditional opportunities for cross-cultural and interperspective dialogues such as those that occur at academic conferences. Again, participants are not required to congregate at a given point in time and space. For people with access to a computer and the Internet, online dialogues can be cost-effective alternatives to the often-expensive conference circuit.

Along with these characteristics and opportunities come challenges and concerns specific to e-mail discussion groups. The most obvious of these is a lack of physical presence and the resulting inability to pick up on social cues based in body language, tones of voice, and the ways people organize themselves within a physical space (Haythornthwaite, 2002). Some listservs experience large volumes of posts—perhaps twenty or thirty in a single day. This may be positive for the sake of dialogue but can result in mailbox "flooding." Another important, but often ignored, constraint of Internet dialogue is that of unequal access and the exclusion of possible participants who do not have convenient access to a computer or the Internet. It deserves repeating that, as access to electronic media becomes increasingly important and valuable, educators at all levels must continue to look for ways to narrow the digital divide that is currently carving a wider gap in the opportunity structure between the socioeconomically privileged and underprivileged. A related concern about e-mail discussion forums is that, despite popular belief, the sexist communication dynamics readily observable offline are replicated almost perfectly online (Castner, 1997; Clark & Gorski, 2002; Herring, 1993). Even in cyberspace, men take up more "space" than women (Blum, 1999; Meyer, 2003). Men post more often than women, and participants are more likely to respond to men's posts than to women's posts.

An e-mail discussion forum can be effective and multicultural only if careful attention is paid to minimizing these constraints.

An Introduction to Multicultural Education E-mail Discussion Groups

The following e-mail discussion groups host active, rich, ongoing dialogues about topics related to multicultural education.

Diversegrad-L *by Morris Jackson*

Changing demographics both internationally and in the United States required a paradigm shift in the knowledge imparted by educators to prepare graduate students for the world of work. Diversity as a specialty in the counseling profession was growing. After some research I determined that traditional means of sharing ideas, thoughts, and feelings about counseling and diversity were inadequate. The world was becoming smaller every day. Becoming a part of the global community was becoming more important every day. Graduate students needed a more viable means to learn about diversity counseling and to stay in communication with their peers living in different parts of the United States and abroad. Listserv technology provided me with a way to assist graduate students, faculty, and other educators to interact and learn from one another about diversity issues.

As an aspiring young professional, I was highly interested in diversity counseling issues. After attending several American Counseling Association conventions, I came to the realization that if one's ideas about diversity did not conform to the prevailing norm, your voice or views about diversity counseling may not be heard. I recalled with delight a conversation I had with a former graduate student about diversity counseling and the Internet. She encouraged me to move forward and create my own listserv. I, in turn, created *Diversegrad-L.*

Diversegrad-L provides a forum through which participants express varied views about diversity counseling issues. There are 275 listserv members who reside in the United States, Canada, Spain, India, Mexico, and Japan. Most members are graduate students and professors working in the counseling field. Others are mental health workers with backgrounds including sociology, psychology, ministry, and education. Because of the diverse membership, a plethora of divergent worldviews are discussed and shared, leading to intellectually challenging exchanges. Often, listserv members' values and belief systems are challenged.

As the owner of the listserv, I read every post. My philosophy is to allow for an open exchange of diverse views. Any intervention by me is motivated by a perceived need to rein in a discussion that has become too personal or emotionally charged. As such, facilitating discussions in which attacking posts are at a minimum and intellectually intriguing posts are at a maximum is an important task. Disagreement in the expression of ideas and thoughts on diversity counseling issues is expected and encouraged. But my ongoing challenge is to involve the silent listserv members who have many different reasons for not posting or participating in the discussion. Other challenges I face include trying to maintain participant interest during the time periods when the discussion slows down and managing situations in which large groups of participants, assigned participation by a professor, simultaneously join or leave the list.

The listserv has been in existence for several years, and the topics posted for discussion have evolved. Initially discussions primarily focused on counseling and diversity issues, but over time the discussions have shifted to issues of diversity in society that may impact and influence not only counseling relationships but the actual development of listserv members' worldview. The most exciting aspect of *Diversegrad-L* is the core of professionals, scholars, and students who have remained members for years, introducing topics and issues that they believe will be valuable to the complete group and participating in the evolution of the forum.

Diversegrad-L provides subscribers the opportunity to increase their knowledge and understanding about diversity issues and how they impact the helping profession. In addition, the listserv helps colleagues share research topics, projects, papers, resources, and conference information significant to diversity counseling. Some members have even collaborated on writing projects and conference presentations.

You can subscribe to *Diversegrad-L* by sending an e-mail to *listserv@ listserv.american.edu* with only the words "Subscribe Diversegrad-L <first name and last name>" in the body of message section. Leave the "Subject" field blank.

MCPAVILION *by Paul C. Gorski*

I created *MCPAVILION* in 1996 at the request of several P-12 teachers who were regular users of the *Multicultural Pavilion* Web site. Though several other multicultural education e-mail forums existed when I created *MCPAVILION*, it seemed that the voices of researchers and academics in those forums overpowered the voices of classroom teachers. I attempted to fill a need by creating a discussion group specifically intended to engage teachers in a collaborative examination of curricular and teaching practice through the exchange of practical classroom experiences and resources. My goal was to provide educators a safe and supportive atmosphere, free of dominating voices and the language, challenges, and criticisms of the academic "elite." I spent much time and energy for three years focusing and refocusing *MCPAVILION* dialogues on classroom practice, challenging contributors of theory- or philosophy-heavy posts to discuss the practical implications of their arguments and ponderings.

It was not until four years into the discussion group's existence that I recognized the constraints and limitations I placed on the exchange of ideas with my practice-only ground rules and facilitation. While attempting to compensate for the age-old gap between multicultural education theory and practice by "rescuing" practitioners from theoretical and philosophical perspectives, I actually widened the gap by actively excluding half of the theory/practice duet. I had attended multicultural education conferences in which the theory or practice orientation of session topics almost perfectly dictated the types of attending participants. I began to wonder whether, with some strategic facilitation, e-mail discussion forums could serve to bridge the seemingly omnipresent wedge.

I found that, as I encouraged the coexistence and interaction of theoretical and practical perspectives on *MCPAVILION*, everybody, including me, was challenged to think about educational and social issues in deeper, more complex ways. I am now convinced that the five or six most active e-mail discussion groups focusing on multicultural education (including those highlighted in this chapter) represent the most successful current and ongoing exchanges on multicultural education, particularly due to their inclusion of voices across the range of diversity and the continuum between theory and practice.

MCPAVILION participants now include teachers and educators at all levels, administrators, activists, students, government workers, librarians, counselors and psychologists, social scientists, teacher educators, child-care providers, and others interested in multicultural education and related issues and topics. Participation has transcended resource sharing and dialogue and has often resulted in the collaborative development of original multicultural teaching and learning resources, including the *Multicultural Song Index* and the *Research Room*, both among the most popular attractions of the *Multicultural Pavilion* Web site.

Currently, nearly 650 participants exchange a total average of twenty messages weekly, though the volume of messages rises and falls regularly. Recent topics other than the role of multicultural education in the math and science classroom have included ethnocentrism in history education and balancing the need for personal awareness and development with curricular and pedagogical transformation.

You can subscribe to *MCPAVILION* through the *Multicultural Pavilion* at *http://www.edchange.org/multicultural/issues.html.*

NAME-MCE *by Bill Howe*

The National Association for Multicultural Education (NAME), the fastest-growing professional organization in the United States that has as its sole objective the advocacy of multicultural education as the foundation philosophy of the nation's educational system from preschool through higher education, manages a Web site (www.nameorg.org) and publishes a quarterly journal and newsletter. In addition, NAME has sponsored a listserv, *NAME-MCE*, since 1993. *NAME-MCE* is a forum for the dissemination of information and the sharing of ideas related to multicultural education. Subscribers to *NAME-MCE* do not have to be NAME members.

There are currently 945 *NAME-MCE* subscribers from fifteen countries. The majority of participants are from higher education (primarily teacher educators) with a significant mixture of P-12 teachers, parents, students and community activists. On average there are about 6 to 7 posts per day.

In a recent survey conducted through *NAME-MCE*, subscribers were asked why they joined the listserv and what they got out of participating. The four most common responses were (1) access to the latest education news including legislation, (2) access to specific information on the theory and practices of multicultural education, (3) access to validation and support, and (4) access to a feeling of connectedness with others in the field. One person wrote, "[*NAME-MCE*] also challenges my thinking, something not always done in Academia." Another participant responded, "This list has provided me with an extensive array of opinions, readings and food for thought on areas of multicultural education that are not discussed in any of my classes... It has provided me the courage to approach this issue in the courses that I teach at both the university and community college level."

Many expressed the value of finding validation and support in a nonhostile environment. According to a subscriber: "It's a great list! As an African American in an all-white Institution, in Appalachia at that, I relish the opportunity to interact with other folks of like mind, even though it is in cyberspace and sometimes controversial." Another wrote, "I work pretty much in isolation, have few diversity peers nearby, and this list provides one source of support for the importance and value of the work; helps me recognize I am not working alone; helps keep me focused, knowledgeable, and energized."

Our international subscribers pointed out the benefit of "reaching across the oceans to stay connected." One international participant remarked, "I am researching multicultural education in Australian schools... and only recently heard of NAME. I joined because I enjoy the interrelational aspects of multicultural listservs, and particularly wanted to be a part of one that focuses on education." Another offered, "I am teaching in middle school at the American International School in Israel, where I am posted for three years. Glancing at the topics and reading occasional postings that are relevant to me is a way of keeping up-to-date on multicultural issues in the U.S. while I am living overseas."

Among the most interesting recent discussions has been one about the purpose of the listserv and the meaning of multicultural education. After a post that seemed to some to be critical of the war effort in Iraq, a few subscribers wrote in to indicate that they felt the posting was "not appropriate for a listserv on multicultural education." This generated a lively and very helpful discussion on the definition of multicultural education.

One participant posted:

education is political. I have a difficult time separating current events, including those of a strong political nature, from the classroom. I believe that to be a "multicultural teacher" one needs to be informed of all events, historical and political, that impact the lives of our students, that is one reason I subscribe to this list... You are right to imply that articles about political views or events are difficult to interpret in a way that translates into a practical application in a classroom so when these articles are presented or sent to the listserv maybe it would be useful if the sender could offer their thoughts of why they are sharing the article on the list and what practical application it might have. This has been a very interesting strand, not very different from the dialogue I hear in my classes about the political nature of education.

Another participant offered:

I think there should be a balanced buffet of issues related to multicultural theory and practice. Although your point is well taken, it is equally important that we balance theory with practice. Perhaps perceiving the two as opposing constructs helps to perpetuate the notion that the two cannot co-exist. In fact, hands-on practice without appropriate theory is as dangerous as theory without explanatory practice. Unfortunately, sometimes, in our efforts to resolve the two, we discard one for the other. Too often, this has been the solution of choice in education. I feel your pain, as classroom teachers, we so often need right-now, real-time solutions to help our students and ourselves get through the day. But don't give up. We need people like you to continue to make sure there's room at the table for everyone.

Some participants have commented that, because there is so much information passing through the NAME listserv, there should be a portal for compiling and storing posts for later reference. Fortunately there are ways to manage this information. On *NAME-MCE* and most listservs you can subscribe to get the digests. This means that instead of receiving six or seven separate e-mails a day you receive one at the beginning of the next day that includes all the postings from the previous day. A good research strategy is to save the digests on your computer. You can then use the Search command in your word processor to seek out areas of interest such as "bilingual education." Subscribers can do this by sending an e-mail to listserv@listserv.umd.edu with the following in the body of the message:

SET NAME-MCE DIGEST

To subscribe to this listserv send an e-mail message to *listserv@listserv. umd.edu* with the subject line blank and the following in the body of the message:

subscribe NAME-MCE your_first_name your_last_name

If you need assistance, contact the Listserv Moderator at *listmoderator@nameorg.org.* For more information about the National Association for Multicultural Education visit the website (*www.nameorg.org*) or e-mail *name@nameorg.org.* You can also write to: NAME National Office, 733 Fifteenth Street, NW — Suite 430, Washington, DC 20005.

NICI-Equity *by Joy Wallace*

In 1994, a forward-thinking educator, Dr. Robert McLaughlin, decided to help a group of New England equity advocates easily keep in touch with one another by establishing a listserv. Most of us had never used a listserv before, but we quickly saw the advantages and eagerly used the technology to plan a workshop and share resources with one another. We collected additional users at our regional equity conference and I was asked to moderate the Equity listserv for the Regional Alliance, an Eisenhower-funded regional consortium. Because the Eisenhower Consortia had a science and mathematics focus, the first Equity listserv featured resources specifically for expanding equity in math and science classrooms.

In 1997 Dr. McLaughlin founded the National Institute for Community Innovation and established the Equity listserv on its server. Over the years, *NICI-Equity* has grown to nearly five hundred subscribers. Its purpose is to provide subscribers with information about educational equity resources including new books, journal articles, workshops, conferences, consultant information, and Web sites. Postings tend to be fairly short and most are reviews of equity resources. I search for these resources every way possible: my reading of *Education Week,* conversations with other equity advocates, Internet searches, and the information I get at conferences and workshops.

Subscribers to *NICI-Equity* all have a connection to educational equity and an interest in fostering educational equity in schools. Subscribers are varied and include college and university professors, special projects staff, nonprofit organizations, teachers and administrators from K-12 schools, regional equity center staff, and consultants.

Many of our subscribers are not heavy technology users. However, since the use of technology is an equity issue, most members attempt to keep apprised of new technology and I believe that all subscribers use Internet resources now. I have seen a marked increase in the use of Internet resources in the past five years.

We conduct evaluations of our listserv and have received important feedback. One participant shared, "I can't tell you how often I use and disseminate the info that you share. Your leadership has provided a great service to equity advocates across the country." Another said, "As an academic and activist I have been enriched constantly thanks to the list." A particularly appreciative participant exclaimed, "I could not do my work without this valuable resource. I appreciate having reviews of new resources sent directly to my e-mail box, and not have to find them myself."

Topics on the listserv must relate to equity in education but cover a wide range of topics such as student testing, lessons about human rights, achievement gaps in schools, teaching in a culturally diverse classroom, cyberfairs for students, NSF-funded resources, disability resources, increasing parent involvement in education, and increasing the participation of underrepresented populations in science, mathematics, and technology.

On average, there are fifteen posts per week, sometimes more, rarely less. *NICI-Equity* is not a conversational list—subscribers look for reviews of excellent resources to be delivered to them—although we have enjoyed some stimulating discussions about controversial topics.

Subscribe by contacting Joy Wallace, moderator, at *joy.Wallace@comcast.net* or by visiting *http://lists.nici-mc2.org/mailman/listinfo*. We recently lost funding from the U.S. Department of Education when a project ended. To keep the listserv alive, we now have an annual subscription fee of $50, although no subscriber is turned away.

ADDITIONAL RESOURCES

The e-mail discussion groups highlighted in this chapter represent a small percentage of those that currently exist, covering topics both related and unrelated to multicultural education. The following Web sites offer resources that help you find, explore, and subscribe to these and other educational listservs.

CataList

http://www.lsoft.com/lists/listref.html

CataList is the official online catalog of listserv discussion groups. Users can do a keyword search to find a relevant group or browse through existing groups by host country or number of subscribers. The site also includes a list owner's guide for people currently facilitating, or interested in initiating, an e-mail discussion group.

EFL/ESL Student Lists

http://www.latrobe.edu.au/www/education/sl/sl.html

This set of discussion groups was created to provide cross-cultural dialogue opportunities among students in English programs around the world.

E-Mail Discussion Lists and Electronic Journals

http://www.ibiblio.org/edweb/lists.html

Part of Andy Carvin's *EdWeb*, a site dedicated to exploring the intersections between educational technology and school reform, this page combines instructional pieces for subscribing to e-mail discussion forums with a list of existing groups.

ERIC Mailing Lists

http://www.askeric.org/Virtual/Listserv_Archives/

ERIC hosts several "virtual communities" focusing on all aspects of education, ranging from campus environments to interdisciplinary teaching. This site includes a list of these e-mail discussion groups as well as short descriptions and subscription information.

Higher Education Forums

http://www.studentaffairs.com/lists/higher.html

StudentAffairs.com includes this extensive list of e-mail discussion groups that focus on issues in higher education ranging from assessment to computer-based education.

Topica: Education

http://www.liszt.com/dir/?cid=4

This is just one among many categories used to organize the thousands of e-mail discussion groups listed on the *Topica* Web site. Use a keyword search function to find listservs on your topics of interest.

Mailing List Manager Commands

http://www.rileyguide.com/mailser.html

James Milles of the Case Western Reserve University Law Library has compiled this collection of e-mail discussion group commands and instructions.

Pitsco KEYPALS

http://www.keypals.com/

Pitsco, Inc., offers this service, connecting teachers, students, and classrooms internationally through an electronic pen pal exchange.

Dr. Bill Howe is Education Consultant for Multicultural Education, Connecticut State Department of Education.

Dr. Morris Jackson is Director of Community Relations and Gift Officer, Office of Development, American University.

Joy Wallace is a consultant in Portland, Oregon.

References

Blum, K. (1999). Gender differences in asynchronous learning in higher education: Learning styles, participation barriers and communication patterns. *Journal of Asynchronous Learning Networks, 1* (3). Available: *http://www.alnresearch.org/Data_Files/articles/full_text/blum.htm.*

Castner, J. (1997). The clash of social categories: What egalitarianism in networked writing classroom? *Computers and Composition, 14,* 257-268.

Clark, C., & Gorski, P. (2002). Multicultural education and the digital divide: Focus on gender. *Multicultural Perspectives, 4* (1), 30-40.

Haythornthwaite, C. (2002). Building social networks via computer networks: Creating and sustaining distributed learning communities. In K. Renninger & W. Shumar (Eds.), *Building virtual communities: Learning and change in cyberspace* (pp. 159-190). New York: Cambridge University Press.

Herring, S. (1993). *Gender and democracy in computer-mediated communication.* Available: *http://dc.smu.edu/dc/classroom/Gender.txt.*

Levin, J., & Cervantes, R. (2002). Understanding the life cycles of network-based learning communities. In K. Renninger & W. Shumar (Eds.), *Building virtual communities: Learning and change in cyberspace* (pp. 269-292). New York: Cambridge University Press.

Meyer, K. (2003). The web's impact on student learning: A review of recent research reveals three areas that can enlighten current online learning practices. *Technological Horizons in Education Journal, 30* (10), 14-19.

CHAPTER 8

Evaluating Educational Web Sites: A Multicultural Approach

M ost of the criteria used to evaluate traditional educational media such as textbooks and films can be directly applied to the evaluation of educational Web sites as well. Some such criteria are accuracy, bias, credibility, appropriateness, accessibility, timeliness, relevance, validity, and the effectiveness of aesthetic aspects. Still, for a variety reasons, deeper considerations for these criteria, along with several new criteria, must be incorporated into current models to holistically evaluate products of this relatively new cybermedium.

For example, unlike films, textbooks, and journals, all of which are usually subject to rigorous review processes before being made widely available to teachers and students, virtually anybody with access to a Web server can create an educational Web site. No entity comparable to a publishing company exists to help ensure the credibility or expertise of educational Web designers or authors. Likewise, no formal review board examines the validity of the information on most educational Web sites. So, while it remains important for educators to constantly perform our own assessments of materials we use in our classrooms, this responsibility is intensified when it comes to Internet media. According to Kathy Schrock (1999), a leading expert of educational Web development, assessment, and critique:

Unlike the media center, there are no media specialists to sort out the valuable information from the substandard information. With more than 350 million documents available on the Web alone, finding relevant information online can be daunting. Therefore, the ability to critically evaluate information is an invaluable skill in this information age.

Other complications to the assessment of Web sites exist within the structure of the medium itself. In no other medium is the line between commercial and informational distinctions so blurry. It is often difficult to ascertain whether a particular site is a purely commercial venture or a purely educational venture. In fact, it may be the case that no site fits the latter extreme. Again, since many Web sites are produced by unfamiliar sources, we, the users, must look deeper to uncover the bias of online educational products. We must ask critical questions: Who produced this Web site? With what motivation? Who is funding the project? Why? Whose voices are being included, whose voices are being excluded, and for what purposes?

In addition, unlike the content of books or films, the information on Web sites is not static. Used responsibly, this can add new dimensions of opportunity to educational Web sites. Information can be updated any time, new information can be added, and old information can be removed. Concurrently, such capabilities introduce the troubling possibility that teachers will send students to a site that once offered a new perspective on World War II, but that now advertises a white supremacist or hate group.

With this new set of challenges, educators and technologists must develop new approaches for evaluating educational Web sites that focus special attention on the characteristics that differentiate the medium from other educational media. These approaches should inform not only our own Web use, but also the ways in which we teach our students to think critically about online resources (Green, 2001). Drawing on multicultural education philosophy as a foundational frame, this chapter proposes a new, multicultural approach for Web site evaluation.

Why a Multicultural Approach for Evaluating Web Sites?

Two related factors highlight the need for a multicultural approach for evaluating educational Web sites. First, despite (or because of) the troubling number of educators who continue to equate it with Black History Month or an annual diversity festival, we must continue to push toward an actualization of multicultural education that examines, critiques, and transforms all aspects of schools and schooling. A tight focus only on curriculum or teaching styles, or any one aspect of education, does not constitute multicultural education, as stated eloquently by James Banks (1993, p. 25):

> *Multicultural education views the school as a social system that consists of highly interrelated parts and variables. Therefore, in order to transform the school to bring about educational equality, all the major components of the school must be substantially changed. A focus on any one variable in the school, such as the formalized curriculum, will not implement multicultural education.*

If we are dedicated to equity and social justice, educational evaluation, like other aspects of education, must be framed with a multicultural perspective.

A second factor necessitating the need for a multicultural approach for evaluating Web sites relates to the potentially powerful intersections between Internet technology and multicultural teaching and learning practices. As I pointed out in Chapter 3, the Web transcends virtually all other educational media in its capacity for facilitating intercultural, interactive and collaborative teaching and learning. Web site evaluation measures must assess Web media in this context, asking, "Does this site take advantage of the multiculturality inherent in the Internet or does it simply reproduce something that can be accomplished through print, film, or other media?"

A short consideration of current approaches for evaluating educational Web sites will provide points of critique and consideration for the development of a new approach.

Current Approaches

For the past several years, university librarians, educational and instructional technologists, and Web developers have created checklists, outlines, and other schema for evaluating Web resources. The range and variation of these models highlight the challenge of creating effective tools for evaluating a phenomenon and medium still in its infancy.

Some models, such as Bruce Leland's *Evaluating Web Sites: A Guide for Writers* (1998), Joe Landsberger's *Evaluating Website Content* (1999), and Elizabeth E. Kirk's *Evaluating Information Found on the Internet* (1999) rely solely on criteria developed for the evaluation of print resources. Though each of these Web authors, in introductions to their models, acknowledges the features differentiating the Web from other media, all fail to include evaluation criteria that focus on these features. Their criteria include authority, currency, bias, accuracy and credibility.

Other existing models for evaluating educational Web sites place emphasis on the unique characteristics, opportunities, and challenges of the medium. The Southern Regional Educational Board's (SREB) *Criteria for Evaluating Web Sites* (2003) and Esther Grassian's *Thinking Critically about World Wide Web Resources* (1999) attempt to narrow the proverbial chasm between education theory and instructional technology by including several items dealing with the effectiveness of a site's educational and graphical design. The staff of McIntyre Library at the University of Wisconsin-Eau Claire (1999) adds a new dimension to the assessment process by including a "Comparability" criterion that asks whether comparable resources can be found in more traditional media, and whether those are more valuable and practical for the intended use. Their *Ten C's for Evaluating Internet Sources* also assesses the extent to which information on a site is updated, an important item for non-static Web media. Schrock's *Teaching Media Literacy in the Age of the Internet* (1999), one of the most comprehensive models, contains a list of twenty-six evaluation criteria for teachers. Many focus on distinct characteristics of the Internet, including:

- ○ Dates: Does the site include a notation about when information was placed online or updated?
- ○ Efficiency: How quickly does the page load on the screen?
- ○ Links: Does the site contain original resources, or just links to other original resources? Are links appropriate?
- ○ Navigability: Is the site's organization obvious?
- ○ Quantity of Information: Is the site interactive, and will it be necessary to return to the site periodically for updated information?
- ○ Requirements: Does the site insist on requirements (such as plug-in software) or registration?
- ○ Uniqueness: Are the unique qualities of the Web a strength (interactivity) or a weakness (blurred distinction between the educational and the commercial) of the site? (pp. 4-6)

These models, by acknowledging and addressing the characteristics that differentiate the Web from other educational media, represent a significant step in the improvement of educational Web site evaluation. But many, including one from The Ohio State University Libraries (2003), incorporate no critical or multicultural items.

Lesley University (2003), Grassian (1999), and Schrock (1999) journey a step further, each introducing at least one criterion that starts to examine important multicultural principles as actualized (or not actualized) in educational sites. All three include an item on accessibility for differently abled users (e.g., text-only versions, large fonts, etc.). Schrock and the McIntyre Library staff at UW-Eau Claire mention the importance of applying critical thinking skills, both for evaluating sites and for preparing students to process information they find on the Web. Lesley University's *Criteria for Evaluating Web Resources* contains an item on "Responsibility," encouraging Web users to consider what hidden motives a Web site author might have for publishing the site.

Still, every model and approach I have examined fails to assess the extent to which educational Web sites utilize the multicultural potentialities of the Internet. Furthermore, they fail to address nearly all multicultural teaching and learning principles: attention to varied learning styles, engagement and inclusion of diverse and divergent perspectives, active and participatory teaching and learning, and others. An approach grounded in these and other principles of multicultural education must reconsider general educational product evaluation criteria and incorporate new criteria that examine the multicultural-educational worth of individual Web sites.

Toward a New Approach — Criteria Categories

Through an understanding of educational evaluation, multicultural education, and the Web as an educational medium, I developed a list of seven criteria categories to help guide a multicultural approach for evaluating educational Web sites:

1. *Relevance and Appropriateness.* In the field of educational technology a tendency exists to use new technology for the sake of using new technology, without a particular need or sense for how it will improve curricula or pedagogy. So while this category may appear to be an obvious first step in assessing a Web site or any educational product, it is also an important point of departure for determining the contextual strength(s) or weakness(es) of a particular medium. It explores the extent to which the medium, content, and target audience of a site are relevant and appropriate to your needs and those of your students.

2. *Credibility*. One cannot assume credibility or expertise in regard to a Web site as readily as with a textbook (although similar questions should be asked about textbook writers). We must be conscious of credibility both in terms of the author's authority and the trustworthiness of a site's content.

3. *Bias Identification*. The focus should not only be on what information is included on a site; we must remember to consider what is *not* included and the related implications. This criteria category critically examines the inclusiveness and exclusiveness of a site.

4. *Accuracy*. The foundation of a multicultural curriculum is accuracy and completeness. This category addresses these intertwined concepts.

5. *Accessibility*. The Internet was originally designed to provide people access to each other and information. If a resource is inaccessible because of coding problems or incompatibility with certain browsers or special-needs users, it fails to meet even the minimum requirements for an effective educational tool. And if a site author or sponsor is inaccessible through the site, she or he fails to take advantage of the inherently interactive nature of Internet technology. This category also reminds us that the supposed "global classroom" is globally exclusive of those who cannot afford to participate or who do not have access for some other reason—an important but often forgotten point of dialogue related to the Internet.

6. *Navigability*. If your students cannot find their way around a site, it will not take long for collective disengagement to ensue.

7. *Multiculturality*. The Web is capable of facilitating educational opportunities consistent with the principles of multicultural teaching and learning to a greater extent than most other media. Educational sites should reflect this capability.

Evaluation Questions

What follows is a set of questions to guide your assessment of educational Web sites from a multicultural perspective. Some will be more relevant than others depending on what type of resources you are looking for and how you plan to use them. I have not included a rating scale because I believe it is more effective to use your own experience in arriving at an overall, holistic sense for whether a particular site will be valuable in your classroom.

CRITERIA CATEGORY	QUESTIONS
Relevance and Appropriateness	1. Is the site's content relevant to your needs? 2. Is the Web medium appropriate and necessary for your needs? 3. Is the target age group clearly indicated and consistent with the age range of your students? 4. Are the mission and the scope of the site clearly indicated and relevant to your purposes? 5. Are graphic images appropriate for your students' age group? 6. Is the content timely and updated reasonably often?
Credibility	1. Is the author of the site clearly indicated? 2. Is the author's experience in the content area sufficient? 3. Is the site author and/or sponsor a known entity? 4. Is there evidence of quality control? 5. Is the site or site author affiliated with an identified educational organization?
Bias Identification	1. Does the site include a statement about the author or sponsoring organization that helps identify potential bias? 2. Is the site authored or sponsored by some person or organization with a known position regarding the content? If not, is their position clearly stated? 3. Is the primary purpose of the site commercial, and if so, how might this interest be informing content? 4. Does the site include forums for users to discuss its content and present divergent perspectives?
Accuracy	1. Does the site contain obvious content errors or omissions? 2. If information on the site is time-sensitive, is it routinely updated to incorporate new and follow-up information? 3. Does the site provide or invite diverse perspectives, or does it rely on a tightly defined single view for understanding its topic? 4. Are sources within the site clearly cited?
Accessibility	1. Is the site free of coding bugs? 2. Does the site load reasonably fast? If students are expected to use the site at home, will it load quickly over a modem connection? 3. Is the author or sponsoring organization accessible to answer your questions, or those of your students, via e-mail or online form? 4. Is contact information provided for the author or sponsoring organization? 5. Does the site take into consideration the needs of differently abled students (e.g., non-frames version and other considerations)?

CRITERIA CATEGORY	QUESTIONS
Navigability	1. Is the site organization intuitive?
	2. Is the necessity of scrolling kept to a minimum?
	3. Is navigation simple and obvious?
	4. Are navigation bars provided to allow users to jump to different places within the site?
Multiculturality	1. Does the site use a variety of media and approaches to effectively engage students with varying learning styles?
	2. Does the site encourage interaction between author and user or among users?
	3. Does the site encourage participation among users through intercultural, interactive, or collaborative opportunities?
	4. Does the site invite critical examination or divergent perspectives through interactive forums or online evaluation instruments?
	5. Does the site provide voice to other perspectives through links or other connections?
	6. Is the site free of material that may be oppressive to one or more groups of students?

References

Banks, J. (1993). Multicultural education: Characteristics and goals. In J. Banks & C. Banks (Eds.), *Multicultural education: Issues and perspectives.* Boston: Allyn & Bacon.

Grassian, E. (1999). *Thinking critically about World Wide Web resources.* Available: *http://www.library.ucla.edu/libraries/college/instruct/web/critical.htm* (December 13, 1999).

Green, T. (2001). Teaching students to critically evaluate web pages. *The Clearing House, 75* (1), 32-34.

Kirk, E. (1999). *Evaluating information found on the Internet.* Available: *http://milton.mse.jhu.edu:8001/research/education/net.html* (December 13, 1999).

Landsberger, J. (1999). *Evaluating website content.* Available: *http://www.iss.stthomas.edu/webtruth/evaluate.htm* (December 13, 1999).

Leland, B. (1998). *Evaluating web sites: A guide for writers.* Available: *http://www.wiu.edu/users/mfbhl/evaluate.htm* (December 13, 1999).

Lesley University. (2003). *Criteria for evaluating web resources.* Available: *http://www.leslely.edu/library/guides/research/evaluating_web.html* (October 6, 2003).

McIntyre Library Staff at University of Wisconsin-Eau Claire. (1999). *Ten c's for evaluating Internet resources.* Available: *http://www.uwec.edu/Admin/Library/Guides/tencs.html* (December 13, 1999).

The Ohio State University Libraries. (2003). *Evaluating web sites.* Available: *http://gateway.lib.ohio-state.edu/tutor/les1/index.html* (October 6, 2003).

Schrock, K. (1999). Teaching media literacy in the age of the Internet. *Classroom Connect,* (December 1998/January 1999), 4-6.

Southern Regional Educational Board. (2003). *Criteria for evaluating web sites.* Available: *http://www.evalutech.sreb.org/criteria/web.asp* (October 6, 2003).

CHAPTER 9

Digging through the Dirt: Locating Contributive Online Resources

I have delivered workshops on using the Internet to complement multicultural teaching practices since 1996. Much has changed in the area of educational technology over the last eight years. In 1996, most schools were not "connected" to the World Wide Web. Most teachers—and most people in general—did not even know what a Web browser was, and if they did, they probably did not know how to find it or open it on a computer. A few educational sites were scattered around the Web, and on a good day they would attract fifteen or twenty visitors. (Top Web sites today attract millions of visitors daily.)

Amid these substantial changes, the chief concern among educators—even those who recognize the educational potential of the Web and remain enthusiastic about finding efficient and effective ways to incorporate online resources into their teaching practices—steadfastly remains the same: It simply takes too long to "dig through the dirt" in hopes of locating the few educationally and multiculturally sound diamonds in the proverbial rough that may (or may not) exist in cyberspace. That is not to say that contributive multicultural education resources do not exist on the Web—they do. As I discussed in Chapter 3, the interactive nature of the Web makes it a powerful tool that can help weave important multicultural teaching ideals into the classroom including interaction, inclusion, and collaboration. Unfortunately, for every content-rich Web site with original, timely educational resources and interactive opportunities, there are literally thousands that fall into one of several other categories, despite pitching themselves as "educational."

The Dirt

One such category includes purely commercial sites. As discussed in the previous chapter, the ever-fading line between educational and commercial Web sites remains one of the great concerns of the education technology community. Hundreds of sites purporting to be educational in nature have virtually no teaching and learning content at all. These sites are often large electronic advertisements for educational or multicultural consulting firms or educational media distributors.

A second category of these sites is comprised of those Web pages that serve only as lists of links to other sites. As I will discuss later in this chapter, some indexes of links to other sites are useful in weeding out uncontributive or outdated resources. But as is the case with many other subject areas, most of the sites on multicultural education are no more than lists of links to other sites. What makes this amusingly frustrating is that all of these lists of links seem to be linked to each other, so a teacher looking for classroom resources can literally spend hours jumping from one list of links to the next, never finding any original material or opportunity for dialogue.

A third category of content-weak "educational" Web sites includes those that have disappeared altogether, either no longer available or moved to a new, unknown location. Have you ever attempted to visit a Web site, the title of which indicates the possibility of wonderful content, only to receive an error message: "The requested document can not be found on the server"? Because Web sites are easily moved or erased, it is not uncommon for many of the sites resulting from an online search to be no longer available. This is the frustration played out in the popular commercials for one of the top Web-based search engine companies: "Any broken links in here?" A related category includes sites that were created and maintained for some amount of time but were later abandoned. Some of these "educational" sites have not been updated in several years, resulting in outdated material, broken links, missing graphics, and little chance that the contact information provided on the site is correct.

Other sites are updated daily with original content, but they must be studied and scrutinized because they have been developed by unknown or unqualified sources. As mentioned earlier, it is important to remember that Web sites—even those that are educational in nature—are not necessarily subject to content review, either by a panel of peers or by the editorial staff at a publishing company.

A set of effective and efficient strategies is needed to help educators avoid the frustration of digging through thousands of sites that fall under these categories in order to find the two or three sites with relevant, contributive, and multicultural content.

Strategies for Searching Success

The three strategies described here will help maximize the efficiency and effectiveness of your quest to find contributive multicultural teaching and learning resources online. Following each of the three is a list of some of the best educational sources on the Web that one would likely find by implementing the respective strategy.

Strategy 1: Turn to Organizations You Know

A simple, quick, and highly effective strategy for finding quality multicultural resources on the Web is to turn to the Web sites of those organizations, publishers, and educational material producers whose products you already find to be valuable in your classroom. Because the Web has become one of the most widely used media and informational sources in the world, a competition has arisen among every organization in every field to develop a strong online presence and win the Internet audience away from competitors. These organizations employ several techniques for attracting Internet users—potential customers—to their Web sites.

A popular strategy among many organizations and corporations traditionally known for producing educational media (including books, CD-ROMs, films, magazines, and journals) is to offer free teaching and learning materials through their sites. Whether offering downloadable maps and activities, online museum exhibits, opportunities to interact with authors, scientists, or researchers, or virtual tours of different parts of the world, organizations and corporations like National Geographic Society, the Discovery Channel, the Public Broadcasting System (PBS), the History Channel, and others have a single goal in mind. They must offer whatever resources are necessary to draw more users to their Web site than land on somebody else's site. These organizations, whose print or video media have been part of our classrooms in the past, and who have an economic interest in providing only high-quality educational materials, are challenging each other to offer more, and better, educational materials via the Internet. So as the competition to offer the most innovative, interactive, teacher- and student-friendly, multimedia educational tools online continues growing hotter, teachers and students are the biggest winners.

In most cases, these sites devote entire subsections to "Teaching Tools" or "Lesson Plans" or "Student Resources." Many host multimedia, interactive learning activities for students. Others offer entire interdisciplinary units around a particular theme or topic. In almost all cases, the teaching and learning resources on these sites are among the best available online.

You can concentrate this strategy further by focusing on organizations that, like PBS, have strong reputations for producing and supporting multicultural programs, resources, and materials.

Strategy 2: Use Site Indexes That Have Started Digging for You

As I prepared to write this chapter, I used *Google*, a popular Web search engine, to search for sites on "multicultural education." The result: About 2,160,000 sites matched my search criteria. While I am thrilled to have found so many sites that mention multicultural education, the prospect of weeding through over two million Web pages to find three or four with meaningful content is a daunting and unattractive one.

A second strategy for maximizing the efficiency and effectiveness of your online time is to avoid search engines that indiscriminately index every available site existing in cyberspace, instead using indexing and search tools that have started the digging process for you by weeding out content-weak Web sites.

As a new crop of Web financiers attempt to tap into the lucrative market currently controlled by search engines and Web indexing sites like *Yahoo!* and *Google*, they, like the educational organizations already mentioned, must find creative ways to draw users away from their more established competitors. And again, as the competition heats up and companies look for innovative and creative ways to make their product more attractive than those of their competitors, the winners are Web users who can devote more energy to searching an index that only includes content-rich, up-to-date, technically sound sites.

About.com and *LookSmart* are two sites that represent this new breed of Web search tool. Both have found their niche by employing legions of individuals with specific content area expertise to literally "mine" the Web for the most content-rich, contributive, and valuable resources on or about that topic. *LookSmart* employs a multilevel indexing scheme that allows users to browse through a series of topic headings that become more specific at each level.

About.com takes this process a step further. It does not simply list groups of Web sites on a given topic. Instead, a team weeds through individual sites, highlighting only the most creditable resources, content, and information within them. Content experts then build "guides" specific to their areas of expertise, organizing links to related resources under several subsection headings. *About.com* guides include "Civil Liberties," "Race Relations," and "Women's Issues."

Other site indexing and search tools follow the example of *LookSmart* and *About.com*, but focus only on sites related to education. One of the best examples of an education-focused site index is *Kathy Shrock's Guide for Educators* (see Figure 9.1). Schrock reviews and organizes educational Web

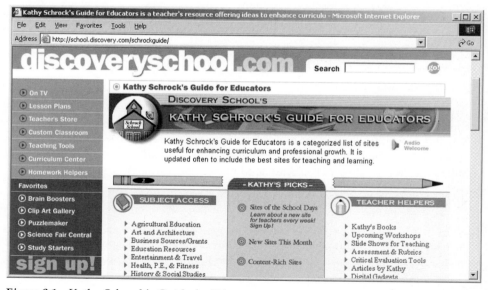

Figure 9.1   Kathy Schrock's Guide for Educators
http://school.discovery.com/schrockguide/

sites by subject area, but also includes useful information including evaluation and search tools.

One weakness of this strategy is that it will necessarily result in a limited selection of resources that may reflect the preferences or biases of a site's creator. Still, it is a useful way of reducing the amount of hit-or-miss searching and exploring needed to locate valuable teaching and learning tools online.

Save time by using these sites, each of which have started the digging process for you.

SITE INDEXES

About.com

http://www.about.com

One of a new breed of Web site search and indexing tools, *About.com* employs topic-specific experts to mine the Internet as well as individual Web sites for the best available resources.

Kathy Schrock's Guide for Educators

http://school.discovery.com/schrockguide/

Schrock, a well-known educational technology guru, has assembled an index of the best education Web sites. Her site, hosted by the Discovery Channel's Web site, is arranged by subject areas.

LookSmart

http://www.looksmart.com

LookSmart, a recent addition to the Web search tool competition, uses a team of Web and content experts to review sites and index only those that pass a rigorous inspection for content and credibility. Subsections of the index include "Community & Cultures" and "International Affairs." A search for "multicultural education" results in a short list and a link to the "Top 10 Most Visited Sites on Multicultural Education."

Special Education Resources on the Internet

http://www.hood.edu/seri/serihome.htm

Also known as *SERI,* this site serves as an index of other sites on special education and related fields. Site categories include "Inclusion Resources" and "Special Education Discussion Groups."

Strategy 3: Use Links Sections of Prominent Web Sites

A third strategy for locating multicultural teaching and learning tools online is to explore the links provided by educational sites through sections titled "Related Sites," "Other Sites," or "Links." The basis for this strategy, like Strategy 2, is to identify a starting point for your search at which somebody has already performed some of the digging and weeding for you. Most educational Web sites provide this point of entry for users. The challenge is to locate "Related Sites" Web pages that do not fall into one of the "Dirt" categories described earlier.

The nature of the Web and hypertext media is such that users of any given site can jump to a different site with a simple mouse click if a link to that different site is provided. As a result, it is in the best interest of site creators, writers, and editors to provide links only to sites that will reflect positively on their own project. Although some may still choose to add a link to virtually any related site, most Web authors and editors of prominent educational sites employ a strict set of criteria for assessing the value of any possible link from their site to another. For example, as the creator and author of the *Multicultural Pavilion* and the *Multicultural Supersite*, I will provide a link to another site if (1) the creator and all contributors to the site are explicitly and clearly identified, AND (2) the site contains quality original educational content, or (3) the site facilitates interaction and dialogue among educators, students, or other users, or (4) the site provides an effective tool for locating other resources on- or offline.

Writers and editors of prominent Web sites also tend to be more conscientious and selective when choosing links, making sure those they include are timely, functional, and up-to-date. This is especially true for sites like the *Diversity Database* and the *Women's Studies Database*, products of the University of Maryland, College Park, both of which are used primarily because of their well-organized links and references to related sites and resources.

This strategy shares limitations with Strategy 2, but employed thoughtfully, can help save time and frustration in your search for contributive online resources. A sample of these resources follows.

Though they are often buried beneath piles of outdated material, broken links, and content-vacant sites, several wonderful resources for supplementing multicultural teaching practices exist on the Web. Employing these and your own strategies, you should be better equipped to more efficiently and effectively mine the Web for the most contributive, most valuable, and most relevant multicultural education resources.

MORE WEB SITES

ORGANIZATIONS YOU KNOW

A&E Classroom

http://www.aetv.com/class/

The Arts and Entertainment network hosts a variety of educational materials including discussion forums and teaching materials.

Crayola Creativity Center

http://www.crayola.com/educators/lessons/index.cfm

The folks at Crayola have developed a series of lesson plans for young students. Themes include "Native Peoples," "Cultures," and "Intergenerational Ideas."

Discovery Channel School

http://school.discovery.com

The Discovery Channel hosts a site featuring resources for teachers, students, and parents. The teacher section includes a collection of lesson plans, many with multicultural themes. The student section has several online learning activities as well as an online history encyclopedia.

History Channel Classroom

http://www.historychannel.com/classroom/classroom.html

The History Channel's Web site offers a plethora of teaching and learning opportunities with periodically changing features. Current features include "The Ellis Island Exhibit" and "The Underground Railroad." A separate section called "Ideas from Our Teachers" highlights specific ways in which teachers have used material from this site.

National Geographic Education Guide

http://www.nationalgeographic.com/education/

National Geographic provides one of the most interactive, educational Web sites available free of charge. The site includes periodically changing features, interactive exhibits, an online world atlas, and other resources for teachers and students to learn more about their own cultures and to explore the rest of the world. A current feature highlights the Underground Railroad.

Nye Labs Online

http://www.billnye.com

Bill Nye, the Science Guy, supplements his popular educational television show with a set of interactive online science labs. Activities are varied and change constantly. Teacher materials and resources are also available.

PBS Online — TeacherSource

http://pbs.org/teachersource/

The Public Broadcasting Service has long been respected for producing effective multi-cultural and educational media. Their *TeacherSource* site further illustrates their dedication to multicultural education by including a database of over one thousand lesson plans, many with multicultural themes. Current features also include teacher guides on topics such as the healing of apartheid wounds in South Africa and a history of African American farmers.

Peace Corps — World Wise Educators

http://www.peacecorps.gov/wws/educators/index.html

The Peace Corps hosts one of the most impressive collections of multicultural teaching and learning resources on the Web. A large collection of lesson plans is highlighted by a section called "Lesson Plans on Looking at Ourselves and Others." This site also facilitates interaction between students and Peace Corps volunteers in the field.

MarcoPolo (MCI Worldcom)

http://www.wcom.com/marcopolo/

Several corporations including MCI Worldcom provide a collection of online educational content produced by content experts. Resources include lesson plans in all subjects and special topics, including "Crossing Borders."

NASA Quest

http://quest.arc.nasa.gov/

NASA's education site hosts interactive projects, timely topic-specific Web chats, and strategies for using the Internet in your classroom. Several forms allow students to interact with NASA engineers, experts, and astronauts. Recent "Hot Topics" include "Women of NASA."

UNICEF: Kids Helping Kids

http://www.unicefusa.org/issues96/sep96/guide/english.html

The U.S. Fund for UNICEF, an organization that advocates the well-being and education of all the world's children, hosts a site with sections including "Respect Differences," "Build a New World," and "Bring Home Peace."

U.S. Geological Survey's Learning Web

http://www.usgs.gov/education/index.html

This site includes a collection of educational materials including lesson plans, classroom materials, and other science-related activities. Students can "Ask the Experts" by directly e-mailing the government's top scientists, study history through maps, or browse image galleries.

World Book Student Resource Center

http://www2.worldbook.com/students/feature_index.asp

The encyclopedia publisher continually adds new features to its online archives. Previous features include "The African American Journey," "The Quest for Equality," and "A Divided Nation."

LINKS SECTIONS OF PROMINENT WEB SITES

American Studies Web: Reference and Research

http://www.georgetown.edu/crossroads/asw/

The American Studies Department at Georgetown University maintains an extensive list of related sites with subtopics that include "Race and Ethnicity," "Gender and Sexuality," and "Sociology and Demography."

Diversity Database

http://www.inform.umd.edu/diversitydb/

Developed by a team of content and technology experts at the University of Maryland, College Park, the *Diversity Database* is a compendium of resources organized by identity dimensions including age, class, race, gender, ability status, religion, and sexual orientation. Listings within each of these sections include books, conference announcements, article citations, Web sites, and course syllabi.

Multicultural Paths—Multicultural Pavilion

http://www.edchange.org/multicultural/sites1.html

Multicultural Paths is an index of multicultural education sites. Entries are divided into categories and subcategories including "Curriculum Transformation," "Homophobia and Education," "Bilingual Education," "Evaluation and Research," and "Digital Divide."

Multicultural SuperLinks—McGraw-Hill Multicultural Supersite

http://www.mhhe.com/socscience/education/multi/links.html

The editor of the *Multicultural Supersite* carefully reviews potential additions to the *SuperLinks* page for content and design before dividing them into categories including "Lesson Plans and Curricular Resources," "Multicultural Organizations and Associations," and "Online Dialogue Forums."

OutProud's Web Resources

http://www.outproud.org/web.html

One of the most popular and extensive Web sites for gay, lesbian, bisexual, and transgender youth also houses one of the best sections of related sites. Categories include "Arts," "Educational Resources," and "Scholarly Resources."

Social Class Page Links

http://www.src.uchicago.edu/SocialClass/links.html

This is one of many resources on the University of Chicago's *Social Class Page.* It includes related links to sites under several categories including "Demography/Sociology" and "Political Science."

Women's Studies Database's Other Web Sites

http://www.inform.umd.edu/EdRes/Topics/WomensStudies/OtherWebSites/

The Women's Studies program at the University of Maryland, College Park, hosts this extensive index of related sites. Subtopics include "Diversity," "Education," "History," "Literature," and "Women of Color."

CHAPTER 10

A Guide to Online Resources: General

The following Web sites are of general multicultural education teaching or scholarly interest.

MULTICULTURAL EDUCATION SITES

Center for Multicultural Education

http://depts.washington.edu/centerme/home.htm

University of Washington faculty developed the Center to coordinate activities and programs related to multicultural education scholarship. The site includes information about model programs and downloadable publications.

Diversity: Issues and Responses

http://goldmine.cde.ca.gov/iasa/diversity.html

Just one section of the California Department of Education site, *Diversity* is a collection of resources, models, and interviews related to diversity education.

Diversity Education Network

http://www.acodden.org/info/index17.html

The European Jewish Information Centre launched this organization and Web site devoted to advocating diversity education throughout Europe.

EdJustice.org

http://edjustice.org/

The Justice Matters Institute in San Francisco hosts this well-organized index of Web resources. The goal of the site is to promote educational equality for all students. Resources on the site include dialogue forums, curriculum ideas, and an events calendar.

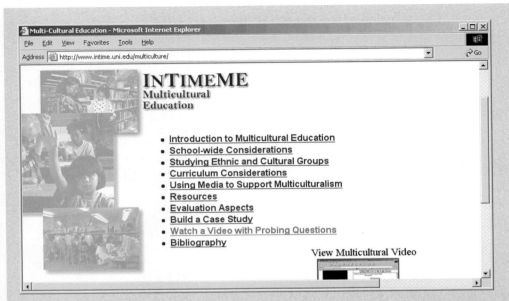

Figure 10.1   InTimeMe
http://www.intime.uni.edu/multiculture/

Inclusive Teaching

http://depts.washington.edu/cidrweb/inclusive/

The University of Washington hosts this site with strategies and hints for providing student-centered, inclusive teaching and learning.

InTimeMe: Multicultural Education (see Figure 10.1)

http://www.intime.uni.edu/multiculture/

InTime (which stands for "Integrating New Technologies into the Methods of Education") helps educators recognize the intersections between technology and multicultural education.

Mid-Atlantic Equity Consortium

http://www.maec.org/

MAEC houses a compendium of equity resources for principals, teachers, counselors, and parents.

Multicultural Pavilion

http://www.edchange.org/multicultural

Multicultural Pavilion provides resources for teachers, educators, and activists to explore and discuss multicultural education; facilitates opportunities for educators to work toward self-awareness and development; and serves as a forum for educators to interact and collaborate toward a critical, transformative approach to multicultural education. The site offers a plethora of theoretical and practical resources including awareness activities, dialogue forums, collections of original essays and research, an intercultural poetry exchange, and a host of collaborative opportunities for teachers and students.

Multicultural Education Supersite

http://www.mhhe.com/multicultural

Hosted by McGraw-Hill's Higher Education Division, the *Multicultural Education Supersite* bridges multicultural education theory and practice by offering a variety of resources including original articles, intercultural classroom activities, an exploration of multicultural curriculum transformation, and book reviews. The site is specifically designed for preservice teachers, inservice teachers, and teacher educators.

New Horizons for Learning: Multicultural Education

http://www.newhorizons.org/strategies/multicultural/front_multicultural.htm

The multicultural education area represents just one of several sets of resources housed within the *New Horizons* Web site. It is primarily a collection of articles and short papers on multicultural education and related topics.

Our Children, Our Communities, and Our Future

http://www.sasked.gov.sk.ca/equity/

This policy framework for education equity was written in 1997 for Saskatchewan educators.

Racism: No Way

http://www.racismnoway.com.au/together/international/index-The.html

This Australia-based site, also known as *International Approaches to Anti-racism Education*, includes classroom activities, a library of readings, and other resources on education equity.

SOFWeb Multicultural Education Home Page

http://www.sofweb.vic.edu.au/lem/multi/index.htm

The state of Victoria's (Australia) Department of Education and Training offers a great policy statement, links, and case studies—all useful resources for teacher preparation.

Teaching Tolerance

http://www.tolerance.org/teach/index.jsp

Though multicultural education challenges us to go beyond tolerance toward equity and social justice, the Southern Poverty Law Center presents some excellent free resources for teachers and students including strategies for responding to bias in the classroom.

ORGANIZATIONS AND ASSOCIATIONS

Alberta Association for Multicultural Education

http://www.albertaassociationformulticulturaleducation.ca/index.htm

AAME advocates dialogues and programs that support multicultural, antiracist education.

All Kinds of Minds

http://www.allkindsofminds.org/index.aspx

This nonprofit provides promising practices, research, and products for the appreciation and validation of learning differences.

Anti-Defamation League: Education

http://www.adl.org/education/

The ADL has a long history of fighting bigotry of all kinds. Their education site includes lesson plans and access to a plethora of free anti-bias classroom resources.

Center for Language Minority Education and Research

http://www.clmer.csulb.edu/

The Center promotes equity in schools for speakers of languages other than English. Browse current issues in education or download powerful presentations related to language equity.

Center for Multilingual Multicultural Research

http://www-rcf.usc.edu/~cmmr/

This Center, located at the University of Southern California, conducts and facilitates research on bilingual, multicultural, and cross-cultural education. It also serves as a starting point for teachers seeking information about these educational approaches.

Center for Research on Education, Diversity, and Excellence

http://www.crede.ucsc.edu/

Through research, publication, and education, CREDE works to assist linguistic and cultural minority students to achieve academically to their highest potentials.

Council for Opportunity in Education

http://www.trioprograms.org/

The Council is a nonprofit organization dedicated to providing all students an equal opportunity to achieve a higher education.

Early Childhood Research Institute on Inclusion

http://www.fpg.unc.edu/~ecrii/

ECRII, a product of five years of research, offers reports and research for administrators determined to practice inclusion in early childhood classrooms.

The Education Alliance

http://www.alliance.brown.edu/

The Alliance, at Brown University, is dedicated to holistic school reform. Their resources are arranged topically, with sections including "Equity and Diversity," "Rural Schools," and "School Reform."

Educators for Social Responsibility

http://www.esrnational.org/home.htm

ESR helps teachers provide a safe learning environment for all students, in part by helping us recognize our roles as social activists. The Web site contains resources pertaining to all levels of education.

Gay, Lesbian, and Straight Education Network

http://www.glsen.org/

GLSEN is a national organization consisting of educators, students, parents, and others working together to address heterosexism and homophobia in schools. The site includes an index of related resources and access to a downloadable journal.

Global Citizens for Change

http://www.citizens4change.org/

Global Citizens for Change helps educators and others put into practice the social changes they would like to see.

NAACP Education Department

http://www.naacp.org/work/education/education.shtml

This progressive organization's education department is dedicated to ensuring that every student receives a quality education. Resources available through the Web site include a "Call for Action," an *Education Advocacy Manual*, and a timeline highlighting the organization's educational activities.

National Association for Bilingual Education

http://www.nabe.org/

This nonprofit was created in the mid-seventies to serve the needs of language minority students in the United States. As both a professional and an advocacy organization, it hosts conferences, conducts research, facilitates professional development, and advocates for legislation to support a growing constituency of students.

National Association for Multicultural Education (see Figure 10.2)

http://www.nameorg.org/

NAME is the largest organization in the world specifically dedicated to the ideals and principles of multicultural education. The site contains information on NAME's national conference, quarterly journal, and national listserv on multicultural issues in education. A highlight of the site is a collection of position statements on topics including high-stakes testing, Title IX, teacher testing, and the digital divide.

National Coalition for Women and Girls in Education

http://www.ncwge.org/

NCWGE, "a nonprofit organization of more than 50 organizations dedicated to improving educational opportunities for girls and women," developed this site to house press releases, research, and resources on gender equity in education.

National Information Center for Children and Youth with Disabilities

http://www.nichcy.org/

This site, offered in both English and Spanish, provides users with information about children with disabilities. It includes a searchable database of related organizations and resources.

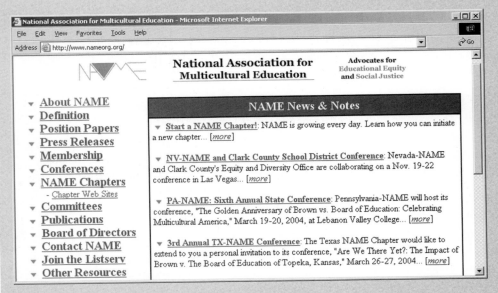

Figure 10.2 National Association for Multicultural Education
http://www.nameorg.org/

National Multicultural Institute

http://www.nmci.org/

First created in the early 1980s to answer a nationwide need for more information and training opportunities related to diversity, NMCI remains one of the leaders in this field through conferences, trainings, and publications.

Resource Center of the Americas

http://www.americas.org/

Based in Minneapolis, Minnesota, the Resource Center promotes human rights and social justice through organizing and educating.

Teaching for Change

http://teachingforchange.org/

Previously the Network of Educators on the Americas, Teaching for Change is a D.C.-based organization that provides easy access to transformational educational resources.

GENERAL TEACHER AND CURRICULAR RESOURCES

Ad Dissection 101: Exposing Media Manipulation (see Figure 10.3)

http://website.education.wisc.edu/rla/ADSITE/index.htm

Mr. Anderson, sophomore English teacher in Verona, Wisconsin, created *Ad Dissection 101* to engage his students in a critical thinking exploration regarding the media.

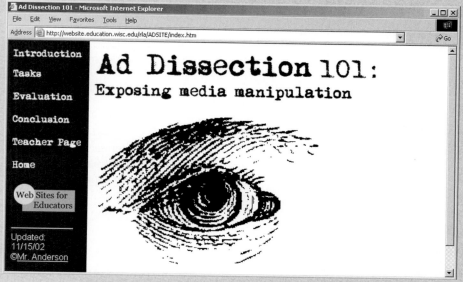

Figure 10.3   Ad Dissection 101

http://website.education.wisc.edu/rla/ADSITE/index.htm

The American Promise

http://www.farmers.com/FarmComm/AmericanPromise/

Sponsored by the Farmers' Insurance Group, PBS Online, and the NCSS, *The American Promise* is devoted to helping educators create democratic schools and classrooms. The site features downloadable resources and lesson plans, teaching guides, and news about related projects.

AskERIC

http://www.askeric.org/

The Educational Information Resource Center offers this large and growing collection of resources for teachers, administrators, and students. The site includes a "Question and Answer" section for educators looking for specific materials; a "Virtual Library" of resources, links, and materials related to a variety of education topics; and a "Lesson Plans" archive with more than one thousand entries.

Blue Web'n

http://www.kn.pacbell.com/wired/bluewebn/

The purpose of *Blue Web'n* is to catalog the best available educational Web sites—particularly those that involve learning activities, lesson plans, and resources for learners. Users are invited to subscribe to a weekly e-mail service to be kept abreast of new educational Web sites.

The Digital Classroom

http://www.archives.gov/

The National Archives and Records Administration puts forth this collection of primary sources and activities for teachers and students. Browse through archives of primary documents and related educational materials and ideas. Another section of the site teaches students how to conduct research using *The Digital Classroom*'s resources.

EdSiteMent

http://edsitement.neh.gov/

This large compendium of resources for teachers and students of the humanities contains original lesson plans as well as links to the best related Web sites. Sponsored by MCI Worldcom, the National Endowment for the Humanities, and the Council of the Great City Schools, *EdSiteMent* covers history, language arts, and foreign languages.

ERIC Clearinghouse on Teaching and Teacher Education

http://www.ericsp.org/

The Educational Information Resource Center includes this set of links to Web resources for teachers and teacher educators.

Federal Resources for Educational Excellence

http://www.ed.gov/free/index.html

More than thirty federal agencies collaborate on a compendium of free educational resources. Content is divided by subject area and includes activities, archives, audio interviews, and other documents.

The Gateway of Educational Materials

http://thegateway.org/index.html

The Gateway is an index of lesson plans, curricular units, and other educational resources available via the Web. Users can search for keywords or by topic area or grade level. A search for "multicultural" returned a list of forty-seven related items.

Global Connections

http://www.pbs.org/wgbh/globalconnections/

PBS sponsors this collection of Web sites that keep educators and others informed of current events around the world. Lesson plans, readings, maps, and timelines are available.

Humanities Interactive

http://www.humanities-interactive.org/a_base.html

The Texas Council for the Humanities Resource Center presents an incredible collection of interactive resources, tools, lesson plans, online exhibits, and other materials about culture, history, and literature.

Inclusion: Yours, Mine, Ours

http://rushservices.com/Inclusion/

Rush Services hosts this collection of resources designed to help teachers more effectively include children with special needs in their classrooms. Register for a free newsletter that includes specific and practical information on classroom inclusion.

K-5 Cyber Trail: Multicultural Curriculum Resources

http://www.wmht.org/trail/explor02.htm

K-5 Cybertrail, an index of sites and materials for educators, includes this section highlighting multicultural resources for elementary school teachers.

LD Online

http://www.ldonline.org/

This interactive guide contains information and resources for students, teachers, and parents on learning disabilities. The site includes first-person accounts, audio clips, discussion forums, and other teaching and learning tools. Teachers are encouraged to submit the work and stories of their own students.

More than Bows and Arrows: Curriculum Materials for Preschoolers

http://www.nativechild.com/

The "Curriculum" section of the *Native Child* Web site contains an array of learning resources with Native American themes. Replace the images of Native Americans that have been fed to students in the past with positive images.

Social Justice Education

http://www.socialjusticeeducation.org/

This organization supports social justice education through curriculum development. Find innovative lesson ideas and tools on the Web site.

TeachersNetwork.org

http://teachnet.org

This nationwide, nonprofit network of educators connects and provides resources to teachers across the country. The network particularly supports teachers who appreciate and strive for innovation in the classroom.

Thinkquest

http://www.thinkquest.org/

Thinkquest sponsors competitions for which students collaborate to build educationally valuable, innovative learning Web sites. The site includes a virtual library of the winning projects.

We Hold These Truths to Be Self-Evident

http://edweb.sdsu.edu/people/cmathison/truths/truths.html

This online activity, created by Carla Mathison and Cathy Pohan of San Diego State University, engages educators in a process of examining whether their school supports educational equity, a welcoming learning environment for all students, and democratic education practices.

ONLINE PUBLICATIONS

Diversity Digest

http://www.diversityweb.org/digest/

The Association of American Colleges and Universities publishes this quarterly newsletter highlighting promising diversity practices in higher education.

Education Policy Analysis Archives

http://epaa.asu.edu/epaa/

EPAA, a generally progressive peer-reviewed online journal, covers policy issues ranging from standardized testing to the conceptualization of "highly qualified teachers."

Electronic Magazine of Multicultural Education

http://www.eastern.edu/publications/emme/

EMME is a purely electronic magazine that publishes curricular tools and ideas, reviews of multicultural media, and scholarly essays on multicultural education. Each issue focuses on a particular theme, the most recent being "Urban Education and Reform."

The Future of Children

http://www.futureofchildren.org/

The Packard Foundation sponsors this journal, fully available online, highlighting research that promotes child advocacy.

Humanising Language Teaching (HLT)

http://www.hltmag.co.uk/index.htm

This UK-based journal combines articles on theory and practice promoting a student-centered approach to language teaching. Common topics include multiple intelligences, bilingual education, and equity.

In Motion

http://www.inmotionmagazine.com/

Produced by NPC Productions, *In Motion* uses a multicultural approach for exploring issues related to democracy. Sections of the magazine include "Affirmative Action," "Education Rights," and "Global Eyes." It is available in both English and Spanish.

International Journal on Multicultural Societies

http://www.unesco.org/most/jmshome.htm

Multiculturalism, migration, and minority rights are the focus of this social science journal sponsored by UNESCO. Topics include language, religion, race, ethnicity, and other social justice issues, all from a global perspective.

Merge

http://www.mergemag.org/

This feminist e-magazine based in Chicago raises awareness about sexism with a strong focus on media messages.

Figure 10.4   New Horizons Online Journal
http://www.newhorizons.org/

Multicultural Review

http://www.mcreview.com/

Though the site is primarily an advertisement for this quarterly journal for all people interested in remaining informed about trends and publications related to cultural diversity and multiculturalism, it also contains each issue's reviews of books, videos, and other educational resources.

New Horizons Online Journal (see Figure 10.4)

http://www.newhorizons.org/

This online journal on progressive educational issues uses quarterly themes. Recent issues have focused on education's role in the twenty-first century, research on ADD/ADHD, the power of storytelling, learning communities, and inclusive schools.

Rethinking Schools Online

http://www.rethinkingschools.org/

The online version of this journal, published by Rethinking Schools, a nonprofit publisher run by activist teachers, contains highlights from the print version. *Rethinking Schools* examines current educational issues and explores progressive solutions to educational problems.

STANDARDS: International Journal of Multicultural Studies

http://www.colorado.edu/journals/standards/

Sponsored by the Office of Diversity and Equity at the University of Colorado, Boulder, *Standards* is a purely electronic journal that combines fiction and nonfiction writing along with resource reviews around topical themes. Recent themes have included "Complexities," "Pride," and "Education."

Urban Educator

http://www.cgcs.org/urbaneducator/

The Council of the Great City Schools runs this online publication covering a variety of issues related to urban education. The site also includes relevant reports and data, press releases, and a guide to promising practices.

Urban Mozaik Magazine

http://www.urbanmozaik.com/index.html

This online and print journal is a celebration of human diversity, working toward a closer multicultural society in North America.

ARTICLES AND ESSAYS

Blinding Sight: A Question of Color

http://www.edchange.org/multicultural/papers/shin.html

Gene-Tey Shin, a teacher and multicultural education trainer, shares his experiences understanding color, color blindness, and education through this personal narrative spanning most of his life.

A Brief History of Multicultural Education

http://www.mhhe.com/socscience/education/multi/philosophy/1history.html

Part of the *Multicultural Supersite*'s Multicultural Philosophy Series, this article by Paul Gorski examines the roots of multicultural education and how its focus has become increasingly progressive and inclusive.

Confronting the Challenge of Diversity in Education

http://www.inmotionmagazine.com/pndivers.html

Pedro Neguera challenges educators to think of pluralism as an opportunity, not a problem, in the classroom.

Cultural Diversity and Academic Achievement

http://www.ncrel.org/sdrs/areas/issues/educatrs/leadrshp/le0bow.htm

Barbara Bowman develops a workable plan to address achievement gaps by preventing their emergence in the first place.

A Cultural Plunge

http://www.edchange.org/multicultural/papers/garyfortune.html

Gary Fortune shares his experience observing a bilingual elementary classroom in San Diego. In narrative form, he implicitly connects his experience feeling like an outsider (he does not speak Spanish) during that single day to that of many students who feel disconnected in schools across the United States every day because English is not their native language.

Defining Multicultural Education

http://www.mhhe.com/socscience/education/multi/define.html

Paul Gorski suggests a holistic definition of multicultural education that focuses on three levels of transformation: (1) the transformation of self; (2) the transformation of schools and schooling; and (3) the transformation of society.

Educating Teachers for Diversity

http://www.ncrel.org/sdrs/areas/issues/educatrs/presrvce/pe300.htm

NCREL's "Critical Issue" paper describes the reform necessary in teacher preparation programs to prepare future educators to effectively teach in increasingly diverse schools.

ERIC Clearinghouse on Urban Education

http://eric-web.tc.columbia.edu/

A host of articles and resources are categorized under headings that include "Community Involvement," "Curriculum and Instruction," "Equity and Cultural Diversity," and "School Reform."

Five Ways to Analyze Classrooms for an Anti-Bias Approach

http://www.nncc.org/Diversity/sac26_anti-bias.analyz.html

Peggy Riehl, family life educator, provides practical strategies for minimizing bias in your classroom.

Gifted Education in a Multicultural Australia

http://www.nexus.edu.au/teachstud/gat/becherv1.htm

Neil E. Bechervaise addresses the failure of Australia's education system to adapt to immigrant populations by exploring immigrant attitudes toward gifted education programs.

Multicultural Education

http://www.edchange.org/multicultural/papers/keith.html

Keith Wilson provides this introductory look at how multicultural education should look.

Multicultural Education: A Blueprint for Action

http://www.newhorizons.org/strategies/multicultural/blueprint/front_blueprint.html

The National Council on Educating Black Children wrote this strategic plan for implementing multicultural education. The article is organized around a chronology of five implementation tasks.

Multicultural Education in Elementary and Secondary Schools

http://www.ed.gov/databases/ERIC_Digests/ed327613.html

Michael Webb composed this article about the implementation of multicultural programs in K-12 schools. He explores the goals of these programs and their effects on students.

The Multicultural Pavilion Research Room

http://www.edchange.org/multicultural/papers.html

This collection of original articles and essays on multicultural education and related topics is one of the most popular sections of the *Multicultural Pavilion* Web site.

Racial and Gender Identity in White Male Multicultural Educators and Facilitators

http://home.earthlink.net/~gorski/dissertation.html

Paul Gorski shares several online chapters from his qualitative dissertation on racial and gender identity development among white men who identify as multicultural educators.

Resegregation in America's Schools

http://www.civilrightsproject.harvard.edu/research/deseg/reseg_schools99.php

Gary Orfield and John Yun of The Civil Rights Project (Harvard University) report trends of the continued and deepening segregation of schools throughout the United States.

Restructuring Education for the 21st Century

http://www.edchange.org/multicultural/papers/caleb/education.html

Caleb Rosado starts with the arguments and research on the need to develop a new, more inclusive, education system, and tackles the question, "how?" He ends the article with three specific methods for implementing educational change.

The Scope of Multicultural Education

http://www.newhorizons.org/strategies/multicultural/hanley.htm

Mary Stone Hanley of Antioch University uses a social change framework to summarize approaches and conceptualizations for multicultural education.

A Synthesis of Scholarship on Multicultural Education

http://www.ncrel.org/sdrs/areas/issues/educatrs/leadrshp/le0gay.htm

Geneva Gay summarizes most of the scholarship on multicultural education.

Teaching with a Multicultural Perspective

http://ericps.ed.uiuc.edu/eece/pubs/digests/1991/gomez91.html

Rey Gomez challenges common myths about the practice of multicultural teaching and learning.

Varieties of Multicultural Education

http://eric-web.tc.columbia.edu/digest/dig98.asp

ERIC's Clearinghouse on Urban Education includes this article by Gary Burnett about different conceptualizations of multicultural education and how understanding them can help all of us develop more effective programs.

What Makes a School Multicultural?

http://www.edchange.org/multicultural/papers/caleb/multicultural.html

Caleb Rosado explores the meaning of "multiculturalism" and how it relates to school change. He moves the conversation into a conceptual framework for multicultural education.

Whites in Multicultural Education: Rethinking Our Role

http://www.enc.org/equity/eqtyres/erg/111354/1354.htm

Gary Howard challenges white educators to think more critically and reflectively about transformative approaches for multicultural education. He does this, in part, by sharing his own powerful and intriguing experiences with multicultural teaching and learning.

Lesson Plan Databases

A to Z Teacher Stuff Thematic Units Index

http://atozteacherstuff.com/themes/

A to Z Teacher Stuff provides a collection of hundreds of resources organized into thematic units. Themes include "Me," "Family," "Around the World," and "Ancient Egypt."

The Academy Curriculum Exchange

http://ofcn.org/cyber.serv/academy/ace/

A consortium of teachers from fourteen states created the core of this lesson plan database. Now *The Academy Curriculum Exchange* houses over seven hundred lesson plans in all subject areas. Many of these have a multicultural flavor, including "Awareness to Culture by Self-Esteem," and "Critical Thinking Skills." Users are encouraged to expand the site by donating their ideas and lesson plans.

Active Citizenship: Empowering America's Youth

http://www.activecitizenship.org/

John Minkler created this curricular unit for grades 7-12 to engage students in lessons about democracy and citizenship.

Apple Lesson Plans Library

http://henson.austin.apple.com/edres/lessonmenu.shtml

The Apple Learning Exchange developed this directory of technology-based lesson plans for all grade levels. Many are multimedia in nature, and nearly all are interactive.

AskERIC Lesson Plans

http://askeric.org/Virtual/Lessons/

More than a thousand lesson plans are housed in this section of ERIC's Web site. These plans have been submitted and reviewed by teachers all over the world and cover all subject areas.

Beads, Bowls, and Tales

http://jeffcoweb.jeffco.k12.co.us/isu/art/beadindex.html

This interdisciplinary multicultural art curriculum unit uses beads to engage students in a variety of learning experiences.

Can Teach

http://www.canteach.ca/

Created for Canadian educators, *Can Teach* houses a large index of lesson plans. A special section allows users to submit their own materials. Resource categories include "Fine Arts," "First Nations," and "Technological Education." Several e-mail discussion groups are also accessible through the site.

Center for Critical Thinking Classroom Materials

http://www.criticalthinking.org/K12/k12class/trc.html

The *Critical Thinking Community* site includes lesson plans and classroom ideas to help K-12 teachers develop critical thinking skills in themselves and their students.

Changing Attitudes in America

http://www.yale.edu/ynhti/curriculum/units/1994/4/94.04.04.x.html

Carolyn Kinder challenges participants to think more critically about equity and social justice issues.

Collaborative Lesson Archive

http://faldo.atmos.uiuc.edu/CLA/

Built by the University of Illinois, the *Collaborative Lesson Archive* is a forum for teachers of all levels (preschool through college) to exchange lesson plans and curricular ideas. Search through the database by grade level, subject, or keyword.

Diversity Learning

http://www.diversitylearning.ca/

Diversity Learning is a Canada-based gateway to hundreds of lesson plans and curricular resources on multiculturalism, gender equity, human rights, and related topics. It is available in French and English.

EdSiteMent Lesson Plans

http://edsitement.neh.gov/lesson_index.asp

EdSiteMent, a Web site designed to help teachers and students locate and use a diversity of educational Internet resources, includes a set of lesson plans. The plans help students learn from multiple perspectives. Topics include "Cultural Change," "Common Visions, Common Voices," and "Perspective on the Slave Narrative."

Educational CyberPlayground Online Curriculum

http://www.edu-cyberpg.com/culdesac/Home_culdesac.html

CyberPlayground provides collaborative, engaging curriculum materials online. Many of these materials have a multicultural edge and nearly all are interdisciplinary.

The Gateway to Educational Materials

http://www.thegateway.org/

GEM, sponsored by the U.S. Department of Education, is a searchable database of lesson plans and curricular materials including all subject areas and grade levels.

Houghton Mifflin Activity Search

http://www.eduplace.com/search/activity.html

Houghton Mifflin's *Education Place* Web site provides a searchable database of more than four hundred classroom activities and lesson plans for kindergarten through eighth grade. Search by subject area or grade level.

Lesson Plans Page

http://www.lessonplanspage.com/

EduScope presents this collection of over eight hundred lesson plans in all subject areas. The site also includes a ten-step guide for writing original lesson plans and a keyword search function.

Media Awareness Network: Teaching Media

http://www.media-awareness.ca/english/index.cfm

The *Media Awareness Network* supplies a collection of lesson plans for encouraging education and critical thinking as it relates to the media. Topics include "Gender Portrayal" and "Stereotyping." Users are also encouraged to contribute their own lesson plan ideas.

New York Times Lesson Plan Archive

http://www.nytimes.com/learning/teachers/lessons/archive.html

The *Times* provides daily lesson plans connecting its contents to classroom learning. This database houses an archive of the plans, many of which are progressively themed.

TeachNet.com

http://www.teachnet.com/

TeachNet includes a collection of lesson plans created and submitted by teachers across the United States. All subject areas and grade levels are represented.

Women's History Teacher's Guide

http://www.feminist.org/research/teach1.html

The Feminist Majority Foundation offers an excellent collection of curricular materials and lesson plans on women's history. Well-developed one-day and five-day plans are available, along with other readings, resources, and learning tools.

MULTICULTURAL CLASSROOM ACTIVITIES

CaMP Coop

http://www.scsv.nevada.edu/~neese/campcoop.html

Denise M. Dalaimo, mediator of the Critical and Multicultural Pedagogy Cooperative, highlights some of the most powerful global, multicultural activities and exercises available online.

EE Link—Multicultural Activities

http://eelink.net/eeactivities-multicultural.html

EE Link, a Web site on environmental education, provides these activities and curricular materials that combine multicultural and environmental concepts.

Exercises to Build Multicultural Awareness

http://www.findarticles.com/cf_0/m1249/3_73/62896135/p1/article.jhtml

Camping Magazine published this online article outlining activities that teach children to think more complexly about diversity.

Gender Equity Activities for Teachers

http://www.sadker.org/ge-teac.htm

Myra Sadker Advocates for Gender Equity, an educational nonprofit, developed this series of classroom activities for students at all levels of education.

Intercultural Activities

http://www.mhhe.com/socscience/education/multi/activities.html

The McGraw-Hill *Multicultural Supersite* includes activities about education equity for teacher educators. Entries include "Student Fishbowl," "The Depth and Breadth of 'Multicultural'," and "Connecting with School Prejudice." Activity descriptions include facilitator notes and a list of necessary materials. Another useful resource on this site is a guide for setting ground rules for dialogue on multicultural issues.

McGraw-Hill Trainer's Toolchest

http://web10.eppg.com/training/toolchest/games.html

McGraw-Hill offers a free collection of games, ice-breakers, and mood setters. Many are designed for a corporate setting, but several can be modified to fit a classroom or in-service environment. Activities include "Learning about Change from Our Experiences," "Stand Up and Be Counted!" and "Assessing Your Skills for Managing Change."

Multicultural Awareness Activities

http://www.edchange.org/multicultural/activityarch.html

The *Multicultural Pavilion* hosts a collection of activities designed to engage students in dialogue on multicultural issues. The activities were developed specifically for K-12 teachers and teacher educators but can be adapted for wider use. They include "Name Stories," "Understanding Prejudice and Discrimination," and "Knowing the Community."

Progressive Technology Integration

Closing the Equity Gap in Technology Access and Use

http://www.netc.org/equity/

The Northwest Educational Technology Consortium provides this guide for teachers dedicated to ensuring equity in technology education. Sections of the guide include "Access Issues," "Access Strategies," and "Curriculum Strategies."

Figure 10.5 Co-nect
http://www.co-nect.net/

Community Learning Network

http://www.cln.org/

The Open Learning Agency developed this site to help K-12 teachers find useful ways for integrating Internet technology into classroom teaching and learning. This site is primarily an index of links to other original resources.

Co-nect (see Figure 10.5)

http://www.co-nect.com/

Co-nect supports school reform by supplying resources on project-based learning, standards-based reform, instructional educational technology, and online learning. A series of projects help teachers find pedagogically sound ways to integrate Internet technology into their curricula.

EdWeb: Exploring Technology and School Reform

http://www.edwebproject.org/

Andy Carvin is the creator and maintainer of *EdWeb*, a site exploring issues and intersections related to school reform and educational technology. Resources include an HTML guide for educators, informational pieces about the role of the Web in education, and a K-12 resource guide.

Integrating the Internet

http://integratingtheinternet.com/

This site helps teachers find online activities and primary sources to use in the classroom. It also offer tips for creating class home pages.

Integrating Technology in the Classroom

http://www.enc.org/focus/topics/edtech/index.htm

The Eisenhower National Clearinghouse (ENC) has assembled a collection of explorations and resources to help teachers find useful and responsible ways to use the Internet and other technologies. The site includes several articles and an index of related resources from ENC.

Increasing Multicultural Awareness Using the Internet

http://showcase.netins.net/web/nwc-iowa/multi/

Floyd Johnson of Northwestern College explores the Internet as a tool for enhancing users' awareness of diversity issues.

Net Day Compass

http://www.netdaycompass.org/

Designed for technology decision makers in K-12 schools, this site is a wide-ranging compendium of education technology resources available online.

Teachers Connect Online

http://www.enc.org/focus/topics/edtech/articles/a08/index.htm

This article by Leah Poynter describes how teachers who use the Internet for personal and professional development find ways to use what they have learned to improve teaching and learning in their classrooms.

Ten Nifty Ways Teachers Can Use Email

http://www.electronic-school.com/0398f5.html

This feature of the *Online Electronic School* authored by James Lerman provides specific strategies for how teachers can use electronic mail to enhance the learning experiences of their students.

SITE INDEXES AND SEARCH TOOLS

The African American Studies Toolkit

http://creativefolk.com/toolkit/reference.html

Gerri Gribi amassed and categorized a selection of resources for educators including biographies, images, timelines, and speeches.

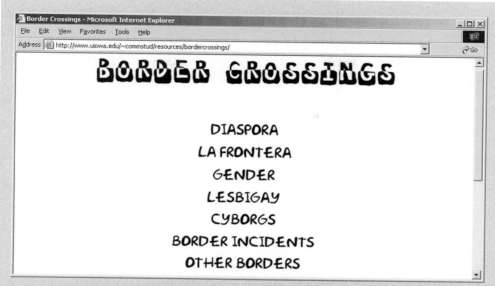

Figure 10.6   Border Crossings
http://www.uiowa.edu/~commstud/resources/bordercrossings/

Awesome Library

http://www.awesomelibrary.org/

Awesome Library has collected and organized thousands of the best K-12 education-related Web sites and provided reviews of many of them. Search or browse by subject, role (teacher, principal, etc.), or topic.

Border Crossings (see Figure 10.6)

http://www.uiowa.edu/~commstud/resources/bordercrossings/

Karla Tonella has been building this site for almost ten years. It is a compendium of resources related to cultural studies and social justice. Categories include "Diaspora," "Border Incidents," and "Gender."

Disability Resources

http://soeweb.syr.edu/thechp/disres.htm

This categorically organized index of sites includes sections on "Community Supports/Inclusion" and "Early Childhood/Children."

Diversity Database

http://www.inform.umd.edu/diversitydb/

Hosted by the University of Maryland, the *Database* is organized by diversity issues. Find conference and job announcements, Web sites, articles, and other resources.

Dr. Labush's Links to Learning

http://www.netrox.net/~labush/

Norman Labush has mined the Internet for the best teaching and learning resources and organized them into an easily navigable Web site. *Links to Learning* has a decidedly, but not completely, elementary school focus.

EduHound

http://www.eduhound.com/

Browse or search through thousands of categorized Web sites related to education. Categories include "Culture & Religion," "Standards & Assessments," and "Kid Sites."

Global Diversity Search Engine

http://www.globaldiversitysearch.net/

The National Multicultural Institute set up a search engine of the best Internet sites and tools related to diversity. You can search in nine languages.

Hall of Multiculturalism

http://www.tenet.edu/halls/multiculturalism.html

The Texas Education Network hosts this index of sites organized around racial and ethnic identities. Categories include "African/African American," "Asian/Asian American," "Indigenous People," "Latino/Chicano/Hispano/Mexican," and "Native American."

History/Social Studies for K-12 Teachers

http://execpc.com/~dboals/boals.html

This extensive, often-updated directory of educational Web sites is organized into categories that include "Non-Western History Sites," "Research/Critical Thinking," and "Diversity Sources."

Instant Access Treasure Chest

http://www.fln.vcu.edu/ld/ld.html

Though this collection of links was created to help foreign language educators effectively reach students with learning disabilities, it can be a useful resource for all educators. Links are divided into categories including "Learning Styles" and "Teaching Students with Learning Disabilities."

Interracial and Multiracial Links

http://multirace.org/multirace.htm

Part of the *Interracial Connection* Web site, this is an index of sites that explore the experiences of bi- and multiracial people in the United States.

Kathy Schrock's Guide for Educators

http://school.discovery.com/schrockguide/

Discovery Channel School sponsors a comprehensive guide of Web resources for teachers.

Lives: The Biography Resource

http://amillionlives.com/

Kenneth P. Lanxner created and continually updates this index of biographical Web sites. Browse the index alphabetically, search for a name, or explore special topics including "African Americans," "Women," "Holocaust Survivors and Rescuers," and "U.S. Civil War."

Multicultural Paths

http://www.edchange.org/multicultural/sites1.html

Multicultural Paths is an index of multicultural education sites. Entries are divided into categories and subcategories including "Curriculum Transformation," "Homophobia and Education," "Bilingual Education," "Evaluation and Research," and "Digital Divide."

Multicultural SuperLinks

http://www.mhhe.com/socscience/education/multi/links.html

The *Multicultural Supersite* offers this directory of multicultural education resources divided into topic and subject area.

OutProud: Explore the World Wide Web

http://www.outproud.org/web.html

OutProud, an organization run by and for lesbian, gay, and questioning youth, offers a guide to related online resources.

Skewl Sites

http://www.skewlsites.com/

This site indexes the best educational Web sites as identified by teachers for teachers. A monthly newsletter informs users about the best new Web sites as they emerge in cyberspace.

Social Class Links

http://www.src.uchicago.edu/SocialClass/links.html

The University of Chicago amassed a list of links to Web sites related to socioeconomic status. A helpful index of online articles supplements these links.

SocioSite

http://www2.fmg.uva.nl/sociosite/

The University of Amsterdam hosts this "social science information system," a guide to Web resources with a progressive twist for sociologists.

Special Education Resources on the Internet (SERI)

http://seriweb.com/

SERI indexes Internet-based resources of interest to teachers, students, parents, and anyone else involved in special education. Sites are organized under several categories including "Special Education Discussion Groups," "Learning Disabilities," and "Inclusion Resources."

Women's Studies Database: Other Sites

http://www.mith2.umd.edu/WomensStudies/OtherWebSites/

The *Database* has been a long-standing and always popular staple of Internet researchers. Its index of other sites has wonderfully progressive topic areas including "Activism and Activist Resources," "Feminist Theory," and "Women of Color."

World History Compass

http://www.worldhistorycompass.com/

Schiller Computing provides this globally focused index of the best history resources on the Web, including Web sites, primary documents, and historical letters and speeches.

Research

City Population

http://www.citypopulation.de/

In both German and English, *City Population* provides research and statistical information on most of the major cities in the world.

CYFERnet

http://www.cyfernet.org/

The Children, Youth and Families Education and Resource Center maintains an extensive collection of research reports on best practices and contemporary issues for young people and their families.

Explorations in Social Inequality

http://www.trinity.edu/~mkearl/strat.html

This Web resource is the highlight of the *Sociological Tour through Cyberspace* site. It provides links, graphs, statistics, and other resources related to inequality and social injustice.

Feminist Research Center

http://www.feminist.org/research/1_public.html

The Feminist Majority Foundation hosts a collection of research materials including data and analyses of sexism-related issues.

Intercultural Development Research Center

http://www.idra.org/default.htm

IDRC, a nonprofit, conducts and collects research for the purpose of advocating equal educational opportunity for all students.

National Center for Educational Statistics

http://nces.ed.gov/

A seemingly endless collection of research reports on a broad range of educational topics are available free of charge at the NCES Web site. They range across topic area, educational issue, and grade level.

U.S. Census Bureau

http://www.census.gov/

The Census Bureau makes nearly all collected information available online through both raw data and statistical reports. Many of these reports are categorized under topics such as "Income," "Housing," "Language Use," and "School Enrollments." You will also find a special section of classroom resources and tools for teachers.

MULTICULTURALISM IN HIGHER EDUCATION

American Association of Colleges for Teacher Education

http://www.aacte.org/Multicultural/default.htm

AACTE's Multicultural/Diversity page highlights current projects, resources, and events for teacher educators.

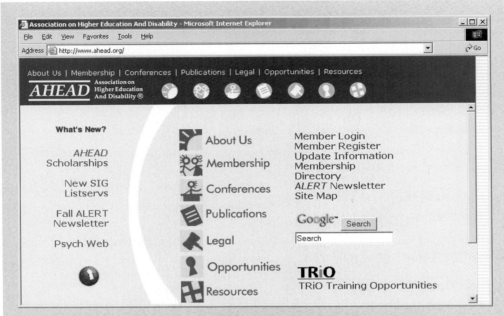

Figure 10.7   Association on Higher Education and Disability
http://www.ahead.org/

American Studies Electronic Crossroads

http://www.georgetown.edu/crossroads/

Crossroads is a networking and curriculum project providing resources for educators. Though the intended focus is American Studies, the site contains many resources adaptable to related areas including the social sciences.

Association on Higher Education and Disability (see Figure 10.7)

http://www.ahead.org/

AHEAD is a national organization based in the United States. The Web site contains information about its publications, conferences, and newsletter.

Compendium of Suggestions for Teaching with Excellence

http://teaching.berkeley.edu/compendium/

Berkeley offers practical and theoretical thinking points for instructors and professors. Sections include "Encouraging Class Discussion" and "Emphasizing Conceptual Understanding."

Diversity and Affirmative Action in Higher Education

http://www.aaup.org/Issues/AffirmativeAction/Archives/aaindex.htm

The American Association of University Professors offers this compendium of articles and research supporting affirmative action.

Diversity Digest

http://www.diversityweb.org/Digest/

Diversity Digest is an online journal highlighting the best practices in higher education. Each quarterly edition focuses on a particular topic. Recent topics have included curriculum transformation, institutional leadership and commitment, and student experience.

Diversity on Campus: Reports from the Field

http://www.naspa.org/resources/reports.cfm

Part of *NASPA Online*, this is a set of reports and findings from research conducted on campuses across the United States. Topics covered in the reports include intergroup interactions, the effects of racial diversity on campus, and campus climate.

DiversityInc.com: Future Work Force

http://www.diversityinc.com/Workforce/FutureWFTOC/futurewftoc.cfm

This online news source focuses primarily on diversity in the corporate United States. The *Future Work Force* section houses all of the publication's higher education articles. Many of these articles highlight promising practices, including the University of Maryland's Student Intercultural Learning Center and Duke University's Cross-Cultural Relations Office.

DiversityWeb

http://www.diversityweb.org

Created and maintained by the Office of Human Relations Programs at the University of Maryland, College Park, and the Association of American Colleges and Universities, with support from the Ford Foundation, *DiversityWeb* serves as a compendium of higher education resources aimed at institutional change. The site is organized around a series of campus priorities including "Institutional Vision, Leadership, and Systemic Change," "Curriculum Transformation," and "Campus Community Connections."

Multicultural Education Pathfinder

http://lweb.tc.columbia.edu/rr/mc/

MilbankWeb compiled this index of multicultural education resources. Listings include e-mail discussion groups, Web sites, print materials, and professional organizations.

Multiculturalism in the Community College Curriculum

http://www.ericfacility.net/ericdigests/ed424898.html

This ERIC Digest, written by Paula Zeszotarski, explains the unique ways in which a multicultural curriculum is of particular importance to community colleges.

National Consortium of Directors of LGBT Resources in Higher Education

http://www.lgbtcampus.org/

The consortium works to achieve equity for all lesbian, gay, bisexual, and transgendered people involved in higher education.

On the Importance of Diversity in Higher Education

http://www.aera.net/about/policy/diverse.htm

The American Educational Research Association published this policy statement supporting the diversification of colleges and universities.

Teaching for Inclusion: Diversity in the College Classroom

http://ctl.unc.edu/tfitoc.html

The Center for Teaching and Learning at the University of North Carolina at Chapel Hill wrote this guide for faculty and staff to critically consider their roles in the inclusion or exclusion of a diversity of students.

Women's International Electronic University

The purpose of *WIEU* is to educate and empower women through the development of cross-cultural and collaborative Internet technology projects. The site contains online courses, dialogue forums, and links to related resources.

CHAPTER 11

A Guide to Online Resources:
Subject-Specific

Resources listed and described in this chapter are organized by school subjects and professional roles. Use these Web sites to strengthen your educational practice and to develop interdisciplinary multicultural education knowledge and skills. Meanwhile, consider what resources you have developed that might be of interest to your colleagues and look for places to share them.

THE ARTS

Art Research & Curriculum

http://www.arcassociates.org/

ARC is a nonprofit dedicated to promoting educational equity and justice through art.

Art Teacher Connection

http://www.artteacherconnection.com/

Bettie Lake offers this collection of resources and innovative strategies for integrating art into thematic units. Special attention is given to how the Internet can be used for this purpose.

Artists Against Racism

http://www.artistsagainstracism.org/AARMain.cfm

AAR, an international nonprofit, connects artists with youth in an attempt to inspire antiracist thinking and action.

ArtsConnectEd

http://artsconnected.org/

The Minnesota Institute of the Arts, the Walker Art Center, and MCI teamed up to build an engaging set of online resources for exploring and creating art.

ArtsEdge

http://artsedge.kennedy-center.org/artsedge.html

The Kennedy Center and the National Endowment for the Arts support a project that aims to provide educators with ways to link arts and education through technology. The site includes a "Curriculum Studio" with specific ideas.

ArtsEdNet

http://www.getty.edu/artsednet/

Developed by the J. Paul Getty Trust, *ArtsEdNet* is a catchall resource attempting to meet the needs of the art education community. It provides resources for art educators and other teachers who want to incorporate art into other subjects. The site includes lesson plans, dialogue forums, and interdisciplinary materials.

Crossing the Threshold

http://www.albany.edu/museum/wwwmuseum/crossing/crossing.htm

This site honors and exhibits the work of thirty-two women artists of the twentieth century.

Cultural Arts Resources for Teachers and Students (CARTS)

http://www.carts.org/index.html

CARTS, sponsored by City Lore and the National Task Force on Folk Arts and Education, aims to strengthen relationships between schools and communities through the sharing of cultural arts ideas and resources. The site includes a list of related Web sites, a discussion area, and descriptions of model cultural arts programs.

The Drama Teacher's Resource Room

http://www3.sk.sympatico.ca/erachi/

Thorton Consulting and Training Services offers this collection of drama resources, lesson plans, and discussion forums.

The Drama Teacher's Resource Room Lesson Plans

http://www3.sk.sympatico.ca/erachi/page2.html

This growing collection of lesson plans adds progressive and dynamic dimensions to drama education. Find a lesson for your class or share one of your lesson plans with other site visitors.

The Incredible Art Department

http://www.princetonol.com/groups/iad/

Ken Rohrer hosts this compendium of resources for arts educators.

The International Society for the Performing Arts

http://www.ispa.org/

ISPA, an international nonprofit, is dedicated to highlighting the social and cultural importance of the arts worldwide.

KinderArt Multicultural Art Lessons

http://www.kinderart.com/multic/

Among *KinderArt*'s extensive collection of art lesson plans is this small array of culturally diverse lesson ideas for kindergarten teachers.

Melissa's Myriad Art Education

http://www.geocities.com/Athens/8020/arted.html

Melissa, an artist and art teacher, shares a variety of resources and lesson plans. Many of the lesson plans she includes are based on multicultural themes.

Multicultural Approaches to Art Learning

http://www.getty.edu/artsednet/resources/Chalmers/

This *ArtsEdNet* site describes strategies for creating and implementing effective multicultural arts curricula. Special attention is given to factors that must be considered in the planning stages of multicultural curriculum transformation in the art classroom.

Multicultural Song Index

http://www.edchange.org/multicultural/arts/songs.html

A collaborative project by teachers, students, and others around the world, the *Multicultural Song Index* encourages educators to use popular music to introduce classroom discussions on prejudice and discrimination. The index contains references and sample lyrics to hundreds of songs that touch on subjects such as racism, sexism, classism, heterosexism, and ageism.

M.U.S.I.C.

http://www.wpe.com/~musici/welcome.html

Musicians United for Songs in the Classroom provides a directory of popular and rock songs that can be used in a variety of educational settings. Also included are specific strategies and resources for using music in the classroom and a dialogue forum called "Rock in the Classroom."

Music Heritage Network (MHN)

http://www.si.umich.edu/CHICO/MHN/

MHN is a virtual community of educators, musicians, and students working together to provide online music-related multicultural curriculum resources. Current features include "Virtual Tours" that introduce users to various cultures through photographs, text, and music.

Professional Cartoonists Index: Teachers Guide

http://cagle.slate.msn.com/teacher/

Daryl Cagle offers a set of resources for introducing the study of political cartoons to K-12 classrooms.

SUAVE Online

http://ww2.csusm.edu/SUAVE/

Socios Unidos para Artes Via Educación takes a multicultural approach to helping teachers integrate (or reintegrate) the arts into the classroom. The site includes curriculum ideas, articles, and related discussion opportunities.

Teaching Art from a Global Perspective

http://www.ed.gov/databases/ERIC_Digests/ed329490.html

This ERIC Digest, written by Enid Zimmerman, explores art education in multinational, multicultural, and community-based contexts.

Women Artists in History

http://www.wendy.com/women/artists.html

Wendy Russ and Carrie Carolin built this index of resources and information about women artists, organized by century.

Women Artists through Time

http://www.uwrf.edu/history/women.html

Browse the work of numerous women artists, arranged chronologically.

World Wide Arts Resources

http://world-arts-resources.com/

This site is a gateway for Internet resources from around the world related to arts and culture. Categories include "Education," "Galleries," and "Exhibits Online."

BILINGUAL EDUCATION AND ENGLISH LANGUAGE LEARNING

Adult Education ESL Teachers Guide

http://humanities.byu.edu/elc/teacher/teacherguidemain

Though developed by C. Ray Graham and Mark M. Walsh expressly for teachers of adult learners, most of the resources and activities described on this site can be adapted for K-12 students.

Bilingual Education from Education Week

http://www.edweek.org/context/topics/issuespage.cfm?id=8

Education Week on the Web offers this special topics section exploring bilingual education and related issues. Among the plethora of resources available through the site are a section describing various bilingual education methods, a series of original articles and essays, and a directory of related Web sites.

Bilingual Research Journal Online

http://brj.asu.edu/

The Southwest Center for Education Equity and Language Diversity hosts an online publication of articles related to social justice and equity for speakers of all languages.

CLAD Web Site

http://coe.sdsu.edu/people/jmora/Default.htm

Jill Mora designed the Cross-*Cultural Language and Academic Development* site to provide quick access to resources related to the philosophy, public policy issues, and methods of educating language minority students.

Dave's ESL Café

http://www.pacificnet.net/~sperling/eslcafe.html

Dave Sperling created, and continues to build, this collection of resources for ESL and EFL students and teachers around the world. The *Café* includes discussion forums, a guide to other Web sites, and ideas for working toward education and change.

The Effectiveness of Bilingual Education

http://www.cal.org/ericcll/faqs/rgos/bi.html

This site serves as an index for other Web and print resources on bilingual education. Links to organizations, monographs, articles, and Web sites are included.

ELTWeb

http://www.eltweb.com/liason/

This well-organized index of English language resources is divided into categories including "Multicultural Issues," "Bilingual Education," and "Immigration."

English Learners: Language and Culture in Education

http://goldmine.cde.ca.gov/el/

A product of the California Department of Education, this site includes news, lesson plans, explorations of current issues and legislation, and other bilingual education resources for teachers and English learners.

ESL and Bilingual Program Models

http://www.cal.org/ericcll/digest/rennie01.html

Jeanne Rennie wrote this exploratory piece on the range of ESL and bilingual education models currently in practice. She provides a list of factors to consider when choosing an appropriate model along with a list of characteristics of effective ESL and bilingual programs.

ESL Lessons, Games, Ideas, and Links

http://members.aol.com/Jakajk/ESLLessons.html

John Korber has assembled a diverse collection of classroom resources and materials. Incorporate these resources into your curriculum, or submit ideas and lesson plans that have been successful for you.

EverythingESL (see Figure 11.1)

http://www.everythingesl.net/

Judie Haynes, the creator of *Everything ESL*, has developed a series of culturally conscious lesson plans and other resources for English language learners. One exciting resource helps students think critically about Christopher Columbus's role in the "founding" of America.

Exploring the World of Meaning of ESL Students

http://www.meaning.ca/articles/meaning_esl_students.html

F. Ishu Ishiyama and Paul T. P. Wong collaborated on an article about considering cultural context in the assessment of ESL students.

Fostering Second Language Development in Young Children

http://www.cal.org/ericcll/digest/ncrcds04.html

National Center for Research on Cultural Diversity and Second Language Learning compiled this ERIC Digest outlining eight pedagogical principles to guide teachers of second language learning students.

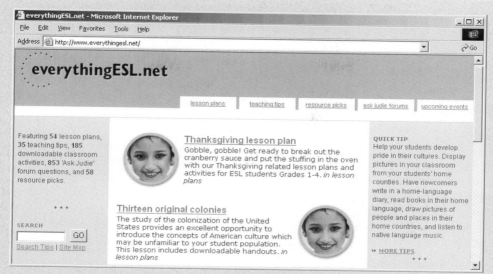

Figure 11.1   everythingESL.net
http://www.everythingesl.net/

A Global Perspective on Bilingualism and Bilingual Education

http://www.cal.org/ericcll/digest/digestglobal.html

G. Richard Tucker of Carnegie Mellon University steps back from a purely U.S. perspective to consider how a wider global perspective would inform the development of effective bilingual education programs. An important section of his paper reminds readers of the sorts of related issues that need further attention and calls for deeper inquiry.

The Internet TESL Journal

http://www.aitech.ac.jp/~iteslj/index.html

This monthly journal combines articles, research papers, lesson plans, classroom handouts, and references to Web sites for teachers of English as a Second Language.

Issues in U.S. Language Policy: Bilingual Education

http://ourworld.compuserve.com/homepages/JWCRAWFORD/biling.htm

James Crawford, well-known advocate for speakers of languages other than English, built this compendium of progressive language policy resources including research and articles.

Karin's ESL Partyland

http://www.eslpartyland.com/

Students and teachers will find a plethora of interesting and engaging teaching and learning resources in *Partyland,* including quizzes, discussion forums, lesson plans, and other educational materials.

Lesson Plans and Resources for ESL, Bilingual, and Foreign Language Teachers

http://www.csun.edu/~hcedu013/eslindex.html

Marty Levine hosts this index of lesson plans and classroom activities. Also included are links to related resources.

Model Strategies in Bilingual Education: Professional Development

http://www.ed.gov/pubs/ModStrat/index.html

This report of the Office of Bilingual Education and Minority Language Affairs, part of the U.S. Department of Education, highlights promising practices in current bilingual education practice and the guiding principles of those practices. Topics addressed include cooperative learning in the bilingual context, preparing new bilingual educators, and promoting students' academic success.

PIZZAZ

http://darkwing.uoregon.edu/~leslieob/pizzaz.html

A site specifically for teachers of English as a Second Language, *PIZZAZ* provides creative writing opportunities for students in an attempt to bring fun into the ESOL classroom. Several activities and lesson plans and links are included.

Ten Common Fallacies about Bilingual Education

http://www.cal.org/ericcll/digest/crawford01.html

In this article, James Crawford attempts to deepen the public understanding of bilingual education by citing a large body of related research that disputes several common myths and misconceptions.

Tower of English

http://towerofenglish.com/

The *Tower of English* is a fun place for ESL students to use and practice English through interaction, writing activities, and collaborative projects. The site has instituted a new pen pal program, linking ESL students interested in sharing their experiences and challenges.

Counseling and Psychology

Ask Your School Psychologist

http://www.bartow.k12.ga.us/psych/psych.html

This site was created to allow school psychologists to share their struggles, issues, and questions with each other through a discussion forum called "PsychoBabble."

Association for Multicultural Counseling and Development

http://www.amcd-aca.org/

This division of the American Counseling Association provides leadership, research, and training in the area of multicultural counseling, with a particular focus on issues of race and ethnicity. Its Web site, *AMCD On Line*, contains organizational, conference, and publication information.

Counselor's Corner: Multicultural Issues

http://members.aol.com/lacillo/multicultural.html

Lori Cillo, a vocational guidance coordinator in Vermont, has compiled this set of resources related to multicultural counseling. The site includes several original articles and links to related sites and organizations.

Diversity at the Pre-college and Undergraduate Levels of Education

http://www.apa.org/ed/divhscollege.html

The American Psychological Association's Web site includes this section of resources and reflections on the need to diversify psychology curricula.

Psychological Science in Cultural Context

http://www.massey.ac.nz/~alock/culture/culture.htm

Kenneth J. Gergen, Andrew Lock, Aydan Gulerce, and Gerishwar Misra offer an intercultural examination of psychological science, critiquing the assumption of a universally correct approach to psychology.

World Counseling Network (WCN)

http://www.counselingnetwork.com/

WCN is an online community of counseling professionals. Though much of the site's purpose is commercial in nature, it also includes a set of discussion forums including chat rooms and bulletin boards.

HEALTH AND MEDICINE

Band-Aides & Blackboards

http://www.faculty.fairfield.edu/fleitas/contents.html

Joan Fleitas, a registered nurse with a doctorate in education, helps us understand the experience of living with a chronic illness. The site is divided into sections for kids, teens, and adults.

Best Practices of Youth Violence Prevention

http://www.cdc.gov/ncipc/dvp/bestpractices.htm

This sourcebook for community action can help educators think complexly about and respond effectively to youth violence in their schools and communities.

Closing the Health Gap

http://www.healthgap.omhrc.gov/

Closing the Health Gap is the Web component of an ongoing campaign to challenge health-care and service gaps across race in the United States.

DiversityRX

http://diversityrx.org/HTML/DIVRX.htm

Striving to promote equitable health care through language and cultural competence, *DiversityRX* offers a collection of online resources such as a Multicultural Health Best Practices report and a database of model programs.

The Mental Illness Education Project

http://www.miepvideos.org/

MIEP develops and distributes resources that challenge the stigmas of people with psychological disabilities. The Web site contains resources to help teachers and students better understand the nature of these illnesses.

Multicultural Health Clearinghouse

http://www.mckinley.uiuc.edu/multiculturalhealth/

The Special Populations Students' Health Concerns Committee at the University of Illinois, Urbana-Champaign, developed this compendium of resources for helping health-care professionals provide the best possible care to a diversity of patients.

Not All Your Patients Are Straight

http://collection.nlc-bnc.ca/100/201/300/cdn_medical_association/cmaj/vol-159/issue-4/0370.htm

This article by Ruth Simpkin was originally published in 1998. It challenges health-care providers to transform the culture around their work so that all people, regardless of sexual orientation, receive equitable treatment.

National Alliance for the Mentally Ill

http://www.nami.org/

NAMI, an advocacy group with more than one thousand U.S. affiliates, provides information, resources, and activism opportunities in support of people with depression, bipolar disorder, and other psychological disabilities.

Transcultural Nursing

http://www.culturediversity.org/

Victor and Kathy Fernandez, both registered nurses, share their experiences and ideas about the complexities and necessities of caring for diverse populations.

HISTORY AND SOCIAL STUDIES

360degrees

http://www.360degrees.org/

Picture Projects hosts a collection of the stories and experiences of inmates, guards, parents, and others who have been impacted by the criminal justice system in the United States.

1492: An Ongoing Voyage

http://metalab.unc.edu/expo/1492.exhibit/Intro.html

This Library of Congress exhibit addresses the questions and controversies surrounding the year 1492 by exploring the cultures existing in the Western Hemisphere before the arrival of European explorers and then examining how these were changed by the explorers' arrival.

African American Holocaust

http://www.maafa.org/

Milford F. Plaines created this important but chilling Web production using photographs, narrative text, and other media to expose the atrocities African Americans have faced in the United States. The presentation is overtly blunt and will lead to deep processing and dialogue.

African Voices

http://www.mnh.si.edu/africanvoices/

The Smithsonian Institute put together a wonderful multimedia and interactive site that deeply explores the history of Africa. Topics include "Africans in Spain," "Slave Trade," and "Colonialism."

American Memory

http://lcweb2.loc.gov/ammem/ammemhome.html

Part of the Library of Congress, *American Memory* houses an online collection of historical documents, maps, motion pictures, photographs, and sound recordings, all organized into content areas including "Art and Architecture," "Education," "History," and "Social Sciences."

American Women in Uniform

http://userpages.aug.com/captbarb/

"Captain Critic" hosts this set of interesting and informative resources about women in the military. Features include "Women in Vietnam," "Women in Combat," and "Myths, Fallacies, and Urban Legends about Military Women."

American Women's History: A Resource Guide

http://frank.mtsu.edu/~kmiddlet/history/women.html

This guide was designed by Ken Middleton to help those searching for information and resources on women's history. Though it is primarily an index of other sites and print materials, *American Women's History* stands out because it is organized by resource type, including "General Reference and Biographical Sources," "Finding Primary Sources: Tools/Formats," and "Digital Collections of Primary Sources."

Anti-Slavery Homepage

http://www.antislavery.org/

Founded in 1839, Anti-Slavery International, the sponsor of this site, is the oldest surviving international human rights organization. The site contains resources and advocacy information for ending slavery and related abuses worldwide.

Asian Nation: The Landscape of Asian America

http://www.asian-nation.org/index.shtml

Asian Nation is a source guide for political, social, and cultural issues in the lives of contemporary Asian Americans.

Beyond Face Value

http://www.lib.lsu.edu/cwc/BeyondFaceValue/index.htm

The U.S. Civil War Center hosts this project revealing depictions of slavery in Confederate currency. View images of the currency along with statements putting the images in historical context.

Black Facts Online

http://www.blackfacts.com/

This online resource guide includes tools for education and research related to African American history. Users can search facts by date.

Black Resistance: Slavery in the U.S.

http://www.afro.com/history/slavery/main.html

Carolyn L. Bennet compiled and wrote a series of stories about the history of slavery and resistance to slavery in the United States. The stories are wonderfully written and illustrated.

Born in Slavery

http://lcweb2.loc.gov/ammem/snhtml/

The Library of Congress offers an online collection of the slave narratives collected between 1936 and 1938 by the Federal Writers' Project.

Children of the Camps: Internment History

http://www.children-of-the-camps.org/history/index.html

Based on the film documentary of the same name, *Children of the Camps* provides a photographic and narrative history of the experiences of the young people who comprised most of the 120,000 Japanese Americans interned after Pearl Harbor. The site also includes copies of important documents like Executive Order 9066, which permitted the internment for the sake of "national defense."

CIA World Factbook

http://www.odci.gov/cia/publications/factbook/index.html

The *Factbook* is a collection of raw data compiled by the CIA on various countries around the world. Each country listing contains subcategories of information, including "Geography," "People," "Government," "Economy," "Communications," "Transportation," "Military," and "Transnational Issues."

Columbus and the Age of Discovery

http://www.millersv.edu/~columbus/

Millersville University of Pennsylvania hosts this collection of more than one thousand articles, speeches, and other documents related to Columbus from a diversity of perspectives.

Cyber Newseum

http://www.newseum.org/cybernewseum/html/index.htm

The Newseum, a museum about the people who research and report the news, put several of its multimedia exhibits online, including "Holocaust: The Untold Story," "Every Four Years," and "The Berlin Wall."

Cybrary of Holocaust

http://remember.org/

A site of *Remember.org*, the "cybrary" gives Web users access to a database of research, books, people, and discussion forums.

A Deeper Shade of History

http://www.seditionists.org/black/bhist.html

This site serves as a clearinghouse for Black History resources, but does so in a way that is not limited to Black History Month or special celebrations. The site includes a "This Week in Black History" feature.

Diotima: Materials for the Study of Gender and Women in the Ancient World

http://www.stoa.org/diotima/

Diotima is an exploration of patterns of gender around the ancient Mediterranean. It provides related articles, course materials, and images. The site also helps facilitate collaboration among educators building curricula around this and related topics.

Documenting the Southeast Asian Refugee Experience

http://www.lib.uci.edu/libraries/collections/sea/seaexhibit/index.html

The University of California's *Southeast Asian Archive* includes this interactive, multimedia exhibit of the experiences, trials, and tribulations of Southeast Asian refugees to the United States.

First Nations Histories

http://www.tolatsga.org/Compacts.html

This site provides an examination of history by and about First Nations peoples.

A First Person History of the Northwest Coast

http://www.hallman.org/indian/.www.html

Bruce Hallman combines maps, photographs, documents, and text to tell the history of the Canadian northwest from a Native American perspective.

Herstory: An Exhibition

http://library.usask.ca/herstory/herstory.html

The Canadian Women's Calendar has been an ongoing feminist project for more than twenty years. This site tells the story of that project and includes images from the calendars.

Historic Audio Archives: Civil Rights

http://webcorp.com/civilrights/

This site presents a collection of audio clips from famous and infamous historical figures, including Nixon, John F. Kennedy, Hitler, Martin Luther King, Jr., Malcolm X, G. Gordon Liddy, and others.

Historical Text Archive

http://historicaltextarchive.com/

Explore history through primary sources with this index of historical texts from around the world. Entries include political, social, governmental, judicial, and legislative documents and are organized by country/region or topic (including "African American" and "Native American").

History and Politics Out Loud

http://www.hpol.org/

Jerry Goldman and Northwestern University host this extraordinary archive of historically significant audio bites. Listen to speeches by Martin Luther King, Jr., Nixon Watergate recordings, and many other materials.

History Matters

http://historymatters.gmu.edu/

A collaborative project between the City University of New York and George Mason University, this site is composed of a large collection of progressive, active teaching and learning resources for high school and undergraduate college students. Read articles, download monthly quizzes, search for classroom activities, and dialogue with other educators on topics of historical importance.

Holocaust Archive Project

http://www.cs.brandeis.edu/~philip/holo.html

By combining discussion forums, art, photography, research, and original documents, this site serves as both a virtual museum and virtual classroom.

Integrating Mexican-American History and Culture into the Social Studies Curriculum

http://www.ericfacility.net/ericdigests/ed348200.html

Kathy Escamilla offers practical suggestions for deep integration of the Mexican American voice and suggests ways of helping teachers do so successfully.

Interactive Border Studies

http://www.humanities-interactive.org/borderstudies/

Border Studies is a collection of multimedia learning resources including nine graphical exhibitions and three slideshows, along with associated classroom activities "presenting the history and culture of the lands and nations bordering Texas and the United States from the 15th Century to the present day." This site was developed by the Texas Humanities Resource Center.

The Japanese American Internment

http://www.geocities.com/Athens/8420/main.html

Photographs, articles, and intriguing quotes make this an interesting educational journey into a too-often not-talked-about piece of American History. It also includes an impressive index of links to important historical sites.

Jim Crow Museum

http://www.ferris.edu/news/jimcrow/menu.htm

Ferris State University offers a virtual tour of its museum of racist memorabilia. Accessible items include racist cartoons and descriptions and depictions of common African American stereotypes.

The Latino History Project

http://www.museumca.org/LHP/

The Oakland Museum of California's Web site includes parts of its exhibits on Latino history, including "Striving for Equality," "Latino Workers," and "Community and Social Life."

Lesbian History Project

http://www-lib.usc.edu/~retter/main.html

Yolanda Retter amasses links to numerous resources, articles, interviews, and bibliographies about lesbians in U.S. history.

Lesson Plans and Resources for Social Studies Teachers

http://www.csun.edu/%7Ehcedu013/index.html

Marty Levine of California State University, Northridge, hosts an index of social studies resources including lesson plans, online activities, e-mail discussion groups, and curriculum frameworks.

Living the Legacy

http://www.legacy98.org/

The National Women's History Project sponsors this site about 150 years of the women's rights movement.

Making of America

http://www.hti.umich.edu/m/moagrp/

This digital library, sponsored by the University of Michigan, houses a collection of primary sources in U.S. social history from the antebellum period through reconstruction.

MidEast Web

http://www.mideastweb.org/history.htm

This collection of resources on Middle East history includes excellent pieces about the Israeli-Palestinian conflict, Palestinian identity, and recent news about the region.

A More Perfect Union

http://americanhistory.si.edu/perfectunion/non-flash/index.html

The Smithsonian explores the lines between national security and human rights through a multimedia exhibit about the Japanese internment.

National Council for the Social Studies: Teacher Resources

http://www.socialstudies.org/resources/

NCSS assembles an extensive collection of organized resources for social studies teachers, including original materials related to "teachable moments."

The National Women's History Project

http://www.nwhp.org/

This, the official Web site of the NWHP, includes an interactive online quiz on women's history and a host of practical suggestions for incorporating the voices and experiences of women into the curriculum.

Native American Documents Project

http://www.csusm.edu/nadp/nadp.htm

California State University, San Marcos, hosts this impressive collection of documents related to Native American experience in the United States. Resources include a list of existing reservations, published reports, letters, chronologies, and maps.

Native American Website for Children

http://www.nhusd.k12.ca.us/ALVE/NativeAmerhome.html/nativeopeningpage.html

With kid-friendly graphics and a simple navigation system, this site actively engages students in a multimedia adventure as they learn about the lives, cultures, and histories of Native American tribes.

Oneida Indian Nation Treaties Project

http://oneida-nation.net/treaties.html

The *Treaties Project* provides all people access to historic treaties to help us better understand an Indian nation's sovereign status.

Our Shared History: African American Heritage

http://www.cr.nps.gov/aahistory/

The National Park Service developed this collection of text and photo exhibits related to African American history. Highlights include a piece about the Underground Railroad and a collection for teachers and students called "Tools for Learning."

Pluralism and Unity

http://www.expo98.msu.edu/

This site was designed to explore conflicts between American identity and the nature of cultural and political pluralism. Among its many resources are historic texts written by Jane Addams, W. E. B. DuBois, Margaret Mead, and Booker T. Washington.

Power, Politics, and Protest

http://learningcurve.pro.gov.uk/politics/suffragettes/

Learning Curve explores the history of women's rights in nineteenth century Britain. The site includes wonderful historical photographs.

Powerful Days in Black and White

http://www.kodak.com/US/en/corp/features/moore/mooreIndex.shtml

Kodak features Charles Moore's photo exhibit from the civil rights movement.

Primary Source

http://www.primarysource.org/

This nonprofit organization supports inclusive, accurate, and interdisciplinary social studies education. The *Primary Source* Web site includes lesson plans, curriculum ideas, and other related resources.

Social Studies and Multicultural Education

http://instech.tusd.k12.az.us/SS/ss.html

Tucson Unified School District provides a compendium of links to multicultural resources by grade level.

Spartacus Educational

http://www.spartacus.schoolnet.co.uk/

This multimedia, online history encyclopedia focuses on specific eras, events, and issues. Entries include "Slavery: 1750-1870," "Investigating the Vietnam War," and "The Trade Union Movement." All entries expand into several subentries focused on relevant people, subtopics, and issues.

Teacher's Guide to the Holocaust

http://fcit.coedu.usf.edu/holocaust/

The Florida Center for Instructional Technology offers an impressive collection of teaching and learning resources, including photographs, movies, music and sound files, art, classroom activities, and historical timelines.

Teaching World History: The Global Human Experience through Time

http://www.ed.gov/databases/ERIC_Digests/ed419772.html

Simone Arias, Marilynn Hitchens, and Heidi Roupp develop a humanistic conceptualization for world history in this article. They explore why world history is important and share effective instructional strategies for history teachers.

The Underground Railroad

http://www.nationalgeographic.com/features/99/railroad/

National Geographic produced this Web site in conjunction with its PBS program on the same topic. This site takes users through an interactive exploration of the Underground Railroad, employing art, artifacts, and text.

U.S. Labor History: Famous Strikes

http://www.state.sd.us/deca/DDN4Learning/ThemeUnits/USLabor/strikes.htm

This online unit about labor history in the United States includes links to information about famous strikes. It also contains a section on "Women in Labor History."

Voices of the Holocaust

http://voices.iit.edu/education.html

The Illinois Institute of Technology has collected and made available a series of interviews with Holocaust survivors. The site also includes audio clips.

War Relocation Authority Camps in Arizona

http://dizzy.library.arizona.edu/images/jpamer/wraintro.html

The University of Arizona library offers this look into the relocation camps through maps, stories, and photographs.

Wide Horizon Education Resources

http://members.aol.com/WEREdu/

Wide Horizon Education Resources is dedicated to providing teachers with creative ideas and resources for teaching world history in middle and high school. Sample lessons and archived editions of the *Wide Horizon* newsletter are available through the site.

Women and the Holocaust

http://www.interlog.com/~mighty/

This site incorporates poetry, art, personal reflections, biographies, and other ways of learning about the unique experiences of women victims of the Holocaust.

Women in World History

http://www.womeninworldhistory.com/

Directed by Lyn Reese, Women in World History provides resources for teachers, students, parents, and others interested in women's experiences in a world history context. The organization's Web site contains information resources, lesson plans, essays, and reviews of classroom materials.

Women's Suffrage

http://www.ipu.org/wmn-e/suffrage.htm

This site is a comprehensive timeline of women's rights around the world.

World History Archives

http://www.hartford-hwp.com/archives/index.html

Dedicated to understanding world history from a working-class perspective, *World History Archives* provides a collection of documents focusing on politics, society, culture, and telecommunications.

LANGUAGE ARTS

The Creative Connections Project

http://www.ccph.com/

Creative Connections developed this language-arts-focused "global exploration" Web site of learning activities. The site houses a variety of interactive, multimedia adventures for students.

CyberGuides: Teacher Guides and Student Activities

http://www.sdcoe.k12.ca.us/score/cyberguide.html

The resources on the *Cyberguides* Web site supplement language arts and literature education. Full educational units are divided into grade level and subject area.

EnglishCLUB.com Teachers' Room

http://teachers.englishclub.com/index.html

EnglishCLUB.com is a connecting place for teachers of English and language arts. Available resources include lesson plans, classroom handouts and activities, articles, and dialogue forums.

Human Languages Page

http://www.ilovelanguages.com/

The *Human Languages Page* is a comprehensive index of Web sites related to the world's languages. Nearly two thousand links are divided into categories such as "Language Lessons" and "Linguistics Resources." The site is offered in English, French, German, Spanish, Portuguese, and Italian.

On-line English Grammar

http://www.edunet.com/english/grammar/index.cfm

Anthony Hughes hosts this "ask the expert" site, encouraging students to send in their questions about English grammar.

Story Arts

http://www.storyarts.org/

Created by author Heather Forest, *Story Arts* is a collection of resources on incorporating storytelling into the K-12 classroom. The site includes lesson plans, a library of stories, articles, links, and a curriculum exchange for language arts teachers.

Teaching with the Web

http://polyglot.lss.wisc.edu/lss/lang/teach.html

Lauren Rosen provides Web-based activities, lesson plans, teaching resources, and collaborative teaching and learning opportunities. Users are encouraged to contribute their ideas and resources.

Thoughts on Not Seeing Oneself

http://www.scils.rutgers.edu/~kvander/Culture/oneself.html

Debbie Reese, an education doctoral student at the University of Illinois, wrote this short piece on the needs of all students to see their cultures and ancestry reflected in books.

Using Multicultural Literature to Teach Reading Processes

http://coe.sdsu.edu/people/jmora/MulticulturalLit/

Jill Kerper Mora of San Diego State University created this online presentation. Topics covered include "Literary Discrimination," "Interpretation in Multicultural Literature," and "Evaluation in Multicultural Literature."

LIBRARIANSHIP

Diversity & Libraries

http://polaris.gseis.ucla.edu/cchu/diversity/

Clara M. Chu of UCLA built this set of resources to help librarians stay informed about the diversity communities around them and to help library educators infuse multiculturalism into their curricula.

Librarians' Index to the Internet

http://lii.org/

The Library of California sponsors a comprehensive index and search tool developed specifically for librarians.

Public Libraries and Cultural Diversity

http://www.ericfacility.net/ericdigests/ed358871.html

Debbie Yumilo Carton composed an ERIC Digest discussing collection development and other multicultural concerns in libraries.

LITERATURE

10 Quick Ways to Analyze Children's Books for Racism and Sexism

http://www.birchlane.davis.ca.us/library/10quick.htm

The Council on Interracial Books for Children lays out simple strategies for making sure our books challenge biases instead of recycling them.

Absolutely Whootie: Stories to Grow By

http://www.storiestogrowby.com/

Whootie the Owl hosts a fun collection of fairly tales from around the world for young children, all with positive messages for growth and openness.

African American Women Writers of the 19th Century

http://digital.nypl.org/schomburg/writers_aa19/toc.html

The New York Public Library offers this online database of literature including poetry, fiction, and autobiography.

Crossing Borders: Multicultural Literature in the Classroom

http://www.ncela.gwu.edu/miscpubs/jeilms/vol15/crossing.htm

Deborah Dietrich and Kathleen S. Ralph composed this essay about effectively and interactively employing multicultural literature.

Cynthia Leitich Smith's Children's Literature Resources

http://www.cynthialeitichsmith.com/index1.htm

This author of children's books is also the creator of an enormous collection of resources, bibliographies, and reviews. The site has a multicultural flavor, including a section on "Multiculturalism" in children's literature.

Feminist Foremothers

http://www.pinn.net/~sunshine/biblio/biblio.html

Sunshine for Women houses a great collection of historic feminist literature, including some of the earliest proclamations of women's rights.

How to Choose the Best Multicultural Books

http://teacher.scholastic.com/products/instructor/multicultural.htm

Scholastic shares strategies for finding truly multicultural books for children. Several different perspectives and guidelines are offered.

Indigenous Australia: Stories of Dreaming

http://www.dreamtime.net.au/dreaming/storylist.htm

The *Australian Museum Online* includes this collection of stories from various indigenous cultures. The site also incorporates a piece about the role of storytelling in indigenous cultures.

Online Books Page

http://digital.library.upenn.edu/books/

John Mark Ockerbloom edits this elaborate database of full-text online books. Browse by topic area, including "Social History, Problems, and Reform," "Human Geography," and "Education."

University of Virginia Electronic Text Center

http://etext.lib.virginia.edu/

This site houses over forty-five thousand full electronic texts along with over fifty thousand related images from the University of Virginia library system. Collections are plentiful and diverse in language, topic, era, and medium. Browse by language, subject, or era. Current holdings categories include "African American," "Native American," "American Civil War," "Women Writers," and "The English Poetry Database."

Vandergrift's Children's Literature Page

http://www.scils.rutgers.edu/~kvander/ChildrenLit/index.html

Kay Vandergrift of Rutgers University has compiled an extensive set of resources on children's literature with special attention to multicultural concerns. Sections include "Gender and Culture in Picture Books," "Powerful Multicultural Images," and "Thought Capsules," a collection of short writings about culture and children's literature from a variety of sources.

Voices from the Gaps

http://voices.cla.umn.edu/

Introduce yourself to the lives and literary works of North American women of color. You can also contribute your own page or publish a book review through the site.

Voices! Intercultural Poetry Exchange

http://www.edchange.org/multicultural/voices.html

The *Multicultural Pavilion* hosts this collection of poetry and prose about culture, identity, and education. Most of the entries are by educators and activists. Visitors are encouraged to participate in the exchange by submitting their writing.

Writing Black

http://www.keele.ac.uk/depts/as/Literature/amlit.black.html

The School of American Studies hosts a directory of online resources by and about African American authors.

MATH

Annotated Bibliography of Multicultural Perspectives in Mathematics Education

http://jwilson.coe.uga.edu/DEPT/Multicultural/MEBib94.html

Patricia S. Wilson, Julio C. Mosquera P., Marilyn E. Strutchens, and Annicia J. Thomas compiled this extensive annotated listing of resources related to multicultural education in the math classroom. Items are divided into three major categories: "Theory," "Research," and "Practice."

Ask Dr. Math

http://mathforum.org/dr.math/

Part of Swarthmore College's *Math Forum*, this site encourages teachers and students to send their questions and challenging problems to a team of expert mathematicians. Another feature of the site, the *Teacher2Teacher* forum, facilitates dialogue among mathematics educators.

Barrier Free Education

http://barrier-free.arch.gatech.edu/

The aim of *Barrier Free Education* is to help students with disabilities gain access to math and science education. The many resources on the site include lab experiments and lessons modified for accessibility, original articles and research, and a related e-mail discussion group.

Biographies of Women Mathematicians

http://www.agnesscott.edu/lriddle/women/women.htm

Larry Riddle of Agnes Scott College maintains this collection of short essays on more than one hundred women mathematicians. Browse through the entries by name or chronology.

The Compatibility of Good Mathematics Tasks with Good Multicultural Teaching Strategies

http://forum.swarthmore.edu/mathed/nctm96/multicultural/grover.questions.html

Barbara W. Grover and Marcia Seeley of the Ohio University and Allegheny Schools Partnership developed this set of questions to help guide math teachers in the process of creating effective lesson plans for a diversity of students and learning styles.

CyberSisters

http://www.cyber-sisters.org/

CyberSisters is a telementoring program created to help middle school girls in math, science, and technology education. Sponsored by the American Association of University Women, the program connects students with mentors all over the country. Both mentors and protégées can register online.

EPA Curriculum Resources & Activities

http://www.epa.gov/teachers/curriculum_resources.htm

A product of the Environmental Protection Agency's Education Center, this site is home to a collection of lesson plans and activities addressing the environment, conservation, and pollution. Many of the activities encourage social action and involvement.

Ethnomathematics

http://www.cs.uidaho.edu/~casey931/seminar/ethno.html

This site by Nancy Casey explores the meaning of "ethnomathematics" and related math teaching and learning issues. Casey also provides a long list of resources that further explore the topic.

Extend Equity and Access in Mathematics Education

http://www.stolaf.edu/other/extend/Access/access.html

This large collection of articles and essays emerged from a roundtable discussion on equity and access in mathematics education in the context of rapidly changing state and local education policy.

Integrating Gender and Equity Reform in Math, Science, and Engineering Instruction

http://www.coe.uga.edu/ingear/

InGEAR houses a collection of curriculum materials promoting excellence and equity in math, science, and engineering education. The site includes specific teaching strategies, online publications and articles, and a collection of classroom activities that address gender issues.

MathNerds

http://www.mathnerds.com/mathnerds/

With a strong commitment to inquiry-based education, the MathNerds are an international volunteer network of mathematicians providing free discovery-based guidance for teachers and students.

Math Teacher Link Message Board

http://mtl.math.uiuc.edu/message_board/

This discussion board was designed for educators to exchange ideas and questions related to math, science, and education. Users are primarily K-12 teachers but also include preservice teachers and others interested in math and science education.

Mathematicians and Education Reform (MER)

http://www.math.uic.edu/MER/pages/

MER is a partnership of mathematicians working for education reform at the K-12, undergraduate, and graduate levels. Learn how to get involved or take advantage of their work and resources on this Web site.

Multicultural Math Fair: Links for Activities

http://forum.swarthmore.edu/alejandre/mathfair/mmflinks.html

The *Math Forum*, hosted by Swarthmore College, includes this collection of mathematics lesson plans and classroom activities built around multicultural themes. Several of the lesson plans are in Spanish.

Multicultural Math Goals

http://people.clarityconnect.com/webpages/terri/multicultural.html

Terri Husted created this page of resources and frameworks for incorporating multicultural teaching and learning into mathematics education. In addition to offering her own set of "goals" for math education, she includes book reviews and links to related sites.

Multicultural Perspectives in Mathematics Education

http://jwilson.coe.uga.edu/DEPT/Multicultural/MathEd.html

University of Georgia's Department of Mathematics hosts this resource directory to help educators understand the role of multicultural teaching and learning in mathematics education. The site includes an annotated bibliography, dissertation references, and Web links.

Native American Geometry

http://www.earthmeasure.com/

This fascinating site gives the history and fundamentals of a Native American tradition of geometry dating about two thousand years.

Plane Math

http://www.planemath.com/

NASA and InfoUse cosponsor a set of interactive activities to help students better understand the mathematics of aeronautics.

Practical Uses of Math and Science (PUMAS)

http://pumas.jpl.nasa.gov/

PUMAS provides thirty-two examples for ways in which math and science lessons can be used in everyday life, effectively drawing on the actual experiences of the students.

Profile of Equitable Mathematics and Science Classroom and Teacher

http://www.col-ed.org/smcnws/equity/profile.html

Joy Wallace of the Columbia Education Center developed this set of equity guidelines for math and science classrooms and teachers. Special attention is given to physical environment, curriculum, language, pedagogy, behavior management, and assessment.

Teaching Mathematics Effectively and Equitably to Females

http://www.enc.org/resources/records/full/0,1240,017214,00.shtm

Katherine Hanson of the Education Development Center explores classroom climate issues for females in mathematics.

Women in Math Project

http://darkwing.uoregon.edu/~wmnmath/

Marie Vitulli of the University of Oregon directs this large collection of resources highlighting women's achievements in math including a directory of publications, a biographical collection, and statistics.

Physical Education and Athletics

Adapted Physical Education

http://www.pecentral.org/adapted/adaptedmenu.html

This section of *P. E. Central* contains resources for teachers working with students with special needs. There is an "Ask the Expert" section through which users pose questions about related issues and suggestions for adapting P.E. activities for students with special needs.

American Indian Sports Team Mascots

http://schools.eastnet.ecu.edu/pitt/ayden/PHYSED8.HTM

AISTM educates all people about the harm and oppression caused by racist team mascots. A guide for educators gives tips for addressing the problem.

The Athletic Experience of Ethnically Diverse Girls

http://eric-web.tc.columbia.edu/digest/dig131.asp

Jeanne Weiller explores how race, ethnicity, and socioeconomic status impact girls' experiences in sports.

Diversity and Inclusion in Physical Education

http://www.cbe.ab.ca/sss/Physed/div-incl.asp

The Calgary Board of Education leads the way for physical education programs by insisting on a framework that centers on diversity and inclusion.

Empowering Women in Sports

http://www.feminist.org/research/sports2.html

The Feminist Majority published this research report on effective ways to support women's athletic pursuits.

Physical Education Lesson Plans

http://schools.eastnet.ecu.edu/pitt/ayden/PHYSED8.HTM

Share P.E. lesson plans. Resources are divided into categories including "Integrated Curriculum" and "Assessments."

Sports and the Disabled

http://www.feminist.org/sports/disability.html

Claudine Sherrill provides a critical analysis of the lack of support for disabled athletes in schools and beyond.

SCIENCE

4000 Years of Women in Science

http://crux.astr.ua.edu/4000ws/4000ws.html

Taking the interdisciplinary approach of combining science education with history education, this site houses photographs, biographies, and references for women who contributed to the fields of science. An interactive quiz is also included.

Access Excellence

http://www.accessexcellence.org/

A site specifically designed for Health and Bioscience teachers and learners, *Access Excellence* is a virtual museum combining informational resources, collaborative opportunities, and dialogue forums for science education reform.

Achieving Gender Equity in the Science Classroom

http://www.brown.edu/Administration/Dean_of_the_College/homepginfo/equity/
Equity_handbook.html

Originally written for college faculty at Brown University, this handbook of specific strategies for ensuring gender equity is in many ways transferable to the K-12 classroom. Some of the specific strategies covered are "Observe Classroom Dynamics," "Switch from a Competitive to a Cooperative Educational Model," and "Fight Narrow Stereotypes of Science."

BEEMNET

http://www.beemnet.com/

The *Brain Exchange Electronic Mentorship Network* sets up exchanges between elementary school classes and neuroscientists. Students are encouraged to publish their responses to the exchange, in writing or art, on the Web site.

Exploratorium

http://www.exploratorium.edu/

An online museum "of science, art, and human perception," this site engages children and adults in interactive explorations of intriguing science questions. Highlights include webcasts, virtual trips, and a learning studio.

The Faces of Science: African Americans in the Sciences

http://www.princeton.edu/~mcbrown/display/faces.html

Mitchell C. Brown hosts this virtual encyclopedia highlighting African American scientists and their work and accomplishments. The site is full of biographies, statistics, and other related informational sources. Biographical entries are organized both alphabetically and by discipline.

Integrating Critical Thinking into the Classroom

http://www.accessexcellence.org/21st/TL/buchanan/

Anne Buchanan wrote this piece on critical thinking in the science classroom for *Access Excellence*. She provides a conceptualization for critical thinking, then provides strategies for incorporating it into the science teaching and learning process.

NASA Quest

http://quest.arc.nasa.gov/

NASA helps bring space and science into the classroom through a series of virtual events, interactive Web pages, and Internet-based space adventures. A "Journal of the Week" gives all of us a glimpse into the lives and work of NASA employees.

Science Playwiths

http://members.ozemail.com.au/~macinnis/scifun/index.htm

Find simple but engaging science experiments using only "junk" you can find around the house.

SPECIAL EDUCATION

Council for Exceptional Children

http://www.cec.sped.org/ab/

CEC is dedicated to providing equitable educational outcomes for students with disabilities, exceptionalities, and giftedness.

Effective Intervention Techniques

http://curry.edschool.virginia.edu/sped/projects/ose/information/interventions.html

This collaborative project by the students from the University of Virginia and East Tennessee State University summarizes scores of studies on effective teaching techniques for exceptional learners.

Gifted Education in a Multicultural Australia

http://www.nexus.edu.au/teachstud/gat/becherv1.htm

Neil E. Bechervaise addresses the failure of Australia's education system to adapt to immigrant populations by exploring immigrant attitudes toward gifted education programs.

Inclusion: Yours, Mine, Ours

http://rushservices.com/Inclusion/homepage.htm

The Florida Inclusion Network sponsors this site to give teachers the support and resources needed to include students with special needs in their classrooms.

LD Online

http://www.ldonline.org/

The Learning Project hosts an excellently organized compendium of resources and strategies on learning disabilities for teachers and parents. The site also includes *KidZone* to help children better understand ADD, ADHD, and other disabilities.

WORLD LANGUAGES

Anacleta's Spanish and World Language Resources

http://anacleta.homestead.com/

A longtime teacher regularly updates this directory of resources for teachers and parents.

FLTeach

http://www.cortland.edu/flteach/

The National Endowment for the Humanities funds this network of foreign language teachers. The site contains articles, dialogues, and other resources and collaborative opportunities.

Foreign Language Resources for Teachers and Students

http://www.geocities.com/Athens/Acropolis/1506/

This site serves as an index of online foreign language education resources. Discussion forums and online newspapers and magazines in various languages are included.

Internet Activities for Foreign Language Classes

http://www.clta.net/lessons/

Lewis Johnson maintains this collection of lesson plans for Spanish, French, Italian, Japanese, and German language students. Many of the lesson plans are culture related.

Language Learning and Technology

http://llt.msu.edu/

This refereed journal for second and foreign language educators disseminates research and information about the intersections of language learning and technology. Each issue is focused on a specific topic and includes articles, reviews, and references related to that topic.

Web Based Activities for Foreign Languages

http://facweb.furman.edu/~pecoy/lessons.htm

Patricia Pecoy has drawn from several other Web sites in producing this index of available foreign language learning activities. Sections include "Vocabulary," "Grammar," and "Information Discovery."

CHAPTER 12

A Guide to Online Resources: Issues and Topics in Multicultural Education

The Web sites highlighted in this chapter expose many specific concerns and inequities that multicultural education aims to address.

ABILITY DIFFERENCES

Disability as Diversity: A Guide for Class Discussion

http://www.apa.org/monitor/feb98/diverse.html

The American Psychological Association's diversity task force published this article about incorporating disability issues into the curriculum.

Disability Rights Education and Defense Fund

http://www.dredf.org/

Advocating for the civil rights of people with disabilities, DREDF provides articles, press releases and other resources through its Web site.

Eliminating Ableism in Education

http://www.rickguidotti.com/about.htm

Thomas Hehir challenges the education community to end the devaluation of disability and work for equity for all students.

Not Dead Yet: The Resistance

http://www.notdeadyet.org/

An activist group of people with disabilities, Not Dead Yet battles against the invisibility and silencing of the disability community.

Positive Exposure

http://www.rickguidotti.com/about.htm

This innovative not-for-profit organization challenges the stigma of ability differences through visual arts.

ACHIEVEMENT GAPS

Closing the Achievement Gap for Educators

http://coe.gasou.edu/gap/

Dan Rea built this Web site to provide educators with information on how to close the gap for all traditionally underserved students. Sections include "School Reform Programs," "Teaching Practices," and "Dropout Prevention."

Education Week on the Web: The Achievement Gap

http://www.edweek.org/sreports/gap.htm

Education Week amassed a collection of reports and articles providing different views on the achievement gap and offers them here.

Facing the Consequences: An Examination of Racial Discrimination in U.S. Public Schools

http://www.arc.org/erase/FTC1intro.html

Outlines how public schools consistently fail to provide quality education to students of color, contributing to the achievement gap.

Movement in the Village

http://www.ncpublicschools.org/schoolimprovement/closingthegap/strategies/movement/

Learn research-based strategies for improving the achievement of all students through a report drafted by the North Carolina Department of Education.

Special Collections: The Achievement Gap

http://www.ncrel.org/info/rc/sc/gapweb.htm

The North Central Regional Educational Laboratory (NCREL) collected several reports and articles about the gap that are available online.

CRITICAL PEDAGOGY

Critical Pedagogy

http://www.criticalmethods.org/s3.mv

Part of a conference Web site, *Critical Pedagogy* provides some conceptualizations and models for critical teaching and learning.

Critical Pedagogy on the Web

http://mingo.info-science.uiowa.edu/~stevens/critped/page1.htm

Read an overview of critical pedagogy and synopses of the work of prominent theorists including Freire and Giroux.

Critical Thinking and Critical Pedagogy

http://faculty.ed.uiuc.edu/burbules/ncb/papers/critical.html

The authors compare and contrast the "critical" nature of critical thinking and critical pedagogy, eventually merging the two.

Radical Pedagogy

http://radicalpedagogy.icaap.org/

An interdisciplinary journal, *Radical Pedagogy* advocates and informs about innovative approaches for teaching and learning that center students and critical thinking.

Rage and Hope

http://www.perfectfit.org/CT/index2.html

This site applies critical pedagogy philosophy to the process of school transformation through an exploration of the work, ideas, and contributions of Michael Apple, Paulo Freire, Henry Giroux, and Peter McLaren.

Teaching Critically as an Act of Praxis and Resistance

http://newton.uor.edu/FacultyFolder/MBoyce/1CRITPED.HTM

Mary E. Boyce instructs us on the theory and philosophy behind critical pedagogy as well as our responsibility to put it into practice.

GENDER AND SEXISM

About-Face

http://www.about-face.org/index.html

Don't fall for the media circus! This organization promotes positive self-esteem in all girls and women through media education.

AdiosBarbie.com

http://www.adiosbarbie.com/

This site provides a critical examination of body image politics and encourages all people to "love your body through thick and think."

Chilly Climate

http://www.chillyclimate.org/index.asp

Explore model programs for gender equity in academia along with relevant statistics and a climate assessment kit.

Expect the Best from a Girl. That's What You'll Get.

http://www.academic.org/

The Office of Communications at Mount Holyoke College describes what parents, teachers, and others can do to show high academic expectations for girls.

Guidelines for Non-Sexist Use of Language

http://www.apa.udel.edu/apa/publications/texts/nonsexist.html

The APA discusses stereotypes and how to break the cycle of sexism in the English language.

National Organization for Men Against Sexism

http://www.nomas.org/sys-tmpl/door/

NOMAS is the oldest pro-feminist men's group in the United States.

Sexism in the Classroom from Grade School to Graduate School

http://www.colorado.edu/gtp/resources/tutor/sexism.html

Myra and David Sadker co-wrote an article naming ways in which sexism is recycled in classrooms across all grade levels.

High-Stakes Testing

Appropriate Use of High-Stakes Testing in Our Nation's Schools

http://www.apa.org/pubinfo/testing.html

The American Psychological Association argues the limitations and dangers of the high-stakes testing craze, suggesting how and for what purposes testing should be used.

The Consortium for Equity in Standards and Testing

http://wwwcsteep.bc.edu/ctest

The Ford Foundation sponsors this consortium as it works to find ways in which standards and assessments can be used more fairly for all students.

Fair Test

http://www.fairtest.org/

Fair Test, the National Center for Fair & Open Testing, advocates an end to the inequities and abuses of standardized testing. Read about related current issues, social action, and reform movements.

High-Stakes Testing Slights Multiculturalism

http://www.rethinkingschools.org/archive/14_03/tale143.shtml

High-stakes testing has become the contemporary threat to multicultural education. Makani Themba-Nixon warns us of the danger.

Students Against Testing

http://www.nomoretests.com/

This student-run Web site includes powerful downloadable flyers, mock standardized tests that illustrate the problems with the testing movement, and fact sheets. This is an excellent and important resource for teacher educators and classroom teachers who want examples of student-led social action.

Teachers College Record: High-Stakes Testing

http://www.tcrecord.org/Collection.asp?CollectionID=57

Browse articles and other resources related to testing in the archives of *TCRecord*. A discussion forum is also available.

No Child Left Behind

NEA Members Speak Out on No Child Left Behind

http://www.nea.org/video/membersspeak.html

View video clips of students and administrators sharing their opinions of NCLB and how it has impacted their work.

No Child Left

http://nochildleft.com/

FNO Press publishes this site that takes a critical, equity-based stand against No Child Left Behind and high-stakes testing.

No Child Left Behind

http://www.ed.gov/nclb/landing.jhtml

This is the U.S. government's primary site for NCLB. Though it has a very propaganda-like feel, the site includes a useful overview of the legislation and research behind it.

A Practical Guide for Talking with Your Community About NCLB

http://www.learningfirst.org/publications/nclbguide/

Most people outside education do not understand the content or implications of No Child Left Behind. The Learning First Alliance provides strategies for engaging parents and other community members in deep discussions about the legislation and what it means to schools and students.

Race, Ethnicity, and Racism

AntiRacismNet

http://www.antiracismnet.org/flash.html

Visit this online international network of anti-racism organizations and practitioners for press releases, action alerts, and other social justice stories and resources.

Bill of Rights for Racially Mixed People

http://www.webcom.com/~intvoice/rights.html

Maria P.P. Root passionately exclaims her rights and in doing so challenges us to better understand the multiracial experience.

Brown vs. Board of Education

http://brownvboard.org/

The Brown Foundation for Education Equity hosts an online exploration of the Brown case and its continuing impact on education policy and practice.

The Civil Rights Project

http://www.civilrightsproject.harvard.edu/

This Harvard-based project aims to reinitiate the civil rights movement through the distribution of information and resources about contemporary civil rights issues.

"Stereotype Threat" and Black Students

http://www.theatlantic.com/issues/99aug/9908stereotype.htm

Claude Steele describes the phenomenon of how low expectations and related stereotypes directly impact the performance of black college students.

Teaching about Whiteness

http://www.uwm.edu/~gjay/Whiteness/Teachwhiteness.html

Gregory Jay recommends activities and exercises for educating students about whiteness and racism.

U.S. Racial Segregation Statistics

http://www.censusscope.org/segregation.html

If you thought segregation was a thing of the past, browse these indices of census information showing the contrary.

SEXUAL ORIENTATION AND HETEROSEXISM

Creating Safe Schools for Lesbian and Gay Students

http://members.tripod.com/~twood/guide.html

Youth Pride, Inc., offers a resource guide for school staff.

GLAAD

http://www.glaad.org/index.php

The Gay and Lesbian Alliance Against Defamation advocates for inclusive media representation of people and events and eliminating homophobia and heterosexism.

Project 10

http://www.project10.org/

This organization provides educational support to lesbian, gay, bisexual, transgender, and questioning youth in public schools. The site contains "Tips for Teachers" and "Tips for Administrators."

The Safe Schools Coalition

http://www.safeschoolscoalition.org/

A public-private partnership, the Coalition provides resources, including handouts and publications, for teachers, students, and others. Many of the site's features are available in both Spanish and English.

Sexual Orientation: Science, Education, and Policy

http://psychology.ucdavis.edu/rainbow/

Gregory Herek provides the content for this site about homophobia, hate crimes, and AIDS stigma.

Socioeconomic Status and Classism

Indicators of Socioeconomic Equity in Technology Programs

http://www.ncrel.org/engauge/framewk/equ/soc/equsocpr.htm

This text-based site examines class inequities related to technology access in and out of schools.

Uncovering Classism

http://www.workforcedevelopmentgroup.com/news_twenty_six.html

This checklist for assessing classism in organizations, though meant for the corporate sector, is very relevant to schools as well.

United for a Fair Economy

http://www.stw.org/

UFE fights for economic equality through research, an activist network, and economics education.

What Research Says about Unequal Funding in Schools

http://www.wested.org/cs/wew/view/rs/694

WestEd offers this downloadable report on classism in public schools.